This Book may be kept

SEVEN DAYS

A fine of 2 CENTS will be charged for each day the Book is kept over time.

L. B. Cat. No. 1137.2

THE JURISDICTION
OF THE CONFESSOR

THE JURISDICTION
OF THE
CONFESSOR
ACCORDING TO THE CODE OF CANON LAW

BY
REV. JAMES P. KELLY, J.C.D.

WITH A PREFACE BY
Rt. Rev. Msgr. PHILIP BERNARDINI, S.T.D., J.U.D.
DEAN OF THE SCHOOL OF CANON LAW
CATHOLIC UNIVERSITY, WASHINGTON, D. C.

New York, Cincinnati, Chicago
BENZIGER BROTHERS
PRINTERS TO THE HOLY APOSTOLIC SEE
1929

Nihil Obstat
>ARTHUR J. SCANLAN, S.T.D.
>*Censor Librorum*

Imprimatur
>✠ PATRICK CARDINAL HAYES
>*Archbishop of New York*

NEW YORK, September 27, 1928.

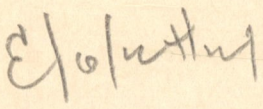

THE JURISDICTION OF THE CONFESSOR : COPYRIGHT, 1929, BY BENZIGER BROTHERS. PRINTED IN THE UNITED STATES OF AMERICA

PREFACE

"There is nothing more excellent, or more useful for the Church of God and the welfare of souls, than the office of confessor." (Conc. Balt. Pl. II, n. 278.) Considering the momentous consequences attendant upon an act of the confessor, there is no office exercised by man laden with graver responsibilities. How important, therefore, that a priest know the exact extent of the powers he is called upon to exercise! Upon the validity of one absolution or dispensation may depend the eternal welfare of an immortal soul.

The various faculties for absolution and dispensation, which the Church grants to the priest in the tribunal of Penance, are scattered throughout the *Codex Juris Canonici*. Doctor Kelly has gathered together these faculties in this scholarly work, and gives a comprehensive and extensive technical analysis of the canons in a way that makes this volume a most valuable reference book for the priest actively engaged in the practice of the confessional, and for the student of Canon Law in the seminary and university.

We congratulate Doctor Kelly for his complete and lucid treatment of the faculties granted by the Code to the confessor, and recommend his volume to all who seek a thorough knowledge of this most important sacerdotal function.

PHILIP BERNARDINI.

CATHOLIC UNIVERSITY
WASHINGTON, D. C.

AUTHOR'S FOREWORD

The codification of Canon Law, undertaken at the command of Pius X in 1904, and promulgated by the Constitution of Benedict XV *Providentissima Mater Ecclesia* on May 27, 1917, has crystallized the legislation of nineteen centuries in the Church. Although there has been no change in the doctrine of the Church from the day of her institution, yet, like any living organization, she has undergone change and development in her discipline. She has been *all things to all men,* an immovable warrior in the defense of truth and a loving mother in the care of her children; down through the centuries she has remained the unchanging Church in a changing world, and yet she has always adapted herself to the ever varying needs of her children.

Accordingly, in her penitential discipline, she has tempered the severity of the public discipline of the first centuries to meet the varying demands of times and circumstances, until the present system of a totally private sacramental discipline of Penance has evolved.

One element of the penitential discipline of the Church constitutes the subject matter of this book. That element is the jurisdiction which a confessor must possess in order to impart valid absolution for sins.

The purpose of this book is to give a clear and concise statement of the nature and extent of the laws governing this important element in the penitential discipline of the Church.

The subject naturally divides itself into two parts.

In Part I the general notion of this jurisdiction is given, the two principal species of the power are discussed, and the evolution of the present law of the Church on this matter is sketched. In Part II are enumerated the individual powers of absolving and dispensing which the Code grants to all priests in some circumstances, to all confessors in other circumstances, and to pastors and missionaries while hearing confessions. The powers for the internal sacramental forum, which are granted to all priests, do not require that the priests be possessed of the faculty *ad audiendas confessiones* in order to use them validly; but the other powers granted by the Code presuppose that the priest is already a confessor, i. e., possessed of habitual ordinary or delegated jurisdiction to hear confessions. These powers, therefore, are granted by the Church in her general law to the priests mentioned above, for use in the internal sacramental forum, and no superior other than the Roman Pontiff can validly restrict or prohibit the use of these powers by the confessor in the exercise of his office.

The author wishes to take this opportunity of expressing his sincere gratitude to the faculty of the School of Canon Law in the Catholic University at Washington, and to the Rev. Joseph C. MacCarthy and the Rev. Jeremiah T. Toomey of St. Joseph's Seminary, Dunwoodie, N. Y., and the Rev. John J. Bingham of New York City, for their valuable aid in the preparation of this work.

JAMES P. KELLY.

ARCHDIOCESE OF NEW YORK
Feast of SS. Peter and Paul
June 29, 1928

CONTENTS

	PAGE
PREFACE BY RT. REV. MSGR. PHILIP BERNARDINI, S.T.D., J.U.D.	V
AUTHOR'S FOREWORD	VII

PART I

PENITENTIAL JURISDICTION IN GENERAL

CHAPTER
I. JURISDICTION IN GENERAL	3
Definition of Jurisdiction	4
Divisions of Jurisdiction	5
II. NECESSITY OF JURISDICTION IN A CONFESSOR (CAN. 872)	8
III. USE OF SECRET (AURICULAR) CONFESSION IN THE CHURCH	12
IV. THE MINISTER OF PENANCE AND HIS JURISDICTION UNDER THE FORMER DISCIPLINE	17
In the First Four Centuries	17
In the Fifth and Sixth Centuries	26
From the Seventh Century to the Council of Trent	27
From the Council of Trent to the Code	33
V. THE PRESENT LAW OF THE CODE	40
Preliminary Remarks	40
ART. I. ORDINARY JURISDICTION (CAN. 873)	42
The Pope, Cardinals, and Local Ordinaries	42
Pastors	43
Quasi-Parochi and Parochial Vicars	46
Canons Penitentiary	50
Exempt Clerical Religious Superiors	50
Cessation of Ordinary Jurisdiction	51

CONTENTS

Art. II. delegated jurisdiction (can. 874)   52
    Manner of Delegating Jurisdiction   54
    Limitation of Delegated Jurisdiction . . .   56
    Cessation of Delegated Jurisdiction . . .   57
    Delegated Jurisdiction of Religious Priests
        and Their Privileges   58
Art. III. reservation (can. 893)   66
    Purpose of Reservation   67
    Effect of Ignorance on Reservation . . .   69
    Division of Reservations   70
    Effect of Reservation on the Orientals . .   72

PART II

PARTICULAR GRANTS OF PENITENTIAL JURISDICTION GIVEN BY THE CODE

Preliminary Remarks   81

Title I

THE PENITENTIAL JURISDICTION GRANTED BY THE CODE TO ALL PRIESTS IN CERTAIN CIRCUMSTANCES

VI. In Danger of Death   90
    Art. I. the power of absolving from sins
        and censures (canons 882, 2252) . . .   90
    The Confessor   92
    The Power   94
    The Conditions   96
    Art. II. the power of dispensing from
        matrimonial impediments (can. 1043) .   99
    The Confessor   100
    The Power   102
    The Conditions   108
    Dispensation from the Form   114

CONTENTS

VII. IN CASES OF COMMON ERROR, DOUBT, AND INADVERTENCE (CANONS 209, 207§2) . . 117
    ART. I. COMMON ERROR 119
        Origin of the Law 119
        The Place of the Error 122
        The Number in Error 123
        The Opinion of Recent Canonists 124
        The Licit use of This Jurisdiction 136
        The Cause Required in Order to Absolve Licitly 140
    ART. II. CASES OF DOUBT 141
    ART. III. INADVERTENCE 145
        Ignorance of Reservation of a Censure . . 146

VIII. THE POWER OF ABSOLVING CARDINALS AND BISHOPS (CANONS 239 §1,2°, 349§1,1°) . 147
    ART. I. THE CONFESSION OF CARDINALS . . . 147
    ART. II. THE CONFESSION OF BISHOPS 149

Title II

PENITENTIAL JURISDICTION GRANTED BY THE CODE TO ALL CONFESSORS IN CERTAIN CIRCUMSTANCES

IX. THE POWERS OF ABSOLVING GRANTED BY THE CODE TO ALL CONFESSORS 152
    ART. I. THE POWER OF ABSOLVING IN CERTAIN CIRCUMSTANCES FROM SINS RESERVED "RATIONE SUI" (CAN. 900) 152
        Cessation of the Reservation of a Sin Reserved "Ratione Sui" 153
    ART. II. THE POWER OF ABSOLVING FROM CENSURES AND SINS RESERVED "RATIONE CENSURAE" (CAN. 2254) 160
        Preliminary Remarks 160
            Explanation of Terms 161
            Reservation of Censures 163
        The Absolution of Reserved Censures in More Urgent Cases 167

CONTENTS

Origin of the Law	168
Extent of the Present Law	169
The Cases	171
The Recourse	172
Territorial Effect of the Reservation of Censures	176
ART. III. MARITIME FACULTIES (CAN. 883)	179
The Power	183
ART. IV. THE POWER OF ABSOLVING RELIGIOUS (CANONS 876, 519, 522, 523)	184
Preliminary Remarks	184
The Confessions of Religious Men	185
The Power of the Confessor	189
The Confessions of Religious Women	191
Origin and Development of This Law	194
Conditions for the Valid and Licit Use of This Power	195
1. Tranquillity of Conscience	195
2. The Approach to the Confessor	196
3. The Jurisdiction Required in the Confessor	198
4. The Place of Confession	198
Conclusion	204
Absolution of a Sick Religious Woman	205
Conditions for the Validity of the Absolution	206
X. THE POWERS OF DISPENSING GRANTED BY THE CODE TO ALL CONFESSORS	210
ART. I. THE POWER OF DISPENSING FROM THE EUCHARISTIC FAST (CAN. 858§2)	210
Conditions	211
ART. II. THE POWER OF DISPENSING FROM MATRIMONIAL IMPEDIMENTS IN URGENT CASES (CAN. 1045)	213
The Confessor	214
The Power	214
The Conditions	217
1. The Forum	218
2. The Urgency	218

CONTENTS

    3. Occult Cases 221
    4. The Approach to the Ordinary ... 227
    5. The Promises in Dispensing from the Impediments of Disparity of Cult and Mixed Religion 228
    6. The Removal of Scandal 231
  Art. III. THE POWER OF DISPENSING FROM IRREGULARITIES ARISING FROM AN OCCULT CRIME (CAN. 990§2) 231
  Art. IV. THE POWER OF DISPENSING FROM VINDICTIVE PENALTIES (CAN. 2290) ... 234
XI. OTHER POWERS GRANTED BY THE CODE TO ALL CONFESSORS 237
  Art. I. THE POWER OF EXTENDING THE PASCHAL TIME (CAN. 859§1) 237
  Art. II. THE POWER OF COMMUTING THE CONDITIONS FOR GAINING AN INDULGENCE (CAN. 935) 238

Title III

THE PENITENTIAL JURISDICTION GRANTED BY THE CODE TO PASTORS AND MISSIONARIES

XII. THE POWER OF ABSOLVING FROM SINS RESERVED "RATIONE SUI" (CAN. 899§3)... 242
  Pastors 242
  Missionaries 244
XIII. THE POWER OF DISPENSING FROM THE LAWS OF FESTAL OBSERVANCE, FAST AND ABSTINENCE GRANTED TO PASTORS (CAN. 1245§1) 245
  Law of Festal Observance 245
  Law of Abstinence 246
  Law of Fasting 247
  Power of Dispensing 248
BIBLIOGRAPHY 251
FORMULARY 256
INDEX 263

PART I
PENITENTIAL JURISDICTION IN GENERAL

CHAPTER I

JURISDICTION IN GENERAL

When Christ established His Church, He constituted it a perfect society having the power of sanctifying, teaching and ruling its members. Accordingly, the ministers of the Church are equipped with a twofold power: the power of orders, for the sanctification of the faithful; and the power of jurisdiction, for their instruction and government. The power of orders is received in sacred ordination and constitutes one a priest, a mediator, capable of bringing man's homage to God, and God's sanctification to man. The power of jurisdiction is received from the commission of one's competent superior, establishing the recipient in authority, furnished with the power of teaching (*magisterium*) by which the intellect is ruled, and with the power of governing (*imperium*) by which the will is ruled.

The respective powers of orders and jurisdiction ordinarily are mutually dependent one upon the other for the valid or at least licit exercise of many ecclesiastical functions, yet they are really distinct and separable. The power of orders usually forms the foundation for the power of jurisdiction, for by ordination one is not only given the power of performing acts that will sanctify man, but also is given an habitual capability of receiving the power of ruling them.

But although the concurrence of both powers in an

ecclesiastical person is required for the exercise of many functions, yet these powers are really distinct and separable, and one may exist without the other. The two powers differ *ratione objecti,* since the power of orders is the power of sanctifying, while the power of jurisdiction is the power of ruling the faithful; they differ *ratione modi acquisitionis,* for the power of orders is acquired only by the sacred rite of ordination, while the power of jurisdiction is acquired by the commission of a superior assigning subjects; they differ *ratione modi quo existunt,* for the power of orders is unlimitable and inamissible, while the power of jurisdiction is able to be restricted and revoked at the will of the superior. Therefore, although the power of orders ordinarily is the basis upon which the power of jurisdiction rests, yet, at least for the valid exercise of this latter power, it is not always necessary that it be based upon the power of orders, for it is possible that a simple cleric, destitute of all power of orders, be elected to the pontifical dignity and enjoy full power of jurisdiction; so also, a deposed or retired bishop still possesses full power of orders and yet lacks all power of jurisdiction. So it is evident that these powers are really distinct, but a cleric deficient in either power could not perform a function requiring the existence of both orders and jurisdiction.

Definition of Jurisdiction

The power of jurisdiction in the Church, then, may be defined as *potestas publica regendi homines baptizatos in ordine ad finem supernaturalem a Deo vel*

JURISDICTION IN GENERAL

ejus Ecclesia concessa, per missionem canonicam vel per deputationem legitimi superioris ecclesiastici.[1]

The following is an explanation of the terms:

Publica—to distinguish it from the private dominative power belonging to the head of imperfect societies such as the family;

Baptizatos—because only such are members of the Church and subjects of ecclesiastical jurisdiction;

In ordine ad finem supernaturalem—for the salvation of man's soul is the end for which the Church exists, and her direct competency in ruling men is limited to the things that pertain to that end;

A Deo vel ejus Ecclesia concessa—for the Pope legitimately elected and having accepted receives his power of jurisdiction immediately from God—all inferior clerics receive their jurisdiction from the Church;[2]

Per missionem canonicam vel per deputationem legitimi superioris ecclesiastici—these are the two means through which jurisdiction can be acquired.

Divisions of Jurisdiction

The power of jurisdiction is divided into many species—taking as the basis of the divisions, the efficacy,

---

[1] Schmalzgrueber, *Jus Ecclesiasticum Universum*, I, tit. XXXI, n. 32; Reiffenstuel, *Jus Canonicum Universum*, I, tit. XXIX, n. 1; Wernz-Vidal, *Jus Canonicum*, II, n. 48; Maroto, *Institutiones Juris Canonici*, n. 573; Vermeersch-Creusen, *Epitome Juris Canonici*, I, n. 200.

[2] Canon 109; Benedict XIV, *De Synodo Dioecesana*, I, tit. I, cap. IV, n. 2; Wernz-Vidal, *op. cit.*, II, n. 579; Vermeersch-Creusen, *op. cit.*, I, n. 399; Cocchi, *Commentarium in Codicem Juris Canonici*, III, n. 249. The opinion that bishops receive their jurisdiction immediately from God in their consecration, is no longer regarded as probable. Cf. Wernz-Vidal, *op. cit.*, II, n. 48.

the object, the extension, and the title to jurisdiction.

Ratione efficaciae—jurisdiction is divided into: jurisdiction for the external forum, or that power which regulates the social actions of the faithful primarily and directly respecting the public good and having its juridical and social effects recognized *coram Ecclesia;* and jurisdiction for the internal forum, or that power which regulates the moral relations of the faithful primarily and directly respecting the private good and having its effects only *coram Deo*.

Jurisdiction for the internal forum is subdivided into: sacramental jurisdiction if it can be exercised only within or upon the occasion of the sacrament of Penance, and extra-sacramental if it can be used outside of the tribunal of Penance.

Ratione objecti—jurisdiction is classified as judicial or voluntary according as this power of rule is exercised with or without a formal judicial process.

Ratione extensionis—jurisdiction is called universal or particular. The former is that power of rule which is all embracing and unrestricted either as regards persons, place, or matter. This jurisdiction is enjoyed only by the Roman Pontiff himself, nor is it shared by the Roman Congregations, which are restricted at least *quoad materiam*. Particular jurisdiction is that power of rule which is limited either to certain people or to a particular place or to definite matter. Such is the jurisdiction possessed by every ecclesiastic inferior to the Roman Pontiff.

Finally, *ratione tituli,* jurisdiction is divided into ordinary and delegated. Ordinary jurisdiction is that power of rule which is attached to an office by law, so that one acquiring that office *eo ipso* acquires the jurisdiction connected with it. This is called *proper* when the office is a principal office, such as a bishopric, and is exercised in one's own name; *vicarius* when the office is accessory, such as a vicariate general, and is exercised in the name of another. All other jurisdiction is called delegated, since it must be derived from the commission of one's competent superior.[3]

Since it is the object of this book to deal only with the jurisdiction of the confessor, it becomes necessary now to limit our inquiry to that jurisdiction which a priest must possess to impart valid absolution for sins. This jurisdiction *ratione objecti* is classified as judicial, for the *forum poenitentiae* is a strict judgment seat wherein the priest is the judge and the penitent is the accuser (*actor*) and the accused (*reus*). The priest in this sacramental tribunal judges the guilt or innocence of the penitent as it appears before God, and his sentence of remission or retention has its effect only before the judgment seat of God; therefore, the jurisdiction over the penitent needed by the priest is merely jurisdiction for the internal sacramental forum. Henceforth, then, we shall be concerned only with jurisdiction for the internal sacramental forum, to the exclusion of all the other species of this power.

[3] Can. 196.

CHAPTER II

NECESSITY OF JURISDICTION IN A CONFESSOR

Ecclesiastical jurisdiction, as has been said, is that public power, which Christ has conferred upon His Church, of ruling the faithful with respect to their supernatural end. This power of ruling is as a genus embracing the threefold specific powers of legislating, judging, and executing, for this triple power is necessary for the attainment of the end of any public authority and is contained in the very nature of a perfect society. Therefore, every judicial act performed by an official of such a society for the attainment of its end is an act of jurisdiction and requires that the official previously be invested with the power of jurisdiction by the society.

The sacrament of Penance is not only a sensible sign instituted by Christ to give grace, as is every sacrament, but it is also by its very nature from the institution of Christ a truly judicial act. Therefore, this sacrament by its very nature requires, for its valid administration, that the minister be possessed not only of the power of orders, by which he is rendered capable of administering the sacraments and sanctifying man, but also that he be possessed of the power of jurisdiction, by which he is rendered capable of performing a judicial act and ruling man for the attainment of the end of the society. The reason, then, that jurisdiction is required in a confessor for the valid administration of the sacrament of Penance is that this sacrament is a truly judicial as well as sacramental action and can be exercised only upon one who is subject to the judge.[1]

One need not examine very closely into the nature of this sacrament as instituted by Christ, to discover that it was intended by the Divine Master to be administered *per modum judicii*. According to the Council of Trent [2] Christ principally instituted this sacrament when he said: "Receive ye the Holy Ghost. Whose sins you shall forgive, they are forgiven them; and whose sins you shall retain, they are retained";[3] for by these words He conferred on the Apostles and their legitimate successors the power of remitting and retaining sins. This power by its nature demands that it be exercised prudently and not indiscriminately. But to be exercised prudently, it must be exercised as a judicial act, investigating the dispositions of the penitent and the matter to be remitted or retained, and also passing a juridical sentence remitting or retaining the sins of the penitent and imposing the satisfaction to be fulfilled. If this sacrament, therefore, must be administered as a judicial act, it is necessary that the confessor be invested with the power of jurisdiction or rule over the subject on whom he passes judgment. So the Council of Trent [4] later states:

Quoniam igitur natura et ratio judicii illud exposcit, ut sententia in subditos dumtaxat fertur, persuasum semper

---
[1] Pesch, *Praelectiones Dogmaticae*, VII, n. 420.
[2] Sess. XIV, *de poenitentia*, c. 1.
[3] John XX, 22.
[4] Sess. IV, *de poenitentia*, c. 7. Cf. also IV Council of Lateran, Ch. XXI; Council of Florence, *Decretum pro Armenis*, apud Denzinger n. 699; St. Thos. *Suppl.*, p. 3ª, q. 8, a. 4.

in Ecclesia Dei fuit et verissimum esse Synodus haec confirmat, nullius momenti absolutionem eam esse debere, quam sacerdos in eum profert, in quam ordinariam aut subdelegatam non habet jurisdictionem.

So it can be seen that the power to forgive sins received by the priest in ordination is a remote power and exists only *in habitu,* inasmuch as in ordination the priest receives from Christ the power of absolving from sin but does not receive subjects over whom he can exercise this power. But jurisdiction is a proximate power, by which the power of forgiving sins received in ordination is brought *ex habitu in actum* and the priest is given the ability to exercise the power conferred upon him in ordination, on the subject now assigned to him.[5] Thus, St. Bonaventure compares the jurisdiction of a confessor to the motive force or the hand which moves a key in a door, so that if this force is lacking, even if the key is present, the door will never be opened.[6] An analogy to the jurisdiction necessary in the confessor may be found in the appointment or election of a civil magistrate, who upon his appointment or election receives the power *in habitu* of interpreting the law and applying it to individual cases; but he cannot exercise this power *in actu* until a definite district has been assigned to him and he takes his oath of office.[7] So also in the sacrament of Penance: the priest receives the power of absolving from sin in ordination, but since this sacramental action is

---

[5] Ferraris, *Prompta Bibliotheca Canonica,* verbum "Confessarius," n. 30. Cf. also Fagnanus, *Commentarium in Libros Decretalium,* lib. V, cap. 12 "Omnis," De Poenitentiis et Remissionibus, n. 84; Billot, *De Ecclesiae Sacramentis,* II, 214.

[6] *Opera Omnia,* pars IV, dist. 19, a. 2, q. 2.

[7] St. Thos. *Suppl.,* p. 3ª, q. 20, a. 1.

at the same time judicial, it can be exercised validly only upon subjects; so until these are assigned to him, the priest can be said to have the power of binding and loosing only *in habitu*.

So Canon 872 of the new Code states the principle that has always been the rule in the Church:

Praeter potestatem ordinis ad validam peccatorum absolutionem requiritur in ministro potestas jurisdictionis, sive ordinaria sive delegata, in poenitentem.

CHAPTER III

USE OF SECRET (AURICULAR) CONFESSION IN THE CHURCH

Because of the varying customs and the obscurity of historical documents in the history of the penitential discipline of the Church, it appears necessary to set forth, in the first place, the fact that secret or auricular confession was in use from the earliest ages of the Church; and, in the second place, the fact that the minister of this sacrament has always been invested with the power of jurisdiction in one form or another, although the early Fathers do not use the word *jurisdiction*, nor do they express their concept of this power in the exact terminology existing today.

The Council of Trent [1] asserts that although the nature of the power of forgiving or retaining sins makes confession by the penitent necessary, yet neither the divine nor any human law prescribes that this confession should be either public or private. Both modes of confessing one's sins are consonant with the requirements of the nature of the sacrament.[2] But the Council in this same chapter asserts that secret sacramental confession (i. e., made for the purpose of obtaining absolution) has been in use from the beginning in the Church and has always been commended by the oldest Fathers.

It is an admitted fact of history that private con-

[1] Sess. XIV, *de poenitentia,* c. 5.
[2] Pesch, *Praelectiones Dogmaticae,* VII, n. 210 seq.

fession was in general use in the Church after the sixth century;[3] therefore any doubt that can be cast upon this institution is confined to the earlier centuries. It will suffice, then, to trace briefly and in summary fashion the evidence for secret confession through the first five centuries of the Church.

Pope St. Leo the Great gives explicit testimony that private confession was in use in the fifth century, when, hearing that some priests read publicly the sins of penitents, he condemns this practice as contrary to the apostolic rule, *cum reatus conscientiarum sufficiat solis sacerdotibus indicare confessione secreta.*[4]

Almost as explicit is the testimony of Basil in the fourth century, who states: *"Mulieres adulterio pollutas, et ob pietatem confitentes, aut quoquomodo convictas publicari patres nostri noluerunt, ne causam mortis praebeamus convictis."*[5] In the same century in the West, Paulinus, the deacon of St. Ambrose, in his life of the Saint, affirms that he heard confessions which are presumed to be secret, since he (Paulinus) adds: *"Causas autem criminum quae illi confitebantur, nulli nisi domino soli, apud quem intercedebat, loquebatur."*[6] This is confirmed by the existence of the office of Canon Penitentiary in the East at least, whose office, according to many, was to hear secret sacramental confessions.[7] If this is true, this practice may be traced back as early as 251 A. D., since this is

---

[3] Watkins, *A History of Penance,* II, p. 755.
[4] Epistola 168, *ad episcopos Companiae,* Migne, P. L. LIV, 1210.
[5] *Epistola Canonica prima,* Can. 34, Migne, P.G. XXXII, 727.
[6] P. L. XIV, 40.
[7] Batiffol, "Les origines de la penitence," in *Etudes d'hist. et de theol. positive,* p. 149; Morinus, *Comm. Hist. de Discip. in Administratione Sac. Poenit.* lib. VI, cap. XXII; Watkins, *op. cit.,* I, p. 353.

the date which Socrates gives as the time when "the Bishops by the ecclesiastical rule appointed in addition the priest penitentiary, etc." [8] A similar office was established by Pope Marcellus at Rome about the year 308 when he assigned twenty-five priests to so-called *titles*. According to the learned editor of the *Liber Pontificalis*, it was part of the duty of these priests to hear confessions and assign penances.[9]

In the second homily on Psalm XXXVII, Origen, writing in the third century, has a passage with regard to the choice of a person to whom one can confess, and the confession is certainly presupposed to be secret: *"Tantummodo circumspice diligentius, cui debeas confiteri peccatum tuum. Proba prius medicum, cui debeas causam languoris exponere . . . et sequaris, si intellexerit et praeviderit, talem esse languorem tuum, qui in conventu totius ecclesiae exponi debeat et curari, ex quo fortassis et ceteri aedificari poterunt et tu ipse facile sanari."* [10] From this passage it can hardly be doubted that Origen speaks of secret confession as distinct from public confession and public penance.[11]

St. Cyprian also gives testimony to the existence of secret confession in the third century when he writes: *"quamvis nullo sacrificii aut libelli facinore constricti, quoniam tamen de hoc vel cogitaverunt, hoc ipsum apud sacerdotes Dei dolenter et simpliciter confitentes, exomologesin conscientiae faciunt, animi sui pondus exponunt . . . ."* [12]

---

[8] Socrates, *Historia Ecclesiastica*, lib. V, cap. 19, P. G. LXVII, 614.
[9] (Ed. Duchesne, 1886), I, 164 seq.
[10] P. G. XII, 1386.
[11] Pesch, *Praelect. Dog.*, VII, n. 213.
[12] *De Lapsis*, c. 28, P. L. IV, 503.

Earlier witnesses for the practice of secret confession could be quoted with some authority, but their testimony is not clear and is open to discordant interpretations. Some authorities interpret these early documents on the confession of sin as referring to the practice of public confession made before the whole community; others interpret them to mean private confession to a priest; while still others assert that these documents allude to the practice of confessing one's sin to God alone. In truth, it cannot be determined to which of these practices the early testimonies bear witness, for most of them can be interpreted as referring to any of the practices mentioned.

But from the testimonies cited above, it can hardly be denied that private confession was in use among both the Greeks and the Latins as early as the third century; and since no trace of any change in this matter can be found, can it not be licitly inferred that this practice has come down from apostolic times as Pope St. Leo teaches? The scarcity of documentary evidence in no way argues against this contention, because many early documents have not come down to us; nor does the lack of explicit testimony repudiate this position, for the early Fathers were forced to write, regulate, and legislate on the more troublesome practice of public penance and public confession and therefore made little reference to the less burdensome and more easily regulated institution of private confession so evidently necessary for the obtaining of absolution.

Therefore, is it not possible to conclude with the Council of Trent that secret auricular confession was in use from the beginning in the Church?

In the first four centuries in the Church, therefore, the procedure seems to have been:

1. A confession of sins by the penitent privately and afterward, in some cases, followed by a public confession;
2. A public exomologesis, or ordered course of public humiliation;
3. A reconciliation or absolution—ordinarily public.

In the two following centuries, the practices of individual churches differed, but practically all the churches retained secret confession; and in the East the tendency was to private penance and private reconciliation, while in the West public penance and public reconciliation were generally maintained.

These general lines were followed until the Celtic system of private confession, private penance, and private reconciliation was introduced on the continent of Europe about the seventh century and gradually clashed with and superseded the ancient system of public penance and public reconciliation.[13]

[13] Watkins, *op. cit.*, II, pp. 770, 771.

CHAPTER IV

THE MINISTER OF PENANCE AND HIS JURISDICTION UNDER THE FORMER DISCIPLINE

In the First Four Centuries

The diversity of practice, the scarcity of explicit statements, and the confusing interpretations of existing documents render it difficult to trace the history of the minister of this sacrament through the early ages of the Church. It can be definitely stated, however, that in the first three centuries in the West the bishop alone, except in cases of emergency, was the minister of reconciliation [1] (i. e., the bishop alone gave the absolution at the end of the period of public penance); but whether or not this was sacramental absolution, or merely ecclesiastical reconciliation, is disputed.[2] But the fact that the bishop alone was the one who reconciled the penitents, except in emergencies, is beyond dispute. It will be sufficient to quote the earliest explicit testimonies to that effect. Tertullian, in his *De Poenitentia,* speaks of the penance that precedes Baptism as inviting the clemency of God, and continues: *"salva illa poenitentiae specie post fidem, quae aut levioribus delictis veniam ab episcopo consequi poterit,*

---
[1] Watkins, *op. cit.,* I, p. 485. Oberhauser, *Jus Ecclesiasticum,* pars II, tit. VI, cap. VII, n. 44. Van Espen, *Operum Juris Eccl. Universi,* pars II, tit. VI, cap. VI, n. 1.
[2] Rauschen, *Eucharist and Penance,* p. 219 seq.

aut majoribus irremissibilibus a Deo solo." [3] It might be mentioned that Tertullian, tending toward Montanism, denies that the Church can forgive certain grave sins.

St. Cyprian, about the year 250, complaining that certain priests communicated with the lapsed before they had fulfilled their penance, gives a valuable insight into the existing procedure, in a letter addressed to the clergy of Carthage:

Nam cum in minoribus peccatis agant peccatores poenitentiam justo tempore, et, secundum disciplinae ordinem, ad exomologesim veniant, et per manus impositionem episcopi et cleri jus communicationis accipiant . . . . nunc crudo tempore, persecutione adhuc perseverante, nondum restituta Ecclesiae ipsius pace, ad communicationem admittuntur et offertur nomine eorum, et nondum poenitentia acta, nondum exomologesi facta, nondum manu eis ab episcopo et clero imposita, Eucharistia illis datur, cum scriptum sit: Qui ederit panem aut biberit calicem Domini indigne, reus erit corporis et sanguinis Domini.[4]

And, again, in his letter addressed to the people, he states:

Audio quosdam de Presbyteris nec Evangelii memores, nec quid ad nos martyres scripserint cogitantes, nec Episcopo honorem sacerdotii sui et cathedrae reservantes, jam cum lapsis communicare coepisse et offerre pro illis, et Eucharistiam dare, quando oporteat ad haec per ordinem perveniri. Nam cum in minoribus delictis, quae non in Deum committuntur, poenitentia agatur justo tempore, et Exhomologesis fiat, inspecta vita ejus qui agit poenitentiam, nec ad communicationem quis venire possit, nisi prius illi ab episcopo et clero manus fuerit

[3] *De Poenitentia,* c. 18, P. L. II, 1017.
[4] *Epistola IX,* P. L. IV, 257.

imposita, quanto magis in his gravissimis et extremis delictis, caute omnia et moderate secundum disciplinam Domini observari oportet.[5]

This same fact, that the bishop was the ordinary minister of reconciliation, is evidenced by all the earliest writers whenever the subject is approached, so that now it is accepted by all scholars.[6]

It is also certain that in the East generally, and in many places in the West, at the end of the third and beginning of the fourth century, it is the priest who heard the secret confessions of sinners before they were admitted to the status of penitents and finally reconciled by the bishop. The earliest evidence of this practice in the East is found in Origen, who, in commenting on Leviticus, states:

Est adhuc et septima, licet dura et laboriosa, per poenitentiam remissio peccatorum, cum lavat peccator in lacrymis stratum suum, et fiunt ei lacrymae suae panes die ac nocte, et cum non erubescit sacerdoti Domini indicare peccatum suum, et quaerere medicinam, secundum eum qui ait: Dixi, Pronuntiabo adversum me injustitiam meam Domino et tu remisisti impietatem cordis mei. In quo impletur et illud, quod Jacobus apostolus dicit: Si quis autem infirmatur, vocet presbyteros Ecclesiae, et imponant ei manus, ungentes eum oleo in nomine Domini, et oratio fidei salvabit infirmum et si in peccatis fuerit, remittentur ei.[7]

Origen here indicates that one submitting to the penitential discipline at Caesarea about the middle of

[5] *Epistola XI*, P. L. IV, 263. Cf. also *Epis. X*, P. L. IV, 260; and *Epis. XXX*, P. L. IV, 313.
[6] Rauschen, *op cit.*, p. 219.
[7] *Hom. 2 in Levit.*, P. G. XII, 417.

the third century, confessed secretly to "the priest of the Lord," who passed judgment upon him and assigned the penance he was to perform. "This procedure," says Watkins, "was probably normal."[8] Whether or not the priest absolved him privately and the subsequent reconciliation by the bishop was only a public reconciliation with the Church, is disputed,[9] but it matters not for our purpose, since at any rate the priest must pass a judgment on the penitent regarding his disposition, etc., and assign a penance to him even if he does not absolve him. Some doubt can be raised as to whether the term *sacerdoti Domini* is to be taken as referring only to bishops or as including priests.

It would not appear from the Latin of Rufinus, in which the passage has come down to us, which position in this matter corresponded with the mind of the ancient author. But Origen's own statement, that in this is fulfilled the instruction of St. James, who speaks certainly of presbyters, argues for the position that he (Origen) includes the presbyters among those who heard the secret confessions of the penitent. This is supported by the fact that Socrates states that at this time, in the East generally, and in Constantinople in particular, *"episcopi poenitentiarium presbyterum albo ecclesiastico adjecerunt ut qui post baptismum lapsi essent, coram presbytero ad eam rem constituto, delicta sua confiterentur"*;[10] and St. Cyprian allows priests in cases of emergency, not only to hear secret con-

[8] *Op. cit.*, I, p. 137.
[9] Rauschen, p. 219 seq.
[10] Socrates, *Historia Ecclesiastica*, lib. V, cap. 19, P. G. LXVII, 614. Sozomen, *Historia Ecclesiastica*, lib. VII, cap. 16, P. G. LXVII, 1458.

fession, but also to reconcile privately.[11] Likewise, half a century later, Pope Marcellus at Rome assigned twenty-five priests to so-called *titles,* and it was part of the duty of these priests, according to Duchesne, to hear secret confessions and assign penances.[12] This practice of allowing the priest to hear the secret confessions, while the bishop alone reconciled publicly, then became more and more general as the years went by, as witnessed by St. Gregory at Nyssa[13] and Innocent I (c. 416 A. D.). The latter states: *"Caeterum de aestimando pondere delictorum sacerdotis est judicare, ut attendat ad confessionem poenitentis et ad fletus atque lacrymas corrigentis; ac tum jubere dimitti, cum viderit congruam satisfactionem. Sane si quis in aegritudinem inciderit, atque usque ad desperationem devenerit, ei est ante tempus Paschae relaxandum, ne de saeculo absque communione discedat."* [14]

It is clear that the word *sacerdos* here includes priests as well as bishops, for in the following paragraph of the same letter Innocent himself draws a distinction between bishop (*episcopus*) and priest (*sacerdos*). When speaking of the holy oil of Chrism, he says: *"quod ab episcopo confectum, non solum sacerdotibus sed et omnibus uti Christianis licet,"* [15] referring, not to the sacrament of Extreme Unction, but to a custom of anointing the sick with holy oil.

Henceforth, it is the common practice to confess secretly to a priest, and even private reconciliation by

[11] *Epistola XII, ad Presbyteros et diaconos,* P. L. IV, 265.
[12] *Liber Pontificalis* (Ed. Duchesne, 1886), I, 164 seq.
[13] *Epistola Canonica ad Letorium,* P. G. XLV, 233.
[14] *Epistola XX, ad Decentium episcopum Eugubinum,* P. L. XX, 559.
[15] *Ibid.*

a priest began to be extended to cases other than extreme emergency.[16]

From these evidences it appears that the bishop always held full power [17] over the administration of the sacrament of Penance, and it would seem that he alone, at first, was the sole minister of this sacrament.[18] When the priest acted even as the partial minister of the sacrament (i. e., as the one who heard the confession, judged the dispositions, and assigned the penance, prescinding from the question as to whether or not he gave absolution), he in this case acted only in virtue of a power delegated to him by the bishop.[19]

This power which the bishop delegated was not the power of orders, for the priest in ordination always has received the power of remitting and retaining sins. The earliest forms of ordination extant bear witness to the transmission to priests of the power of forgiving and retaining sins. The *Canones Hippolyti* have, in the prayer used for the consecration of a bishop, the following words: "Grant to him, O Lord, the episcopate and a clement spirit and the power to remit sins." Changing only the word "episcopate,"

---

[16] Thomassinus, *Vetus et Nova Ecclesiae Disciplina,* pars I, lib. II, cap. XXIII, n. 14.

[17] C. 5, C. XXVI, q. 6: Aurelius episcopus (Cartagenensi, 390) dixit: "Si quisquam in periculo fuerit constitutus—si episcopus absens fuerit, debet utique presbyter consulere episcopum et sic periclitantem ejus precepto reconciliare." Item ex concilio Cartagenensi II, Can. 4: "Ab universis Episcopis dictum est . . . reconciliare quemquam in publica Missa presbyteris inconsulto episcopo, non licere."

[18] Watkins, *op. cit.,* I, p. 485 seq. Oberhauser, *Jus Eccl.,* pars II, tit. VI, cap, VII, n. 44. Van Espen, *Operum Juris Eccl. Universi,* pars II, tit. VI, cap. VI, n. 1.

[19] Oberhauser, *op. cit.,* pars II, tit. VI, cap. VII, n. 60.

the Canons appoint the same forms to be used in the ordination of the presbyter.[20]

If the presbyter in ordination received the power of remitting and retaining sins, the power which was delegated to him by the bishop, enabling him to hear sacramental confessions, was nothing more or less than the power of jurisdiction, the public power of ruling the faithful in respect to their supernatural end, the power of passing judgment on a subject. Thus, it was not because they lacked the power of orders, but because they lacked the power of jurisdiction, that St. Cyprian complains, in his letter to the people of Carthage, quoted above, that those presbyters who reconciled the *lapsed* have not reserved to the bishop, "the honor of his priesthood and chair"—"*nec Episcopo honorem sacerdotii sui et cathedrae reservantes.*" [21]

So, also, it is of the power of jurisdiction that Canon 30 of the Council of Hippo, in 393, speaks, when it ruled that priests cannot absolve (i.e., reconcile) any penitent without the consent of the bishop, except when the bishop is absent and in case of necessity.[22] Evidently the priest did not lack the power to absolve, since he needed only the consent of the bishop, but what he lacked was the power of jurisdiction, or the authority to pass judgment upon the penitent.

From these evidences, it seems quite certain that the principle of jurisdiction and its necessity in a confessor was recognized even in the early Church

[20] Watkins, *op. cit.*, I, p. 484.
[21] *Epistola, XI*, P. L. IV, 263.
[22] Mansi, *Sacrorum Conciliorum Nova et Amplissima Collectio*, III, 923.

notwithstanding its divergent and varying discipline. There is no justification, therefore, for the statement of Lea, that up to the twelfth century "there is no trace of the existence of jurisdiction as a recognized principle." [23] This author apparently maliciously contends that the idea of jurisdiction as necessary in a confessor is a product of Scholasticism; and he seems to have deliberately set out to make the beginning of the restriction of jurisdiction appear to be the origin of the idea of penitential jurisdiction. It is true that the clear notion of this power existing today, had its birth in the mind of the Schoolmen, who applied to it, as to many other points of canonical law and practice, a definite terminology; but from what has been shown in the foregoing pages, it can hardly be doubted that even in its earliest age the Church has recognized the necessity of jurisdiction in the confessor.

Traces of the fundamental division of this power into ordinary and delegated jurisdiction can be found even in the very early ages of the Church, although not expressed in the scholastic terminology of the twelfth century. Certainly the power exercised by the bishop over the sacramental tribunal corresponds quite accurately with our modern notion of ordinary jurisdiction; and the license granted to priests to hear the sacramental confessions of the faithful, to pass judgment on their dispositions, and to assign penances to them, to say nothing of the power granted to absolve (reconcile) sinners privately in some circumstances, is nothing other than the delegated power of jurisdic-

[23] *A History of Auricular Confession and Indulgences,* Vol. I, ch. x, p. 274.

tion. If the power granted to the priests penitentiaries in the East and to the priests of the *titles* at Rome, does not correspond exactly to our modern notion of ordinary jurisdiction (even if vicarious), still it is something very much akin to it and perhaps is the first evidence of such a division in the history of penitential jurisdiction.

John Morinus [24] is of the opinion that in the early Church there existed no clear distinction between the external forum and the internal, and that therefore in the early Church censures and public penance were identical. Devoti declares that this opinion is altogether false and contrary to the ancient discipline of the Church, quoting many authorities and examples to prove that public penance was distinct from censures in the early Church, and *"ecclesiam semper habuisse forum exterius ab interiori et poenitentiali distinctum."* [25] The latter opinion, that such a distinction was recognized very early in the Church, seems more in keeping with the early discipline and subsequent development. This opinion is also supported by the fact that as early as 390, there appeared the expression *jure fori et jure poli,* used by Aurelius, bishop of Carthage.[26] Hence, it appears very probable that some distinction of fora was recognized in the early Church, and consequently it seems probable that very early in the history of the Church the power of jurisdiction was divided into jurisdiction for the external and internal fora, and naturally the jurisdiction

---

[24] *Commentarius Historicus de Discip. in Administratione Sac. Poenit.,* lib. V, cap. XXVI, n. 19.
[25] Devoti, *Institutionum Canonicarum,* III, tit. I, § 13, n. 1.
[26] C. 43, C. XVII, q. 4.

required in the minister of the sacrament of Penance was merely jurisdiction for the internal forum.

In the Fifth and Sixth Centuries

During the next two centuries in the East, the tendency toward a totally private discipline of penance, noticed earlier, grew more and more general until hardly any trace of the old discipline of public penance and public reconciliation remained. Monasteries of holy monks, living under very strict discipline, flourished, while the secular clergy, leading loose lives, began to lose their hold on the people. Accordingly, in stress of conscience the lay people began to seek advice from the holy monastics and to make their sacramental confessions to them.[27] These monks received their jurisdiction from the bishop at ordination,[28] and the practice continued under the bishops' sanction until it grew into a custom. But this custom developed into an abuse whereby monks who were never ordained priests essayed to hear sacramental confessions, so that the Council in Trullo, in 680 A. D., was forced to declare: *"Nota quod qui sine Episcopali permissione hominum confessiones excipiunt sacrati monachi, male faciunt, multo autem magis non sacrati. Ii enim nec cum permissione Episcopi possunt tale quidquam exercere."* [29]

In the West, the old system of private confession to a priest, who assigned a penance which now might be semi-private, but not without some marks of pub-

[27] Rauschen, *Eucharist and Penance*, p. 247.
[28] Thomassinus, *op. cit.*, pars I, lib. II, cap. XII, n. 9.
[29] *Ibid., loc. cit.*

licity, with final reconciliation performed publicly by the bishop, still remained generally in force.[30] But, during this period in the British Isles there sprung up a wholly private system of penitential discipline which included private confession, private satisfaction, and private absolution. As yet this system had not spread to the continent, but in the following century, the seventh, traces of this system are found in Europe, spreading from the religious houses founded by the Celtic monastics.[31]

From the Seventh Century to the Council of Trent

The use of this private system of penance spread rapidly through Europe during the next two centuries and finally supplanted the old system. The principle of private penance for occult sins and public penance for public sins then became the rule, and this marks the intermediate stage between the old discipline and the subsequent system of a wholly private discipline. This developed into the first step toward episcopal reservations, since only the bishop could grant reconciliation to public penitents.[32] Thus, the penitential jurisdiction of priests began to be restricted *quoad materiam* about the beginning of the ninth century.

With the more definite establishment of parishes about the seventh century, the parish priest received jurisdiction for hearing the sacramental confessions

[30] Watkins, *op. cit.*, II, p. 751 seq.
[31] *Ibid.*, p. 758 seq.
[32] Thomassinus, *op. cit.*, pars I, lib. II, cap XI, n. 6, and cap. XII, n. 1; Dargin, *Reserved Cases*, p. 7; Oberhauser, *op. cit.*, pars II, tit. VI, cap. VI, n. 44.

of his subjects by the very assignment to the benefice.[33] But since the monastics had not the care of souls committed to them, they could only exercise the priestly power of binding and loosing by delegation from the bishop.[34] The parish priest then came to be regarded as the only one who had jurisdiction over his parishioners, so that the parishioner was limited in his choice of a confessor to his parish priest or to another only with the permission of his pastor. This practice continued and became the rule. Ahyto, bishop of Basil in 810, prescribed that those setting out on a journey should confess to their own parish priest, *"quia a proprio episcopo suo aut sacerdote ligandi aut exsolvendi sunt, non ab extraneo."*[35] This same legislation is found in the *De Disciplinis Ecclesiasticis Regionis Prumiensis Abbatis* of the same century, wherein it states that

Presbyteri debent admonere plebem sibi subjectam ut omnis qui se sentit mortifero peccati vulnere sauciatum . . . ad proprium sacerdotem venire festinet . . . et humiliter confiteatur.[36]

Down through the later centuries this was the practice almost everywhere. It is found in the *dictum Gratiani* to the chapter "Adicimus," where it is stated:

Quod vero penitentiam dare prohibentus, inde est quod nulli sacerdotum licet parochianorum alterius ligare vel solvere.[37]

---

[33] Van Espen, *op. cit.,* pars II, tit. VI, cap. VI, n. 2; Badii,*Institutiones Juris Canonici,* I, note to n. 43.
[34] Ferraris, *Prompta Bibliotheca,* verbum "Approbatio," n. 102.
[35] P. L. CXV, 14.
[36] P. L. CXXXII, 245; cf. also *ibid.,* 253, and XCVII, 845.
[37] C. 19, C. XVI, q. 1.

This legislation restricting the jurisdiction of the confessor culminated in the famous decree of the fourth Council of Lateran in 1215 *Omnis utriusque sexus*,[38] prescribing annual confession to one's "*proprius sacerdos.*"

This decree made general law what before was universal practice. For many centuries parish priests had been forbidden to hear the sacramental confession of any but their own subjects, and the subjects in turn were unable to be absolved by any one but their own pastor. If one wished to confess to another, he must obtain the license of his own pastor or the bishop, and the one to whom he confessed then received delegated jurisdiction over this penitent from his proper pastor or bishop. Concurrent with this practice, the custom had arisen whereby one could obtain the privilege of electing his own confessor; and he who was elected, *ipso facto* obtained jurisdiction over this particular penitent. It was to this custom that Boniface VIII (1294-1308) referred when he declared:

Si episcopus suo subdito concesserit, ut sibi possit idoneum eligere confessorem: ille quem is eligerit, in casibus qui eidem episcopo specialiter reservantur, nullam habet penitus potestatem, quum in generali concessione illa non veniant, quae non esset quis verisimiliter in specie concessurus. Nulla quoque potest consuetudine introduci quod aliquis praeter sui superioris licentiam confessorem sibi eligere valeat, qui cum possit solvere vel ligare.[39]

As this practice and legislation developed, it more and more restricted the power of the monastics. They were forbidden to hear the confessions of any but those

[38] C. 12, X, *De Poenit. et Remiss.*, V. 38.
[39] C. 2, *De Poenit. et Remiss.*, V. 10, in VI.

of their own Order. So the forty-sixth chapter of the sixth Synod of Paris in 829 had explicitly ruled to this effect:

> Porro si sacerdotibus, id nonnisi in ecclesia coram sancto altari, astantibus haud procul testibus faciant. Nullo modo quippe videtur nobis convenire, ut Monachus, relicto monasterio suo, idcirco sanctimonialium monasterio adeat, ut confitentibus peccata sua modum poenitentiae imponat. Nec etiam illud videtur nobis congruum ut clerici et laici episcoporum et presbyterorum canonicorum judicia declinantes; monasteria monachorum expetant, ut ibi sacerdotibus monachis confessionem peccatorum suorum faciant; praesertim cum eisdem sacerdotibus monachis id facere fas non fit, exceptis his dumtaxat, qui sub monastico ordine secum in monasteriis degunt. Illis namque est confessio peccatorum facienda, a quibus subinde et modus poenitentiae et consilium salutis capiatur, et a quibus post tempora poenitentiae peracta, secundum canonicam institutionem, si episcopus jusserit, reconciliatio mercatur.[40]

This, Thomassinus states, marked the beginning of the long and bitter fight between the monastics and the seculars regarding the ministry of Penance. This disagreement continued through the following centuries and culminated, about the thirteenth century, in the granting of penitential jurisdiction over all the faithful to the Mendicants in the form of Papal privileges.[41]

These privileges subsequently were claimed by all regulars through communication. The first of these privileges seems to have been given by Gregory IX

---
[40] Mansi, *op. cit.*, XIV, 565.
[41] Van Espen, *op. cit.*, pars II, tit. VI, cap. V, n. 10.

in 1227 in a bull addressed to the *Praelates constituti per Angliam,* exhorting them

ut Fratres Praedicatores benigne recipiant, et populos sibi commissos sedulo admoneant, ut ex ore ipsorum verbi Dei semen devote suscipiant, et confiteantur, cum ipsis auctoritate nostra liceat confessiones audire, ac poenitentias injungere.[42]

These grants were continued and enlarged by subsequent pontiffs, but this served only to make the dispute more bitter between the bishops and pastors on the one hand, and the monastics on the other. Boniface VIII, hoping to end the discord, issued his constitution *Super Cathedram,*[43] ruling that the superiors of the Order should designate those to whom the office of confessor was to be granted, and that these in turn should seek the license of the prelates in whose dioceses they were to exercise their privilege. But if the prelates refused this permission, it would be valid and licit to proceed without it.

In his constitution *Inter cunctas,* Benedict XI[44] took away the restrictions of Boniface and allowed the monks to administer the sacrament of Penance anywhere without seeking any further permission of the bishops or pastors in whose territory they ministered. Clement V[45] restored the restrictions of Boniface once more, and the fight continued down to the Council of Trent.[46]

When these privileges became widespread, the people

[42] *Ibid.*
[43] C. 2, *De Sepul.,* III, 6, Extrav. Com.
[44] C. 1, *De Priv.,* V. 7, Extrav. Com.
[45] C. 2, *De Sepul.,* III, 7, Clem.
[46] Van Espen, *op. cit.,* pars II, tit. VI, cap. 5, n. 10.

naturally thought that the restrictions of the fourth Lateran Council, requiring their confession to their *"proprius sacerdos,"* were no longer in force. So Martin IV (1281) had to declare that it was still necessary for each one to confess at least once in the year, during the Paschal season, to his own parish priest, or obtain his license to confess to another.[47] The implication was that at all other times one could confess to any other who had jurisdiction over him, i. e., from the Pope, his bishop, or his pastor. This was the first official sanction given to the new custom of confessing to one other than one's own pastor. But even the obligation to confess to one's proper pastor at least during Easter time, began soon to be disregarded. In 1475, Sixtus IV declared that the Mendicants should not preach that parishioners are not obliged to confess to their own parish priest at least during the Paschal time.[48] From this time down to 1516, various local councils and synods exhorted pastors to grant without difficulty the license to subjects to confess to another approved priest.[49] The practice then seems to have fallen into desuetude, and the obligation of confessing to one's proper pastor to have been abolished by custom, when the people began to confess to other approved confessors even during the Paschal time with the tacit or presumed permission of their pastor.[50] In 1516, Leo X appears to have condoned this obligation when he declared that those who confessed to priests approved by the Ordinary,

[47] *Ibid.* n. 14.
[48] C. 2, *De Treuga et Pace,* I, 9, Extrav. Com.
[49] Van Espen, *op. cit.,* pars II, tit. VI, cap. V, n. 25.
[50] Oberhauser, *op cit.,* pars II, tit. VI, cap. VII, n. 58.

or even to those unduly refused approval, must be thought to have satisfied the Paschal precept.[51]

The Council of Trent, although confirming the obligation of annual confession, is silent regarding that phase of the precept demanding the administration by one's own pastor.[52] St. Alphonsus, finally, mentions that at his time there is no obligation to confess to one's own pastor at any time.[53]

From the Council of Trent to the Code

The great reforming council held at Trent in 1545 summarized the former legislation and instituted some important changes in the existing discipline. It decreed that the absolution of the priest was not a *"nudum ministerium . . . sed ad instar actus judicialis quo ab ipso velut a judice sententia pronunciatur."* [54] Therefore, absolution given by a priest *"qui non habet ordinariam aut subdelegatam jurisdictionem, esse nullius momento."* [55] The Council further points out that this jurisdiction could be limited in different ways: *quoad materiam,* so that certain graver crimes were reserved to the judgment of the bishop;[56] and *quoad personas,* so that a confessor could absolve only those over whom he had jurisdiction.[57]

This jurisdiction over penitents was acquired for-

[51] Leo X, const. *Dum intra mentis,* 19 dec. 1516, § 6, Fontes n. 72.
[52] Sess. XIV, *de poenitentia,* c. 5; cf also Clemens X, const. *Superna,* 21 jun. 1670, § 5, Fontes n. 246.
[53] *Theologia Moralis,* VI, n. 574.
[54] Sess. XIV, *de poenitentia,* c. 6.
[55] *Ibid.,* c. 7.
[56] *Ibid.*
[57] *Ibid.*

merly by seculars either by the assignment of a parochial benefice or by the delegation of the bishop or pastor of the penitent. It was acquired by regulars over all penitents from the grants of the Popes; but hitherto, to use it, he must notify the bishop of the place where he is to hear confessions, though, whether the bishop consents or not, he may validly and licitly exercise his power.[58] But the Council now rules:

Quamvis presbyteri in sua Ordinatione a peccatis absolvendi potestatem accipiant, decernit tamen sancta Synodus nullum, etiam regularem, posse confessiones saecularium, etiam sacerdotum audire, nec ad id idoneum reputari, nisi aut parochiale beneficium aut ab episcopis per examen, si illis videbitur esse necessarium, aut alias idoneus judicetur, et approbationem, quae gratis detur, obtineat: privilegiis et consuetudine quacumque, etiam immemorabili, non obstantibus.[59]

Similar legislation had been decreed by Leo X, but it was not so absolute in its scope or character.[60]

Now the license of the bishop of former ages became known as approbation and required the bishop to judge the fitness of the priest before granting his approval. This approbation differed from the conferring of jurisdiction, for the former was an act of the intellect authentically declaring a priest fit to hear confessions, while the latter was an act of the will by which the superior gave the priest power over certain subjects.[61] The conferring of jurisdiction has always

[58] C. 2, *De Sepul.*, III, 7, in Clem.
[59] Sess. XXIII, *De Reform,* c. 15.
[60] Leo X, const. *Dum intra mentis,* 19 dec. 1516, n. 6, Fontes n. 72.
[61] Ferraris, *Prompta Bibliotheca,* verbum "Approbatio," nn. 1, 2, 3. Benedict. XIV, ep. encycl. *Apostolicum Ministerium,* 30 maii 1753, § 8, Fontes n. 425.

presupposed the approval by the bishop of the priest's fitness, for this is required by the natural law; but the legislation of Trent, for purposes of reformation, emphasized the necessity of approbation, although both approbation and the conferring of jurisdiction usually were given simultaneously by the bishop. Because of this practice of granting approbation and jurisdiction at the same time, the two became so identified that the terms were almost regarded as synonymous.

Still, the two terms theoretically were distinct, for it was possible that the bishop should judge a priest fit to hear confessions and yet not actually assign any subjects to him. But in reality this would hardly ever occur, because of the practice of conferring both together. Theoretically there was another case in which the distinction became apparent, for the regulars still claimed that they received their jurisdiction over all penitents from the Pope, through their own superiors, in virtue of the Papal privileges; but now, for the validity of their absolutions, they also needed the approbation of the bishop in whose diocese they heard confessions. However, there was really no practical difference between approbation and jurisdiction.[62]

The legislation of Trent therefore can be seen to have effected many changes in the old discipline. First, for the validity of their absolutions, regulars hearing the confession of seculars now needed the approbation of the bishop of the place where they acted as confessors, even though they had obtained jurisdiction

[62] Ferraris, *op. et loc. cit.*, nn. 4, 5.

over all penitents from the Pope. The former discipline had obliged them merely to apply to the bishop for permission, and, having applied, they could validly and licitly exercise their office even if refused. Secondly, secular priests having a parochial benefice, *eo ipso* were regarded as approved, but could exercise the power of binding and loosing only upon their own subjects, since over these alone they had ordinary jurisdiction. Thirdly, the pastor could no longer delegate any other priest to hear the confession of his subject, as was formerly done when he gave permission to his subjects to confess to another; but now when he gave such permission, if it were ever sought, it was understood that the subject must confess to one who had been approved by the bishop for his diocese and to him only could the pastor give jurisdiction over this penitent.[63] Finally, all seculars, other than pastors, must obtain delegated jurisdiction and approbation from the bishop in whose diocese they are to hear confessions.

Thus, it can be seen that Trent left the whole administration of the sacrament of Penance in the hands of the bishop, regardless of whether the confessor was a secular priest or a regular. The approbation of the bishop was wholly territorial and was of no value outside of the territory of the approving bishop, so that a priest approved in one diocese could not hear confessions in another diocese without the approbation of the bishop of the diocese in which he was exer-

---

[63] Barbosa, *De Officiis et Potestate Episcopi*, pars II, alleg. 25; De Lugo, *Disputationes Scholasticae et Morales*, Disp. XXI, sect. 1, § 6.

cising his office. This was confirmed by Gregory XV,[64] Urban VIII,[65] and Clement X,[66] who even forbade regulars to hear the confession of a penitent outside his diocese who was a subject of the bishop who had approved him.

But in the diocese in which he was approved, a regular could absolve a penitent from any other diocese who came to him, because he had jurisdiction from the Pope which was not restricted to the confines of a definite territory.[67] Clement X[68] even allowed such a regular to absolve penitents of another diocese from cases reserved in their own diocese but not in the diocese of confession, as long as they did not leave their own diocese *in fraudem reservationis*.

If the Council of Trent made quite definite the extent of the power of the regulars, it cannot be said to have also definitized the power of the secular clergy, and soon many difficulties arose from this source. The parish priest needed no further approbation for hearing the confessions of his subjects than the assignment to his benefice, for he thereby obtained ordinary jurisdiction and it was presupposed that he was judged fit to hear confessions by the bishop when he was given the care of souls. So it was commonly conceded that a pastor could hear the confessions of his parishioners even outside the confines of his parish and diocese, since these were still his subjects and for these he

[64] Greg. XV, const. *Inscrutabili*, 5 febr. 1622, n. 1, Fontes n. 199.
[65] Urban VIII, const. *Cum sicut accepimus*, 12 sept. 1628, Fontes n. 208.
[66] Clemens X, const. *Superna*, 21 jun. 1670, n. 4, Fontes n. 246.
[67] Fagnanus, *Commentarium in libros Decretalium*, cap. "Omnis," de Poenit. et Remiss., n. 79.
[68] Clemens X, const. *Superna*, 21 jun. 1670, n. 7, Fontes n. 246.

38   JURISDICTION OF THE CONFESSOR

remained approved.[69] Other priests not having a parochial benefice needed to receive approbation and delegated jurisdiction from the bishop. This was usually granted for the whole diocese of the bishop.[70] This presented the situation of having pastors capable of absolving only their own parishioners, while others could hear and absolve penitents of the whole diocese. The custom then arose of regarding one with a parochial benefice in a diocese as approved for the whole diocese, and therefore capable of hearing confessions anywhere within his own diocese as long as he received jurisdiction over the members of the parish where he heard confessions from the pastor of that place.[71] This custom had the tacit approbation of the bishops and even the explicit approval of the Synod of Namur in 1659.[72] This custom remained in force in many places even up to the promulgation of the new Code of Canon Law.[73] Some theologians extended this practice so that a pastor from one diocese could be invited by a pastor into another diocese to hear confessions, and the extraneous priest needed to obtain no further approbation from the bishop of the place, since these theologians regarded him as approved for the whole Church.[74]

Since a pastor had jurisdiction only over his own parishioners, a difficulty arose as to the source of his jurisdiction over others who might present themselves

---

[69] Thomassinus, *Vet. et Nov. Eccl. Discip.*, pars IV, lib. I, cap. LXIX, n. 10.
[70] Van Espen, *Op. Jur. Eccl. Univ.*, pars II, tit. VI, cap. VI, n. 9.
[71] *Ibid., op. et loc. cit.*; St. Alphon. VI, n. 544.
[72] Tit. V, cap. VII, apud Mansi, XXXVI, 359.
[73] Sabetti-Barrett, *Compendium Theologiae Moralis*, p. 739; Motry, *Diocesan Faculties*, p. 92 seq.
[74] St. Alphon. VI, n. 544.

to him in his own parish. Most theologians claimed that he acquired this jurisdiction implicitly either from the Pope or their respective bishops, since these superiors tolerated the custom of penitents confessing to any approved confessor without obtaining any explicit license from their own pastor.[75]

The legislation of Trent marks the end of the development of the legislation regarding the jurisdiction of the confessor up to the promulgation of the new Code. Henceforth, official pronouncements of the Holy See took the form of interpretations of the laws of the Council of Trent or answers to difficulties presented to the Roman Congregations. But in general these same principles obtained until the promulgation of the new Code.

[75] St. Alphon., VI, n. 569.

CHAPTER V

THE PRESENT LAW OF THE CODE

PRELIMINARY REMARKS

Before setting forth the present law on penitential jurisdiction, it is necessary to note that the Code is silent on one point that was greatly stressed by the Council of Trent, viz., the approbation of the bishop. Under the laws of Trent, this approbation, together with the power of orders and the power of jurisdiction, formed the three essential elements of a valid absolution from sin. The reason for this legislation was that Trent wished to place in the hands of the bishop full control over the administration of the sacrament of Penance so as better to effect the reformation of the clergy. This purpose, then, necessitated their requiring, for valid absolution, an explicit judgment by the bishop regarding the fitness of the confessor for his office because not all who heard confessions in his diocese were obliged to obtain their jurisdiction from that Ordinary, as, e.g., regulars who had obtained jurisdiction over all the faithful from the Pope.[1]

The Code, in ruling that all priests, both secular and religious, who do not receive ordinary jurisdiction by reason of their office, must obtain delegated

[1] St. Alphon., VI, n. 542.

jurisdiction for hearing the confessions of secular people from the Ordinary of the place where the confessions are heard, leaves the same control of the administration of this sacrament in the hands of the bishop, and yet eliminates the necessity of any explicit approbation regarding the fitness of the priest for the office of confessor. Of course, the bishop still remains obliged by the natural law to assure himself of the fitness of the priest before granting him jurisdiction, and this obligation is expressly laid down in the Code.[2] But that explicit judgment of the bishop regarding the fitness of the priest, which was technically known as approbation, and which was regarded as an essential element for the validity of sacramental absolution, henceforth is no longer necessary. It now suffices that the confessor possess ordinary jurisdiction or jurisdiction delegated by the Ordinary of the place where he is exercising his office. Having this jurisdiction, his absolutions are valid even though the bishop knew that he was unfit to hear confessions and thereby sinned in conferring jurisdiction upon him.[3] Therefore, in places where the Code uses such expressions as *"ad audiendas confessiones approbati in aliquo loco,"*[4] and *"ad confessiones non approbati,"*[5] the word *approbati* is to be understood to mean "possessed of jurisdiction."[6]

[2] Can. 877.
[3] *Irish Eccl. Record*, Series V., Vol. XI (1918), p. 15.
[4] Can. 881, § 1.
[5] Can. 882.
[6] Vermeersch-Creusen, *Epitome*, II, n. 143; Cappello, *De Sacramentis*, II, n. 376; Motry, *Diocesan Faculties*, p. 96; Genicot-Salsmans, *Theo. Mor.*, II. n. 326.

ARTICLE I

Ordinary Jurisdiction

The Code has not changed the traditional notion of ordinary jurisdiction and describes it as that jurisdiction which is annexed to an office by law.[7]

Canon 873 of the Code enumerates those who have ordinary jurisdiction for hearing confessions. The canon reads:

§ 1. Ordinaria jurisdictione ad confessiones excipiendas pro universa Ecclesia, praeter Romanum Pontificem, potiuntur S. R. E. Cardinales; pro suo quisque territorio Ordinarius loci, et parochus aliique qui loco parochi sunt.

§ 2. Hac eadem jurisdictione gaudent etiam canonicus poenitentiarius ecclesiae quoque collegiatae, ad normam can. 401, § 1, et Superiores religiosi exempti pro suis subditis, ad normam constitutionum.

§ 3. Haec jurisdictio cessat amissione officii, ad normam can. 183, et, post sententiam condemnatoriam vel declaratoriam, excommunicatione, suspensione ab officio, interdicto.

The Pope, Cardinals, and Local Ordinaries

The Pope and members of the College of Cardinals have ordinary jurisdiction for the internal sacramental forum over all the faithful and may grant valid absolution from sin everywhere in the world to any member of the Church. The local Ordinary has this same jurisdiction over all those within the limits of his own territory, and a pastor and those who take the

[7] Can. 197, § 1.

place of the pastor have this power over those within the parish.

Canon 198 enumerates those who are included under the term *Ordinarius loci*. These are the Roman Pontiff, for the whole world; and for their respective territories, residential Bishops, Abbots, and Prelates *nullius,* and their Vicars General, Administrators, Vicars and Prefects Apostolic, and those who succeed all these in ruling the territory, e.g., the Vicar Capitular or Administrator of a diocese. The *Vicarius delegatus* appointed by a Vicar or Prefect Apostolic is also to be included among these.[8]

According to Canon 199, § 1, anyone having ordinary jurisdiction may delegate it in whole or in part to another, so that the above mentioned *Ordinarii locorum* may delegate to others their jurisdiction for hearing confessions within their territory; but those delegated, in turn may not subdelegate this power to others except when the Ordinary has expressly given this concession.[9]

Pastors

A priest or moral person to whom a parish with the care of souls is given *in titulum,* to be administered under the authority of the local Ordinary, is canonically titled a *pastor,*[10] and a pastor enjoys ordinary jurisdiction for hearing confessions within his own territory.[11]

---

[8] S. C. de Prop. Fide., litt. encycl., 8 dec. 1919, *A. A. S.* XII (1920), 120.
[9] Can. 199, § 4.
[10] Can. 451, § 1.
[11] Can. 873, § 1.

Although the Code does not state so explicitly, it is certain that a pastor cannot delegate his jurisdiction for hearing confessions even though his jurisdiction is ordinary. This could be deduced from the fact that he is not enumerated among those who are permitted to delegate jurisdiction for hearing confessions.[12] Yet some doubt about the question remained. All doubt, however, was dispelled when this was authentically decided, on October 16, 1919, by the Pontifical Commission for Interpreting the Code.[13] The Commission declared that pastors and those taking the place of pastors, without the special concession of the local Ordinary were unable to delegate their jurisdiction for hearing confessions either to secular or religious priests; nor could a pastor or his vicar extend the jurisdiction of an already approved priest beyond the confines of place or persons within which his jurisdiction was circumscribed according to the norm of Canon 879, § 1. A pastor, therefore, although he has ordinary jurisdiction for the internal forum over those who have a domicile or quasi-domicile in his parish, cannot delegate another priest to hear the confessions of these subjects. Yet anyone having ordinary jurisdiction, including the pastor, may absolve a subject anywhere in the world.[14]

The question naturally arises, from whence does a pastor receive his jurisdiction over those who are not parishioners but who present themselves for absolution before his tribunal in his parish church? Over these a pastor receives what seems to be delegated juris-

[12] Cf. Can. 874.
[13] *A. A. S.* XI (1919), 477.
[14] Can. 881, § 2.

diction *a jure,* for Canon 881, § 1, states that all priests of either clergy, approved for hearing confessions in any place and possessed of ordinary or delegated jurisdiction, validly and licitly absolve both *vagi* and *peregrini* from another diocese or parish, as well as Catholics of an Oriental rite who present themselves to their tribunal.

But since it is usual for those receiving delegated jurisdiction from the local Ordinary to receive it for the whole territory of the Ordinary, is a pastor to be considered as less privileged than they, and restricted to his own parish? Is it not possible for a pastor to absolve validly a penitent other than his own parishioner outside his parish but within his own diocese? It has already been pointed out that after Trent the custom arose whereby one having a parochial benefice in a diocese was regarded as approved for the whole diocese, and therefore capable of validly absolving penitents anywhere within his own diocese as long as he received delegated jurisdiction over the members of the parish from the pastor of the place where he heard confessions.[15] But the Code has abolished the necessity of explicit approbation by the bishop, and requires only the presence of the power of jurisdiction. It also prohibits a pastor from delegating jurisdiction for hearing confessions to another. Is the aforementioned custom still in force, and, if it is, from whence do such pastors now derive their jurisdiction? Most theologians and canonists regard this custom as still existing and having the force of law, since Canon 874, § 1, contains no reprobating clause,

[15] Supra, p. 37.

and Canon 5 permits such centenary customs to exist.[16] Under the law of the Code, therefore, if a pastor does not receive delegated jurisdiction for the whole diocese from the local Ordinary or from the diocesan statutes, it would seem that he receives this jurisdiction *a jure,* i. e., from this custom having the force of law.[17] He is capable, therefore, of absolving validly any penitents other than his own parishioners outside his parish but within his diocese and, for the liceity of his action, needs only the permission of the pastor of the place where he hears confessions.

Quasi-Parochi and Parochial Vicars

Among those whom Canon 873, § 1, includes as having ordinary jurisdiction for the internal sacramental forum are pastors *aliique qui loco parochi sunt.* Besides a pastor properly so called, Canon 451, § 2, regards the following as equal to pastors, with all their rights and obligations, and as included in law under the name of *parochus:*

1. A *quasi-parochus,* i. e., the rector of a church in a vicariate or prefecture apostolic;[18]
2. Parochial vicars, if they are equipped with full parochial powers.

Chapter X of the same Title VIII of the second book of the Code enumerates those who are included under the name of parochial vicars. These are: the

---

[16] Vermeersch, *Theo. Mor.,* III, n. 445; Noldin, *De Sacramentis,* III, n. 340.
[17] Cappello, *De Sac.,* II, n. 384, -4.
[18] Can. 216, § 3.

THE PRESENT LAW OF THE CODE

vicarius curatus, or he who has been appointed by the bishop to the actual care of souls in a parish church which is joined to a moral person, such as a religious house or capitular church, the *parochus habitualis* of which church is the moral person; [19] the *vicarius oeconomus,* or he who has been appointed by the Ordinary to rule a vacant parish until the assignment of a new *parochus*—known among us as the administrator;[20] also the first assistant, or, if there is no assistant, the pastor of the nearest parish, who, upon the vacancy of the neighboring parish, assumes charge until the administrator has been appointed by the Ordinary;[21] the *vicarius substitutus,* who fills the pastor's place when he is to be absent beyond a week;[22] the *vicarius adjutor,* who in all things supplies the place of a *parochus* unable to fulfill his duties because of old age, blindness, or some other permanent disability;[23] finally, the *vicarius cooperator,* who is given to a *parochus* unable to handle the care of souls alone in his parish because of the great number of people or some such cause.[24] These are known in this country as assistants.

There is no doubt that the *quasi-parochus,* and all the parochial vicars when enjoying full parochial power, except the *vicarius cooperator,* are included under Canon 873, § 1, as acquiring ordinary jurisdiction for the internal sacramental forum, for each of these really is in *loco parochi.*

[19] Can. 471.
[20] Can. 472, § 1.
[21] Can. 472, § 2.
[22] Can. 474.
[23] Can. 475.
[24] Can. 476.

Fanfani is of the opinion that if the *vicarius cooperator* has full power of substituting for the pastor in all things, he enjoys by virtue of his office ordinary jurisdiction for hearing the confessions of the parishioners of the parish. In support of this position he argues that Canon 873, § 1, concedes ordinary jurisdiction to the pastor *"aliisque qui loco parochi sunt"*; and Canon 451, § 2, regards *"vicarii paroeciales si plena potestate paroeciali sunt praediti aequiparantur parochis . . . et parochorum nomine in jure veniunt"*; and under the chapter enumerating the parochial vicars are included the *vicarii cooperatores*.[25] Fanfani, then, seems to be of the opinion that the phrase *"qui loco parochi sunt"* of Canon 873, § 1, is equivalent to and of the same significance as the phrase *"parochorum nomine in jure veniunt"* of Canon 451, § 2.

However, it seems that it is the mind of the legislator not to include the *vicarii cooperatores* among those *qui loco parochi sunt* and who enjoy ordinary jurisdiction for hearing confessions; for, even though they may be equipped with full parochial power, yet their rights and obligations are derived from the diocesan statutes, the letters of the Ordinary, and the commission of the pastor, and not *ex jure vi officii*.[26] It would appear, then, that their jurisdiction for hearing confessions *ratione tituli* must be classified as delegated and not ordinary, since *ipso jure* their jurisdiction is not connected with their office.[27] This position also seems to be supported by the fact that Canon

[25] Fanfani, *De Jure Parochorum*, n. 251, B. 6; Bargilliat, *Praelectiones Juris Canonici*, II, n. 1174.
[26] Can. 476, § 6.
[27] Can. 197, § 1.

475, § 2, makes the distinction for the *vicarius adjutor* whereby, if he supplies the place of the pastor in all things, he enjoys all the rights and offices of the pastor (with one exception); and if he does not take the place of the pastor in all things, his rights and obligations are derived from his letters of deputation. On the other hand, Canon 476, § 6, makes no distinction, and states that the rights and obligations of the *vicarius cooperator* are derived from the diocesan statutes, the letters of the Ordinary, and the commission of the pastor; so that, even if he is equipped with full parochial power, still this is derived from these three sources and not *ex jure vi officii*. However, if this full parochial power is granted to assistants by the diocesan statutes, then he might be considered as enjoying this power *ex jure vi officii* and his jurisdiction for the internal sacramental forum might be considered ordinary. But *ex jure communi*, it does not appear as if the *vicarius cooperator* enjoys ordinary jurisdiction for hearing confessions, because his jurisdiction is not attached by law to his office, as is required by Canon 197, § 1, in order that jurisdiction be considered ordinary. Furthermore, the *vicarius cooperator* does not really act *in loco parochi* in the proper sense of the words as do the other *vicarii paroeciales;* for the *vicarius cooperator* merely helps the pastor in his work, whereas the other *vicarii paroeciales* act in the absence of the pastor. Therefore, it seems more proper to say that *ex jure communi* the *vicarii cooperatores* have only delegated jurisdiction for the internal sacramental forum, while the pastor, and the other *vicarii paroeciales* when they enjoy full parochial power and really act *in loco parochi,* possess ordinary penitential jurisdiction.

Canons Penitentiary

The Canon Penitentiary of a cathedral or collegiate church also enjoys ordinary jurisdiction for the internal sacramental forum, but, like the pastor, he is forbidden to delegate it.[28] To this office is attached the power of absolving diocesans even outside the diocese, and others within the diocese, *a peccatis et a censuris Episcopo reservatis.*[29] The canon does not distinguish between those reservations established by the Code and those which the Ordinary himself has established, so on the principle *ubi lex non distinguit nec nos distinguere debemus,*[30] there is no reason for excluding those reserved *a jure* to the Ordinary or those which a bishop reserves to himself by decree or by diocesan statute. On the same principle, a Canon Penitentiary enjoys the power of absolving from censures which a national or provincial synod reserves to the bishop, e. g., the excommunication attached to attempted marriage after a civil divorce, which the Third Plenary Council of Baltimore has reserved to the bishop.[31]

Exempt Clerical Religious Superiors

The exempt clerical religious superior also enjoys the same ordinary penitential jurisdiction, but only for

[28] Canons 873, § 2, and 401, § 1.
[29] Can. 401, § 1.
[30] Wernz, *Jus Decretalium,* I, n, 131.
[31] *Acta et Decreta Conc. Plen. Baltimorensis III,* n. 124.

THE PRESENT LAW OF THE CODE

his own subjects, not for secular people. There is no doubt that the major superiors, titled as Ordinaries in Canon 198 and enumerated under Canon 488, n. 8, enjoy this power. These major superiors are: Abbots primate and Abbots superior of Monastic Congregations, Abbots of Monasteries *sui juris*, the Supreme Moderators of other non-monastic religious societies, Provincials and the vicars of these who have the equivalent of provincial power. Local superiors of exempt religious houses also enjoy this ordinary jurisdiction for the internal forum when they take the place of a pastor for their subjects.[32] The subjects of exempt clerical religious superiors include, not only the religious themselves, but also the novices, postulants, servants, and any others who remain night and day in the religious house either as students, guests, or for the sake of their health.[33]

Cessation of Ordinary Jurisdiction

This ordinary jurisdiction for hearing confessions ceases with the loss of the office to which the jurisdiction is attached. Ecclesiastical offices are lost: by resignation accepted by the superior, by deprivation made known to the office holder, by removal, by transfer, and by the lapse of the time defined in the appointment.[34] It also ceases when the office holder is placed under the censure of excommunication, suspension from office, or interdict, by a condemnatory or declaratory sentence. Therefore, one incurring such a censure

[32] Cappello, *op cit.*, II, n. 386.
[33] Canons 875, § 1, and 514, § 1.
[34] Can. 183, § 1.

ipso facto which does not require a declaratory sentence, or one incurring one of these censures which does require such a sentence, before that sentence is pronounced may validly absolve one of his subjects, for he has not yet lost his jurisdiction.[35] Besides suspension from office, other suspensions by their nature, when inflicted by a condemnatory or declaratory sentence, deprive one of the power of absolving validly. Such suspensions are: suspension from jurisdiction, since jurisdiction is necessary for a valid absolution; suspension *a divinis;* suspension *ab ordinibus;* suspension *a sacris ordinibus;* suspension *ab audiendis confessionibus;* since all of these deprive one of the right to exercise his power of orders validly.[36] Other suspensions do not invalidate the absolution of a priest unless this is explicitly or equivalently stated in the decree of suspension, for penalties must be benignly interpreted.[37] The suspended cleric therefore is to be regarded as deprived only of those powers which are expressly mentioned in the decree of suspension.

ARTICLE II

Delegated Jurisdiction

The delegated jurisdiction for hearing confessions, which a priest must obtain in order to impart valid absolution from sin, is nothing more than the power of ruling the penitents as subjects, or the authority to pass judgment upon them. This, as has been pointed

---

[35] Vermeersch-Creusen, *Epitome, II,* n. 144, *3;* Cappello, *op. cit.,* II, n. 389, *3.* Cf. also Canons 2265, § 2, and 2283.
[36] Canons 2284, 2279, § 2; Cappello, *op. cit.,* II, n. 390.
[37] Can. 2219, § 1.

out, is required by the judicial character of the sacrament of Penance. This jurisdiction is usually delegated among the faculties given by a bishop to his priests. The terms *jurisdiction* and *faculties* are sometimes regarded as synonymous, but improperly, for *faculties* is a wider term within which *jurisdiction for confessions* is included among other concessions of the bishop, jurisdictional and otherwise.[1] The only *faculty* therefore which a priest who has not ordinary jurisdiction must obtain in order to absolve validly from sin is the *faculty to hear confessions,* or the power of jurisdiction over the penitents for the internal sacramental forum.

The present law regarding delegated power of penitential jurisdiction is given in Canon 874, which reads as follows:

§ 1. Jurisdictionem delegatam ad recipiendas confessiones quorumlibet sive saecularium sive religiosorum confert sacerdotibus tum saecularibus tum religiosis etiam exemptis Ordinarius loci in quo confessiones excipiuntur; sacerdotes autem religiosi, eadem ne utantur sine licentia saltem praesumpta sui Superioris, firmo tamen praescripto can. 519.

§ 2. Locorum Ordinarii jurisdictionem ad audiendas confessiones habitualiter ne concedant religiosis qui a proprio Superiore non praesentantur; iis vero qui a proprio Superiore praesentantur, sine gravi causa eam ne denegent, firmo tamen praescripto can. 877.

The local Ordinary may delegate jurisdiction to hear the confessions of any person in his territory, secular or religious, even exempt; and he may delegate this

[1] Motry, *Diocesan Faculties,* p. 7 seq.

jurisdiction to any priest, secular or religious, even exempt. He is the one and only source from whence jurisdiction for hearing the confessions of secular people, both clerical and lay, and non-exempt religious men and all religious women, may be obtained by any priest, either secular or religious.[2] But the Major Superiors [3] of an exempt clerical religious society, as well as the local Ordinary, may confer jurisdiction on either a secular or a religious priest, even one of another religious society, to hear the confessions of his own subjects.[4]

The prohibition expressed in this canon whereby religious priests are forbidden to exercise the jurisdiction conferred by the local Ordinary without the license of their own superiors, does not affect the validity of the absolution granted without this license, but only the liceity of the priest's action.[5]

Manner of Delegating Jurisdiction

Delegated jurisdiction must be conceded either in writing or expressly by word, otherwise the delegation is invalid, and the subsequent absolutions of the supposedly delegated confessor are invalid,[6] except in those cases in which the Church supplies the missing

---

[2] Vermeersch, *Theo. Mor.*, III, 447; *Commentarium pro Religiosis*, III (1922), p. 77.

[3] Canons 198 and 488, § 8.

[4] Can. 875, § 1. The subjects of the religious superior, for whom he may delegate penitential jurisdiction, include, not only the religious, the novices, and the postulants but also those enumerated above who remain night and day in the religious house. Cf. p. 51.

[5] Noldin, III, n. 341, *3b; Irish Eccl. Record*, Series V, Vol. XI (1918), p. 16.

[6] Can. 879, § 1.

jurisdiction. The word *expressly* used here has not the same meaning as the word *explicitly*. The canon does not require an explicit formula of concession, but merely an expressed formula. Therefore, an implicit grant of jurisdiction suffices for the validity of absolution from sin; e. g., if the bishop sends a priest to give a mission at a certain place, implicitly this priest receives jurisdiction for hearing confessions in that place.[7]

When no petition for jurisdiction has been made, the presumed concession of the faculties certainly does not suffice, for no delegation of jurisdiction has really taken place. When the petition for jurisdiction has been made, some are of the opinion that one who is morally certain that the bishop has received his petition and has sent an affirmative answer, although this mandate has not yet reached him, may validly absolve and in an urgent case even licitly.[8] This opinion seems probable as long as the priest is morally certain that the delegation of jurisdiction has already been made. This resolves itself into the question as to what kind of knowledge regarding the conferring of jurisdiction is necessary. Is it necessary to have been authentically notified of the concession, or is private knowledge of the concession sufficient? Most theologians hold that, under the Code, authentic knowledge is not required, for, they argue, Canon 37 states that a rescript is valid before its acceptance, and Canon 38 rules that rescripts which grant a favor without the intervention of an executor take effect from the moment the letters

[7] Cappello, *op. cit.*, II, n. 398.
[8] Vermeersch-Creusen, *Epitome,* II, n. 149; Capello, *op. et loc. cit.*

were given.[9] Therefore, jurisdiction takes effect at the moment it is granted and one who is morally certain of the concession, no matter by what sort of knowledge he arrived at this certainty, may validly, and with sufficient reason licitly, use the jurisdiction. Likewise, almost all modern theologians and canonists admit that notification of the concession of jurisdiction made over the telephone or by telegraph is sufficient.[10]

Limitation of Delegated Jurisdiction

Delegated jurisdiction can be circumscribed by certain limits [11] and *per se* it is necessary to exercise the jurisdiction strictly within these limits for the validity of the subsequent absolutions. These limitations may affect: the time within which a priest may hear confessions; the place at which he may exercise that office; the class of people whom he may absolve; or the matter from which he may absolve. It has been said that these limitations *per se* affect the validity of his absolution, because there are certain cases in which the Church supplies the deficient jurisdiction. These will be discussed later.[12]

In delegating jurisdiction, however, the local Ordinary cannot restrict the power of absolving or of dispensing which the common law gives to simple confessors; e. g., the Ordinary cannot prohibit a confessor from hearing the confessions of religious, men or

---

[9] Vermeersch, *Theo. Mor.*, III, n. 453; Cappello, *De Sac.* II, n. 392; Arregui, note to n. 599.
[10] Vermeersch-Creusen, *Epitome,* II, n. 149; Cappello, *op. cit.,* II, n. 398.
[11] Can. 878, § 1.
[12] Infra, p. 117 seq.

women, who approach him for the tranquillity of their consciences, according to the norms of Canons 519 and 522 respectively. If the Ordinary does restrict a power given by common law, his restriction is invalid, and any approved priest may validly and licitly absolve contrary to the restriction of the Ordinary. But even within his rights, the Ordinary should not restrict the jurisdiction that he delegates to confessors,[13] without a reasonable cause, but if he does so restrict the jurisdiction that he delegates, the limitations thus placed are valid although illicit, and the delegated priest cannot validly absolve from cases falling within the illicit restriction of his jurisdiction.[14]

Cessation of Delegated Jurisdiction

Delegated jurisdiction ceases: upon the fulfillment of the mandate; upon the lapse of the time defined in the concession; upon the exhaustion of the number of cases for which the jurisdiction was granted; when the final cause of the delegation ceases; by the revocation of the one delegating directly made known to the one delegated;[15] by the renunciation of the one delegated directly made known to the one delegating and accepted by him.[16] It does not cease, however, when the one delegating relinquishes his office, except when this is expressly stated in the concession, or when the power was conceded only for hearing the confession of some particular person expressly

[13] Can. 878, § 2.
[14] *Irish Eccl. Record*, Series V, Vol. XIV (1919), p. 322.
[15] *Ibid. loc. cit.*
[16] Canons 207, § 1 and 61, and Vermeersch-Creusen, *op cit.*, I, n, 147.

determined in the rescript, and *res adhuc integra sit,* i. e., the confession has not yet been heard; or has been finished; but if the confession has been heard and absolution deferred, *res non est integra,* and the delegation does not cease. Finally, jurisdiction conceded *ad beneplacitum nostrum* or *donec vixero,* or *durante meo munere* ceases with the loss of office of the one delegating, but not jurisdiction conceded *usque ad revocationem,* or *ad beneplacitum.*

Delegated Jurisdiction of Religious Priests and Their Privileges

Canon 874, § 1, has changed the discipline existing before the Code at least as regards the source of the jurisdiction of religious priests over secular people.[17] At various times since the thirteenth century the Holy See has granted jurisdiction over all the faithful to the priests of one Religious Order or another in the form of privileges.[18] As time went on, these privileges were extended to other Orders and Congregations through communication, so that in the sixteenth century almost all religious priests claimed that they received jurisdiction over all the faithful from the Pope, through their own superiors. These Papal privileges included the privilege of absolving from all sins and censures, even those reserved to the Holy See and to the bishop. The Council of Trent nullified the utility of these privileges as a source of jurisdiction

---
[17] Vermeersch, *Theo. Mor.,* III, n. 447; Melo, *De Exemptione Regularium,* p. 100; *Irish Eccl. Record,* Series V, Vol. XI (1918), p. 17.

[18] C. 2, *De Sepul.,* III, 6, Extrav. Com.; C. 1, *De Priv.* V, 7, Extrav. Com.; C. 2, *De Sepul.,* III, 7, Clem.

for these confessors when the Council insisted that all priests, even regulars, in order to absolve validly from sin, must obtain the approbation of the bishop of the place where they heard confessions.[19] The Code abolishes the necessity of episcopal approbation and requires only the presence of jurisdiction for valid absolution. It is now necessary for all priests, both secular and religious, who have not an office to which is attached ordinary jurisdiction for the internal sacramental forum, to obtain delegated jurisdiction to hear the confessions of secular people from the Ordinary of the place where the confessions are to be heard. This legislation, therefore, abolishes at least one phase of the ancient privileges of the regulars, and constitutes the local Ordinary as the only source from whence they may obtain jurisdiction to hear the confessions of secular people.[20]

However, the question as to whether or not the religious priests have the power of absolving secular people from reserved sins and censures in virtue of these privileges, still remains. As has been stated, the Papal privileges granted to the regulars included also the power to absolve from all reserved sins and censures. But these privileges alternately were amplified and restricted by the various Pontiffs,[21] so that at the time of St. Alphonsus the question whether or not regulars had the power of absolving from Papal reservations was a matter of dispute among theologians. That prince of moralists declares that at his time there were

[19] Sess. XXV, *De Reform.*, c. 15; Alex. VII, 18 mart. 1666, *Prop. Dam.*, § 36, apud Denzinger, § 1136.
[20] Vermeersch, *Theo. Mor.*, III, n. 447; *Comm. pro Religiosis,* III (1922), p. 77.
[21] Supra, p. 30.

two opinions: the one denying this power to regulars he calls probable; and the one affirming, he calls more probable.[22]

Those denying this power to regulars argued that in a decree issued by the *S. Cong. S. R. E. Cardinalium in negotiis Episcoporum et Regularium,* Paul V had revoked the privilege in these words:

> Ac insuper ut nulli ex sacerdotibus praedictis (scilicet saecularibus et regularibus) quibuscumque privilegiis, indultis et facultatibus suffulti ab excommunicationibus vel casibus eisdem ordinariis vel sedi apostolicae reservatis, praeterquam in articulo mortis, absolvere audeant vel praesumant.[23]

Those affirming the possession of these faculties by the regulars, however, held that the prohibition of Paul V affected only certain cases reserved by his predecessor Clement VIII.[24] These opinions concerned only Papal cases or reservations made by the Holy See restricting the power of absolving in these cases either to itself or to the local Ordinary.

Regarding cases which the local Ordinary reserved to himself, before the Council of Trent regulars were conceded the power of absolving from these, since they received their jurisdiction over all the faithful from the Roman Pontiffs through their own superiors, and therefore their jurisdiction was not subject to the restrictions of the local Ordinary. But when the Council of Trent insisted upon the necessity of episcopal approbation for the validity of the absolution even of regu-

---
[22] St. Alphon., VII, n. 96.
[23] Chokier, *Tractatus de Jurisdictione Ordinarii in Exemptos,* p. 340; Vicentia, *De Privilegiis Regularium,* p. 61.
[24] St. Alphon., VII, n. 96.

THE PRESENT LAW OF THE CODE

lars, it was disputed whether or not regulars were approved for such cases. In 1602 Clement VIII [25] prohibited regulars in Italy from absolving from cases which the bishop reserved to himself. Later this prohibition was extended to the whole world by the same Pontiff. The opinion holding that the regulars still possessed such a privilege finally was condemned by Alexander VII in 1665, in the words: *"Mendicantes possunt absolvere a casibus episcopis reservatis, non obtenta ad id episcoporum facultate."* [26] Thereafter their inability to absolve from cases which the bishop reserved to himself was certain.

On October 12, 1869, Pius IX issued his constitution *Apostolicae Sedis,* revising the legislation on censures and their reservation; and in this constitution he revoked any privilege that regulars may have had, giving them the power to absolve from censures and, consequently, the sin connected with them, which were reserved to the Holy See.[27] Undaunted, the regulars still claimed the privilege of absolving from censures reserved by common law to the local Ordinary.[28] Up to the publication of the Code, some theologians upheld the existence of this privilege,[29] and others denied it.[30]

Since the publication of the Code, it is certain from Canon 874, § 1, that the religious no longer obtain any jurisdiction over secular people by virtue of their

---

[25] Chokier, *op. cit.,* p. 338-339; Vicentia, *op. cit.,* p. 60.
[26] Alexander VII, 24 sept. 1665, *Prop. Dam.* § 12, apud Denzinger, § 1112; cf. also St. Alphon., VII, n. 98.
[27] Fontes, n. 552.
[28] Lehmkuhl, *Theologia Moralis,* II, n. 968.
[29] *Ibid., loc. cit.;* Bucceroni, *Casus Conscientiae* (6th ed., 1918), I, n. 277; La Croix, *Theologia Moralis,* VI, n. 1628.
[30] D'Annibale, *Summula Theologiae Moralis,* I, n. 344.

former privileges.[31] In view of this, it would appear that the legislator intends to abolish also the alleged privilege of the religious of absolving from reserved cases, since he abolishes the privilege which was the foundation stone of their claim. It is certainly the spirit of the Code, if not the very letter, that all priests, secular and religious, must obtain all their jurisdiction to hear confessions from the local Ordinary. Yet, in virtue of Canons 4 and 209, the use of this dubious privilege cannot be denied to the religious confessor until the Holy See definitely determines the matter, since Canon 874, § 1, contains no clause abrogating former privileges and customs.[32]

However, according to some authors,[33] the use of this privilege among others under the Code, is restricted to those religious confessors whose Order received the privilege directly from the Holy See, to the exclusion of those other religious confessors whose institute received the privilege through communication. This opinion is based upon an interpretation of Canon 613, § 1. The canon in question reads:

[31] Vermeersch, *Theo. Mor.*, III, n. 447; Melo, *De Exemptione Regularium*, p. 100.

[32] Canon 4: "Jura aliis quaesita, itemque privilegia atque indulta quae, ab Apostolica Sede ad haec usque tempora personis sive physicis sive moralibus concessa, in usu adhuc sunt nec revocata, integra manent, nisi hujus Codicis canonibus expresse revocentur."

Canon 209: "In errore communi aut in dubio positivo et probabili sive juris sive facti, jurisdictionem supplet Ecclesia pro foro tum externo tum interno."

[33] Blat, *Commentarium in Textum Juris Canonici*, II, n. 689; Biederlack-Fuehrich, *De Religiosis Codicis Juris Canonici*, n. 145; Chelodi, *Jus de Personis*, n. 280; Leitner, *Handbuch des katholischen Kirchenrechts*, III, § 3, n. 8; Cicognani, *Commentarium in Codicem Juris Canonici*, p. 279; *Il Monitore Ecclesiastico*, XXX (1918), 194, 366-7; Roelker, *Principles of Privilege*, p. 52.

THE PRESENT LAW OF THE CODE

Quaelibet religio iis tantum privilegiis gaudet, quae vel hoc in Codice continentur, vel a Sede Apostolica directe eidem concessa fuerint, exclusa in posterum qualibet communicatione.

These canonists interpret the law, according to the evident signification of the words, to mean that each institute enjoys those privileges only which are
1. Either contained in the Code;
2. Or may have been directly conceded to it by the Apostolic See, every communication of privilege therefore being henceforth excluded.

This interpretation, then, insists that religious no longer possess those privileges which they had obtained before the Code by communication. The supporters of this opinion maintain that Canon 613, § 1, as a particular law for the religious, contains the revocation of communicated privileges required by the more general prescriptions of Canon 4. This latter canon demands express revocation by the canons of the Code for the cessation of a privilege which has been in force up to this time. Accordingly, these authorities maintain that Canon 613, § 1, expressly revokes those privileges which religious have obtained in the past through communication, because Canon 613, § 1, evidently intends a *taxative* enumeration of the privileges which the religious possess under the new law, and definitely enumerates only those contained in the Code and those which may have been directly conceded by the Holy See. Accepting this interpretation, it would seem that Canon 613, § 1, merely gives another evidence that it is the mind of the legislator to reduce the number of privileges possessed by religious. This tendency on the part of the legislator certainly is noticeable in the history at least of the one particular privilege with which we are concerned.

Other authors,[34] however, interpret Canon 613, § 1, to mean that the religious societies possess those privileges which are contained in the Code, those which they have received in the past in any way, and those which shall have been directly conceded by the Holy See in the future, which latter privileges cannot be communicated. The perfect subjunctive form, *concessa fuerint*, is taken here as implying potentiality, which *per se* prescinds from any question of time, but here refers to the future.[35] Therefore, according to these authorities, the religious enjoy

1. Those privileges contained in the Code;
2. Those privileges which shall have been directly conceded to them in the future by the Holy See;
3. Those privileges which they have received in the past both by direct concession and by communication, for they hold that these are not revoked by Canon 613, § 1, and are therefore still in force in virtue of Canon 4.

The object of every commentator should be to discover the mind of the legislator, for the law itself is nothing other than the expression of his will. To this end, Canon 18 states that ecclesiastical laws must be understood according to the proper signification of the words, considered in their text and context. The

---

[34] Prümmer, *Manuale Juris Canonici*, praenotamen ad g. 239; Vermeersch-Creusen, *Epit.* I, n. 615; Brandys, *Kirchliches Rechtsbuch*, n. 89; *Com. pro Religiosis*, III (1922), p. 205. Fanfani, *De Jure Religiosorum*, p. 362.

[35] *Com. pro Religiosis*, III (1922), p. 212.

proper signification of the perfect tense is to denote action begun in the past and continued in the present. It is true that the subjunctive mood may be used to express potentiality; but when used in the perfect tense, is not the natural signification of the words rather the expression of potential action begun in the past and continued in the present? Therefore, does it not seem to be erroneously or at least gratuitously asserted that here the potentiality refers to the future, excluding the past and the present?

The interpretation of this group of authors, moreover, is contrary to the sense of the first clause of Canon 613, § 1, *"Quaelibet religio iis tantum privilegiis gaudet,"* which, if it has any meaning, is *taxative*. This is the juridical value attributed to the word *tantum* by Barbosa.[36] If the legislator intended that this canon contain a *taxative* enumeration of the privileges of the religious under the new law, then a religious institute enjoys only those privileges which are contained in the Code or which have been conceded directly by the Holy See.

It seems evident, therefore, that the Code intends to exclude those privileges which were obtained by religious before 1918 by communication. In theory, therefore, only that religious priest whose society obtained this privilege by direct concession of the Holy See, can absolve from a censure which is reserved by common law to the Ordinary; and, in view of the stormy career of this privilege, even this is doubtful and, in our opinion, opposed to the mind of the

[36] Barbosa, CCCCII, n. 2, in *Tractatu de Dictionibus usu frequentioribus,* apud *Tractatus Varii.*

legislator as expressed in the Code. In practice, however, in virtue of Canon 209 and in deference to the authority of the canonists upholding the milder view, even those religious priests whose institute received the privilege by communication, may absolve from these reserved censures until the Holy See declares otherwise. If we accept the word of the reliable *Monitore Ecclesiastico,* this consummation, devoutly to be wished, ought soon to be forthcoming, for the *Monitore* declares, without giving its authority for the statement: "We know that the application of Canon 613, § 1, is suspended until the Sacred Congregation for Religious finishes its work of revising the privileges of the various religious institutes."[37]

ARTICLE III

Reservation

Canon 893 describes what is known as the reservation of certain cases whereby jurisdiction for these cases is restricted to the tribunals of the one reserving the case or the one to whom he reserves it. Accordingly, the jurisdiction of all inferior confessors is limited, so that they are not authorized to pass any judgment on such cases and therefore cannot validly absolve. The canon reads:

§ 1. Qui ordinario jure possunt audiendi confessiones potestatem concedere aut ferre censuras, possunt quoque, excepto Vicario Capitulari et Vicario Generali sine mandato speciali, nonnullos casus ad

[37] *Il Monitore Ecclesiastico,* XXX(1918), p. 366.

suum avocare judicium, inferioribus absolvendi potestatem limitantes.

§ 2. Haec avocatio dicitur *reservatio casuum*.

§ 3. Quod attinet ad reservationem censurarum, servatur praescriptum can. 2246, 2247.

This legislation has its counterpart in civil law, inasmuch as the jurisdiction of lower courts is likewise limited to certain cases, and therefore these courts are unable to try crimes of a more serious or heinous character; e. g., the jurisdiction of a simple district or municipal court is so restricted that it is unable to pass judgment on the crime of murder.

Thus, the reservation of cases directly affects the court or the confessor by limiting the power of passing judgment on certain cases, and only indirectly affects the delinquent or the penitent inasmuch as he presents himself to a confessor whose jurisdiction is restricted and who, in consequence, is unable to absolve him.

Purpose of Reservation

The purpose of this restriction of the jurisdiction of inferior tribunals in the civil law is to bring more serious cases before a higher tribunal, which is better qualified, by reason of its position, experience, and learning, to render a just and equitable decision and to provide for the good of the community. It is quite certain now that the purpose of reservation in ecclesiastical law is almost the same as it is in the civil law, and therefore is called medicinal and not penal. It is not to punish the delinquent that the more serious crimes are reserved to the higher tribunal, but rather that a proper remedy may be supplied and the best interests of ecclesiastical discipline provided for, by those best qualified to handle such cases.

The Code does not state explicitly that the purpose of reservation is medicinal, but it provides ample evidence to support this conclusion. In the first place, the Code does not list reservation among the canonical penalties, and declares that only those penalties are in force which are contained in the Code.[1] In the description of reservation given in Canon 893, the object of reservation is shown to be the withholding of jurisdiction over some cases so that it will be necessary for the case to be brought before the tribunal of the superior either by the penitent or by a confessor. This may occasion delay in obtaining absolution; but is this delay the object of reservation and intended as a punishment for the sin? The delay in the disposal of a serious crime occasioned by the incapacity of lower courts in civil law is not the object of the restriction of their jurisdiction; neither is it the object of reservation in ecclesiastical law. The Code gives no further positive hint as to the reason for reserving cases to the tribunal of the superiors, but the instruction of the Sacred Congregation of the Holy Office issued on July 13, 1916, the salient points of which are incorporated in the Code, states that if the Ordinaries strive to form learned and pious and prudent confessors throughout their dioceses to whom they can suggest the remedies which are calculated to check the spread of these vices, and which they themselves would use if the penitents were sent to them, then

[1] Can. 6, n. 5.

the hardships inevitable to reservation will be avoided and the desired effect gained.[2] Evidently, therefore, the hardship of delayed absolution is not the object of reservation, but the suggesting of the proper remedy for rooting out the vice is the purpose of calling these serious cases to the tribunal of the superior. And this is medicinal or disciplinary, and not penal.

Effect of Ignorance on Reservation

The question to be discussed, is not the effect of ignorance of the sinfulness of the act nor the effect of ignorance of the censure if one is attached to the sin, but the effect of ignorance of the reservation. Ignorance of the sinfulness of the act certainly excuses from the reservation, since no sin whatsoever has been committed; consequently there is no sin to reserve. Likewise, ignorance of the censure excuses one from incurring it; so if the sin is reserved only because of the reserved censure attached to it, when the censure is not incurred, the sin is not reserved. But when the penitent knows the sinfulness of the action and knows he has incurred the censure if the sin is reserved *ratione censurae,* but is ignorant merely of the reservation—ignorant only of the fact that a simple confessor cannot absolve from the sin or censure—does this ignorance excuse him from incurring the reservation? If the purpose of the reservation were penal, then the penitent's ignorance merely of the reservation of the sin would excuse him from the reservation, for it is not becoming to inflict a penalty on one who does not know of the penalty. Since the purpose of

[2] S. C. S. Off., inst., 13 jul. 1916, par. 8, *A. A. S.,* VIII (1916), 313.

reservation is disciplinary, ignorance of the reservation does not excuse from it. For, one's ignorance that his sin needs to be placed before a higher tribunal does not take away that need, which is not dependent on the penitent's ignorance, but is created by the serious character of his sin.[3] Therefore, it is certain that ignorance merely of the reservation does not excuse from it, and the case remains reserved and the confessor is without power to absolve from it whenever the penitent knows the sinfulness of the act, and, if a censure is attached, knows that he has incurred the censure, but is ignorant merely of the confessor's lack of power to absolve him.[4]

Division of Reservations

The term *reserved case* used in Canon 893, § 1, is a generic term including within its scope three species of reservations:

1. The reservation of the sin itself;
2. The reservation of a censure attached to a sin;
3. The reservation of both the sin and a censure attached to it.

The sin itself, therefore, may be reserved without having any censure attached to it, and it is then said to be reserved *ratione sui*. The sin may have attached to

---

[3] Genicot-Salsmans, *Theo. Moral.*, II, n. 309; Vermeersch-Creusen, *Eptome*, II, n. 99; Dargin, *Reserved Cases*, p. 13; Cappello, *De Sac.*, II, n. 507.

[4] It is possible for the superior to declare that reservation is penal and that the sin will not be reserved, and consequently the confessor's power will not be restricted, unless the penitent knows of the reservation, e.g., Benedict. XIV, const., *Sacramentum Poenitentiae*, § 3, Documentum V, apud *Codicem*.

it a reserved censure, which impedes the reception of the sacraments; in this case the sin cannot be absolved until the censure is removed, and the sin is said to be reserved *ratione censurae*. Finally, the sin itself may be reserved and at the same time have attached to it a reserved censure impeding the reception of the sacraments, so that the sin is said to be reserved both *ratione sui* and *ratione censurae*.

In the first case, the reservation directly affects the sin, and the jurisdiction of the confessor which has been restricted is the jurisdiction to absolve from the sin. In the second case, the reservation directly affects the censure and only indirectly affects the sin, and the jurisdiction of the confessor which has been restricted is the jurisdiction to absolve from the censure, so that if the censure is not incurred or has been removed by absolution, the sin is no longer reserved, and any confessor may absolve from the sin. In the third case, the reservation directly affects both the sin and the censure, and the jurisdiction of the confessor which is restricted is the jurisdiction to absolve from both the sin and the censure, so that if the censure is not incurred or has been removed, the sin still remains reserved and the jurisdiction of the simple confessor is still restricted, so that he cannot absolve from that sin.

This is the fundamental division of reserved cases as treated in the Code. Accordingly, the prescriptions of the canons of the Code on the absolution from reserved cases apply to both episcopal and Papal cases unless the contrary is specified. All the reservations contained in the Code, save one, are reserved *ratione censurae;* the lone exception to the rule is the sin of false accusation of an innocent confessor of the crime of solicitation, made to ecclesiastical judges. This sin is reserved both *ratione sui* and *ratione censurae*.[5]

Effect of Reservation on the Orientals

The very first canon of the Code states that the legislation contained in the Code is intended only for the Latin Church and does not affect the churches of the Oriental rites except when these are mentioned, or the matter of the law is such, that of its very nature it affects also the members of the various Oriental rites. Accordingly, unless Orientals are specifically mentioned therein, the reservations of sin and censure established by the Code do not affect priests of the Oriental rites in the exercise of their jurisdiction, nor the faithful of these rites at least as regards the reservation of sins reserved *ratione censurae,* since they are not subject to the censures established by the Code and therefore do not incur these penalties.

Orientals are specifically mentioned as being subject to the following reservations of sins and censures which impede the reception of the sacraments:

1. The sin, reserved *ratione sui,* in Canon 894, of falsely accusing an innocent confessor before ecclesiastical judges of the crime of solicitation in confession;[6]

[5] Canons 894 and 2363.
[6] Canon 6, n. 2; and Benedictus XIV, const., *Sacramentum Poenitentiae,* 1 jun. 1741, Documentum V, apud *Codicem;* const. *Etsi Pastoralis,* 26 maii 1742, § 9, n. 5, Fontes, n. 328; S. C. S. Off., 13 jun. 1710, Fontes, n. 775; S. C. de Prop. Fide, 26 aug. 1775, Collect. n 509; 6 aug. 1885, Collect. n. 1640.

2. The censure of excommunication, reserved *speciali modo* to the Holy See, inflicted by Canon 2363 on those guilty of this crime of falsely accusing an innocent confessor of the crime of solicitation in confession, even when this accusation is made merely to a superior;[7]
3. The censure of excommunication, reserved *speciali modo* to the Holy See, inflicted by Canon 2314 on all apostates, heretics, and schismatics;[8]
4. The censure of excommunication reserved *simpliciter* to the Holy See, inflicted by Canon 2335 on those giving their names to Masonic sects or associations of this kind which plot against the Church and the legitimate civil authority.[9]

These are the only reserved cases established by the Code to which Orientals are certainly subject. They may seem to be subject to other censures *ex natura rei*,[10] but this cannot be established as certain, so that they must be excused from incurring such censures.[11] Maroto is of the opinion that Orientals are subject to all the penal laws of the Code, because these laws respect the public order.[12] Accordingly, he would have Orientals incur all the censures established by the Code and consequently be subject to their reservation. But this opinion does not seem true, since all laws are made for the public order, and Orientals would therefore be subject to all the laws of the Code, contrary

---
[7] *Ibid.*
[8] S. C. de Prop. Fide, 6 aug. 1889, Collect. n. 1640.
[9] *Ibid.*
[10] E.g., Canons 2318 and 2367.
[11] Can. 2219, § 1.
[12] Maroto, *Institutiones Juris Canonici* (3rd ed., 1921), I, n. 198.

to the prescriptions of Canon 1. Therefore, it seems that Orientals *per se* are not subject to the reservations of the Code (except those mentioned above), nor to the reservations of the Latin Ordinaries in whose territory they dwell.

In the United States, however, the members of the various Oriental rites are governed by special regulations. On May 29, 1925, the Congregation for the Oriental Churches, in a letter to the Apostolic Delegate, informed him that all Orientals who have not their own proper Ordinary in this country are to be regarded as subject in all things to the Latin Ordinary in whose territory they dwell.[13] Therefore, it seems that they must be regarded as subject to the whole discipline in force in that territory. As a consequence, both priests and faithful of the various Oriental rites would seem to be subject to all the reservations of sins and censures in force in the territory, regardless of whether the reservation was established by the Holy See or by the local Latin Ordinary.

But for the Greek-Ruthenians living in the United States the Holy See has appointed two Ordinaries of their own rite to whom alone they are subject.[14] Therefore, *per se* Greek-Ruthenians in this country are subject only to those reservations established by the Code which have been enumerated above, and the reserva-

---

[13] "Quindi egli come tutti gli altri Orientali che non abbiano un proprio Ordinario, in America deve in tutto e per tutto stare soggetto all'Ordinario del luogo nel quale risiede, ne potra ivi o altrove esercitare facolta eventualmente accordate dal suo Patriarca o Ordinario, i quali fuori del rispettivo territorio non hanno alcuna giurisdizione sul Clero e sui fedeli salvo nei casi provvisti dal Diritto Comune."

[14] S. C. de Prop. Fide, 17 aug. 1914, *A. A. S.*, VI (1914), 458; S. C. Consist., 20 maii 1924, *A. A. S.*, XVI (1924), 243.

THE PRESENT LAW OF THE CODE

tions of their own proper Ordinary, and they are not subject to the reservations established by the local Latin Ordinaries in whose territory they live. Yet, they may confess to a priest of the Latin rite, who receives his jurisdiction from the Latin Ordinary, and the faithful of the Latin rite may confess to a priest of the Greek-Ruthenian rite, who receives his jurisdiction from his own Oriental Ordinary.[15]

Difficulties immediately are in evidence, since reservation directly affects the jurisdiction of the priest by limiting his power to absolve. There is no difficulty about the one sin reserved *ratione sui* by the Code,[16] since the Orientals are also subject to this reservation. But when a Latin Ordinary reserves a sin *ratione sui,* a priest of the Latin rite cannot absolve a Greek-Ruthenian penitent from this sin even though *per se* this penitent is not subject to the reservations of the Latin Ordinary, because reservation directly affects the confessor by restricting his power to absolve. On the other hand, a Greek-Ruthenian priest could absolve a penitent of the Latin rite from this sin even though this penitent is subject to the reservation, because his jurisdiction over this sin is not restricted by the reservation of the Latin Ordinary. When the Greek-Ruthenian Ordinary reserves a sin *ratione sui,* a similar difficulty is also present.

Further difficulties arise regarding sins reserved *ratione censurae,* for when the censure is not incurred, the sin is not reserved. Suppose, therefore, that a Greek-Ruthenian penitent confesses a sin to a priest

[15] Can. 881, § 1 and S. C. de Prop. Fide, 17 aug. 1914, n. 22, *A. A. S.,* VI (1914), 462.
[16] Can. 894.

of the Latin rite, to which sin the Code has annexed a reserved censure impeding the reception of the sacraments, other than one to which Orientals are subject. The penitent does not incur the censure, and the sin therefore is not reserved, and the Latin confessor can absolve the penitent from his sin. The same is true when the local Latin Ordinary has attached to the sin a reserved censure impeding the reception of the sacraments. Similar difficulties arise when a penitent of the Latin rite confesses to a Greek-Ruthenian priest a sin to which the Code or the local Latin Ordinary has attached a reserved censure which impedes the reception of the sacraments. These entanglements would cause serious confusion in practice, forcing the priest to ascertain the rite to which each penitent belongs who confesses a reserved sin.

Accordingly, the Holy See, in establishing Ordinaries for the Greek-Ruthenians in this country, has provided that:

Fideles Latini, etiamsi adsit presbyter Latini ritus, apud sacerdotem Graeco-Ruthenum ab Ordinario suo adprobatum, peccata sua confiteri et beneficium sacramentalis absolutionis valide et licite obtinere possunt. Item, fideles Graeco-Rutheni peccata sua confiteri possunt apud sacerdotem Latinum ab Episcopo suo adprobatum. Presbyteri vero Latini absolvere non poterunt fideles Graeco-Rutheni ritus a censuris et casibus reservatis ab Ordinario Graeco-Rutheni statutis, absque venia ejusdem. Vicissim idem dicatur de presbyteris Graeco-Ruthenis quoad censuras et reservationes statutas ab Ordinariis Latini ritus.[17]

[17] S. C. de Prop. Fide, 17 aug. 1914, n. 22, *A. A. S.,* VI (1914), 462. This regulation was renewed indefinitely by the S. Cong. pro Eccl. Orient. on June 21, 1924, according to a letter sent out by the Apostolic Delegate to all Ordinaries.

It must be noted that, by this regulation, it is the Roman Congregation which is restricting the jurisdiction of the Latin and Ruthenian confessors respectively, for the Latin Ordinary would have no right to restrict the Ruthenian confessor by his reservations nor would the Ruthenian Ordinary have a right to restrict the jurisdiction of the Latin confessor by his reservations.

Does this regulation include only those reservations which the respective Ordinaries have established, to the exclusion of those established by the Code? Or does it also include the reservations established by the Code, to which Orientals ordinarily are not subject? If these Papal reservations, to which Orientals ordinarily are not subject, are not included in this regulation, then a Greek-Ruthenian priest can absolve a penitent of the Latin rite from any censure reserved by the Code, except those mentioned above, for the priest is not subject to the Code and therefore his jurisdiction is not restricted. Likewise, a priest of the Latin rite can absolve a Greek-Ruthenian penitent from any of the sins to which a reserved censure, other than one of those enumerated above, is attached by the Code, for the penitent does not incur the censure and therefore the sin is not reserved.

Technically, the above regulation applies only to those reservations established by the respective Ordinaries, but the only reason that can be alleged for the regulation, is to avoid the difficulties mentioned above, which arise from the reservation of censures established by the Code, as well as from the reservations of sins and of censures established by the respective Ordinaries. In view of this, it would seem to be the intention of the legislator to include all the reservations in force in the place, whether established by the Code or by the respective Ordinaries, in order that there might be complete uniformity of discipline. However, since the wording of the regulation is so clear, one could not be condemned for following the milder interpretation, and absolutions given in virtue of this interpretation would be certainly valid.[18]

[18] Can. 209.

PART II

PARTICULAR GRANTS OF PENITENTIAL JURISDICTION GIVEN BY THE CODE

PRELIMINARY REMARKS

The remaining portion of this book will treat of the particular powers of absolving and of dispensing which the general law of the Church contained in the Code of Canon Law gives to all confessors at certain times, prescinding altogether from any particular powers or faculties which individual priests may have obtained by delegation from the Roman Pontiff, or their own bishop, or their exempt religious superior.

In order to impart valid absolution from sin, every priest must be possessed of jurisdiction for the internal sacramental forum. This jurisdiction is nothing more than the authority to pass judgment on the penitent as a subject. It is obtained:

1. By one's canonical institution in an ecclesiastical office to which this jurisdiction has been attached by law itself, e. g., by one's canonical installation in a parochial benefice; or
2. By delegation from a competent superior, e. g., by obtaining the faculty of hearing confessions from the local Ordinary. Priests having this ordinary or delegated jurisdiction, but not having any specially delegated faculties, are called *simple confessors*.

The Code of Canon Law grants to all *priests,* in some circumstances, certain powers of absolving and of dispensing. The Code also grants to all *confessors,* in other circumstances, other powers of absolving and of dispensing.

The powers granted by the Code to all *priests* do

82 JURISDICTION OF THE CONFESSOR

not require that the priest have any habitual ordinary or delegated jurisdiction in order to use the power thus granted. The circumstances in which these powers are granted, and the nature of the powers conceded, are as follows:

ALL PRIESTS

1. *In Danger of Death* — The power of absolving from all sins and censures.[1] The power of dispensing from all impediments to Matrimony established by ecclesiastical law, except the impediment created by the order of Priesthood and affinity in the direct line arising from a consummated marriage.[2]

2. *In Common Error and in Positive and Probable Doubt* — Any power of jurisdiction, general or particular.[3]

3. *Confessions of Cardinals and Their Household* — The power to absolve from any sins or censures except those reserved *specialissimo modo* to the Holy See and those annexed to the violation of a secret of the Holy Office, when chosen by a Cardinal to hear his confession or the confession of one of his household.[4]

4. *Confessions of Bishops and Their Household* — The power to absolve from any sins or censures or at least those reserved to the local Ordinary, when chosen by a Bishop to hear his confession or the confession of one of his household.[5]

The powers which the Code grants in certain circumstances to *confessors* require that the priest already be

[1] Canons 882 and 2252. [3] Can. 209. [5] Can. 349, § 1, n. 1.
[2] Canons 1043 and 1044. [4] Can. 239, § 1, n. 2.

possessed of either ordinary or delegated jurisdiction to hear confessions, in order to avail himself of the powers thus granted. These powers then form a kind of supplement to the jurisdiction he has already obtained. Some of these powers are granted to all *confessors;* others are granted only to those who hold a certain office, such as a pastor. The circumstances in which the Code grants certain powers of jurisdiction to *all confessors,* and the nature of these powers are as follows:

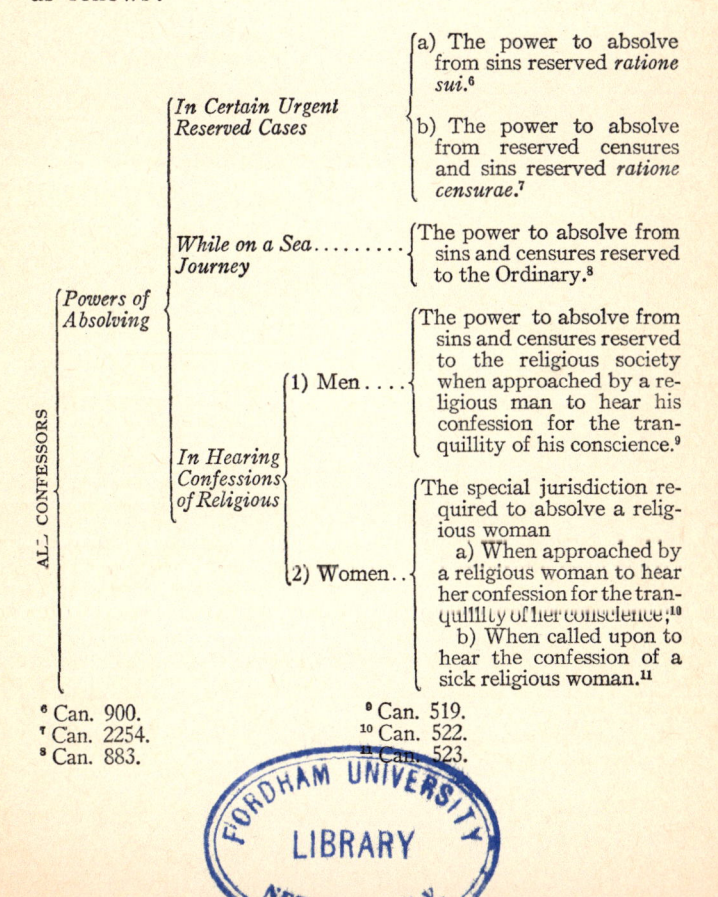

ALL CONFESSORS
- *Powers of Absolving*
  - *In Certain Urgent Reserved Cases*
    - a) The power to absolve from sins reserved *ratione sui*.[6]
    - b) The power to absolve from reserved censures and sins reserved *ratione censurae*.[7]
  - *While on a Sea Journey* — The power to absolve from sins and censures reserved to the Ordinary.[8]
  - *In Hearing Confessions of Religious*
    - 1) Men — The power to absolve from sins and censures reserved to the religious society when approached by a religious man to hear his confession for the tranquillity of his conscience.[9]
    - 2) Women — The special jurisdiction required to absolve a religious woman
      a) When approached by a religious woman to hear her confession for the tranquillity of her conscience;[10]
      b) When called upon to hear the confession of a sick religious woman.[11]

[6] Can. 900.
[7] Can. 2254.
[8] Can. 883.
[9] Can. 519.
[10] Can. 522.
[11] Can. 523.

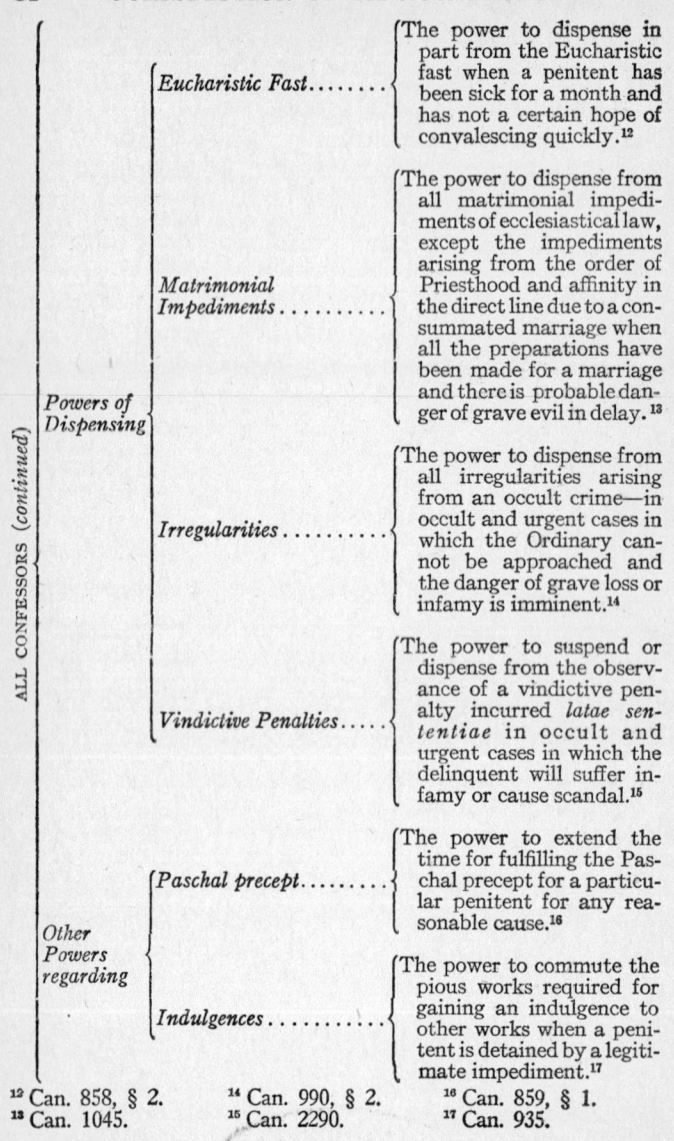

JURISDICTION OF THE CONFESSOR

ALL CONFESSORS *(continued)*

Powers of Dispensing

- *Eucharistic Fast* — The power to dispense in part from the Eucharistic fast when a penitent has been sick for a month and has not a certain hope of convalescing quickly.[12]

- *Matrimonial Impediments* — The power to dispense from all matrimonial impediments of ecclesiastical law, except the impediments arising from the order of Priesthood and affinity in the direct line due to a consummated marriage when all the preparations have been made for a marriage and there is probable danger of grave evil in delay.[13]

- *Irregularities* — The power to dispense from all irregularities arising from an occult crime—in occult and urgent cases in which the Ordinary cannot be approached and the danger of grave loss or infamy is imminent.[14]

- *Vindictive Penalties* — The power to suspend or dispense from the observance of a vindictive penalty incurred *latae sententiae* in occult and urgent cases in which the delinquent will suffer infamy or cause scandal.[15]

Other Powers regarding

- *Paschal precept* — The power to extend the time for fulfilling the Paschal precept for a particular penitent for any reasonable cause.[16]

- *Indulgences* — The power to commute the pious works required for gaining an indulgence to other works when a penitent is detained by a legitimate impediment.[17]

---

[12] Can. 858, § 2.
[13] Can. 1045.
[14] Can. 990, § 2.
[15] Can. 2290.
[16] Can. 859, § 1.
[17] Can. 935.

PRESENT LAW OF THE CODE 85

The circumstances in which the Code grants special powers to confessors who hold a particular office, and the nature of such powers, are as follows:

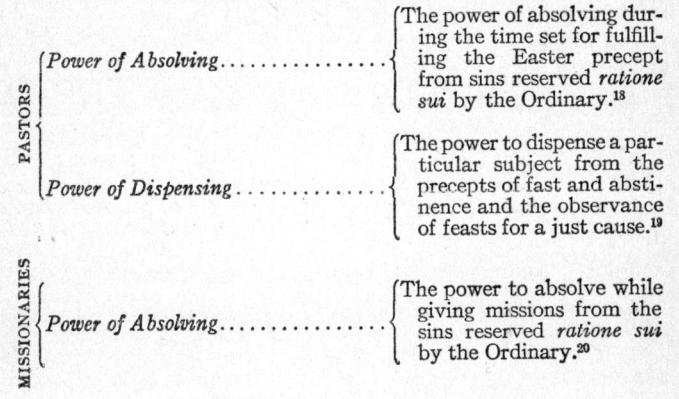

PASTORS	Power of Absolving	The power of absolving during the time set for fulfilling the Easter precept from sins reserved *ratione sui* by the Ordinary.[18]
	Power of Dispensing	The power to dispense a particular subject from the precepts of fast and abstinence and the observance of feasts for a just cause.[19]
MISSIONARIES	Power of Absolving	The power to absolve while giving missions from the sins reserved *ratione sui* by the Ordinary.[20]

This jurisdiction, which the Code grants in these extraordinary circumstances, when it is not annexed to an office in the strict sense of the term,[21] seems best called delegated by law (*delegata a jure*);[22] for the office of confessor is not an ecclesiastical office in the strict sense, and in some cases jurisdiction is granted by the Code to priests who do not hold even the office of confessor.[23] Therefore this jurisdiction cannot be said to be ordinary. Nor can it be said to be delegated *ab homine*, since it is not granted immediately and personally by a superior to an individual. However, it must be admitted that there is some doubt as to whether

---

[18] Can. 899, § 3.
[19] Can. 1245.
[20] Can. 899, § 3.
[21] Can. 145.
[22] Cappello, *De Sac.*, II, 400; Wernz-Vidal, *Jus Can.*, II, n. 373; Vermeersch-Creusen, *Epit.*, I, n. 277; Maroto, *Instit. Jur. Can.*, I, n. 705.
[23] E.g., in danger of death; cf. Canons 882, 2252, 1044.

or not there is such a thing as jurisdiction delegated by law. But in view of the definition of ordinary jurisdiction, given in Canon 197 § 1, and in view of the definition of an ecclesiastical office given in Canon 145, it is difficult to understand how such jurisdiction as this can be called anything else.

At any rate, these powers are conferred upon priests and confessors, according to the circumstances, for use in the internal sacramental forum, by the Code itself, or, more properly, by the Roman Pontiff, whose will is expressed in the Code. No superior, therefore, other than the Roman Pontiff can validly or licitly deny a priest the right to use any power conceded to him by common law provided the circumstances required by the law are present. Therefore if a superior, other than the Roman Pontiff, attempts to limit these powers granted by the Code, he acts illicitly and his limitation may be ignored. For example, if a bishop should prohibit his priests from absolving from a certain censure even in danger of death, the bishop would act illicitly, and any priest could validly and licitly absolve from the censure in danger of death, contrary to the prohibition of the bishop. However, it must be noted that this mode of procedure can be followed only when the lesser superior attempts to limit a power granted by the Code. A confessor could neither validly nor licitly proceed when a superior has limited a faculty which he himself has delegated even though his limitation is illicit. For example, if a bishop gave his priests the faculty of absolving from the censure attached to the crime of abortion provided the penitent revealed the identity of the one performing the operation, a confessor could not validly absolve from that censure without fulfilling that condition, even though the condition upon which the faculty was granted is illicit. Of course, the confessor should not carry out the illicit condition either, but rather treat the matter as any other reserved censure for which he has no specially delegated faculties.

The list of powers given above constitutes a complete enumeration of all the faculties granted by the Code for use in the internal sacramental forum. Any other faculty which a confessor possesses is derived from some other source. Other faculties are acquired by virtue of the possession of an office to which local law or custom has attached some power, or by virtue of delegation from a superior. It is our purpose now to examine each of the faculties individually which have been granted by the Code for use in the internal sacramental forum.

In examining into these powers individually, it is necessary to keep in mind the distinction between the validity of an action and the liceity of the action. Not every absolution or dispensation which can be granted validly is licit, although every invalid absolution or dispensation is at the same time illicit. There are cases where the law delegates jurisdiction to the confessor and renders his absolution valid because of the supreme interest of the Church in the good of souls;[24] but the priest is prohibited from using this jurisdiction except in extreme necessity, so that if he uses the jurisdiction without necessity, the confessor absolves validly but is guilty of sin, for he acts illicitly; e. g., the absolution

[24] "Bonum animarum est lex suprema ecclesiae."

of a dying accomplice by the guilty priest when another priest, to whom the accomplice would and could confess, is present or could be summoned easily. Therefore, in using the faculties granted by the Code to the confessor in these extraordinary circumstances, the priest must bear in mind that there are two aspects of his action with which he must be concerned: the validity of his absolution or dispensation, and the liceity of his action.[25]

[25] Wernz-Vidal, *op. cit.*, II, n. 378.

Title I

THE PENITENTIAL JURISDICTION GIVEN BY THE CODE TO ALL PRIESTS IN CERTAIN CIRCUMSTANCES

The powers of absolving and the powers of dispensing in the internal sacramental forum which the Code grants to *all priests* in certain circumstances, will be the subject matter of this title. When the circumstances specified in the ensuing canons are verified, it is not necessary that the priest be possessed of the faculty to hear confessions in the place, in order that his absolution or dispensation may be valid, for the Code grants the necessary jurisdiction in these circumstances to all who are marked with the character of priestly orders.

CHAPTER VI

IN DANGER OF DEATH

The first circumstance in which the Code grants penitential jurisdiction to all priests is when a penitent is in danger of death. In this emergency the Code grants to any priest the power of absolving any penitent from every sin and censure, and the power of dispensing any penitent from every matrimonial impediment of ecclesiastical law except two—the impediment arising from priestly orders, and the impediment of affinity in the direct line, arising from a consummated marriage. Each of these powers will be examined in detail.

ARTICLE I

THE POWER OF ABSOLVING FROM SINS AND CENSURES

Verumtamen pie admodum, ne hac ipsa occasione aliquis pereat, in eadem Ecclesia Dei custoditum semper fuit, ut nulla sit reservatio in articulo mortis, atque ideo omnes sacerdotes quoslibet poenitentes a quibusvis peccatis et censuris absolvere possunt.

Thus states the Council of Trent.[1] Testimony of the truth of this assertion may be found in almost every collection of ecclesiastical laws available.[2] Even as

---
[1] Sess. XIV, *de poenitentia*, c. 7.
[2] Cf. C. 1, *de privilegiis*, V, 7, in Extrav., Com.; C. 14, C. XXVI, q. 6; IV Conc. Carthag., c. 76, apud Mansi, III, n. 957.

early as the first general council, held at Nicaea in 325, the Church has expressed similar sentiments.[3]

The Code, in Canon 882, continues to voice this unvaried solicitude of the Church for the salvation of souls, and provides that:

> In periculo mortis omnes sacerdotes, licet ad confessiones non approbati, valide et licite absolvunt quoslibet poenitentes a quibusvis peccatis aut censuris, quantumvis reservatis et notoriis, etiamsi praesens sit sacerdos approbatus, salvo praescripto can. 884, 2252.

Strictly speaking, the meaning of the expression *in periculo mortis* differs greatly from the meaning of the expression *in articulo mortis,* for the former includes any circumstance in which it can be prudently feared that death will soon occur, whereas the latter phrase merely signifies the very last moment of life, or the occasion when death is imminent and inevitable. Canonists and theologians, however, have come to regard the two phrases as synonymous,[4] and the Holy See has repeatedly used them promiscuously,[5] so that there is no doubt that in law they have the same force. To use the faculty granted by Canon 882, therefore, it is not necessary that the penitent be on the very brink of the grave, nor was this necessary before the promulgation of the Code, notwithstanding the expression used by

---

[3] Conc. Nicaenum, Can. 13, apud Denzinger-Bannwart, n. 57.

[4] St. Alphon. VI, nn. 560, 561; Lugo, Disp. XVIII, n. 21; Ferraris, *Prompta Bibliotheca,* verbum "Jurisdictio," n. 28; D'Annibale, *Summula,* I, n. 38; Genicot-Salsmans, *Instit.,* II, n. 332; Cappello, *De Sac.,* II, n. 408; Vermeersch-Creusen, *Epit.,* II, n. 306.

[5] S. C. S. Off. (*Kentucky*), 9 maii 1821, Fontes n. 860; S. C. S. Off. (*Cincinnat.*), 13 sept. 1859, Fontes n. 955, Pius IX, const. *Apostolicae Sedis,* 12 oct. 1869, § 1, n. 12, Fontes n. 552.

the Council of Trent;[6] but it suffices that there exist in the moral estimation of the priest a prudent fear that the penitent may die within a short time.

If the priest doubts whether or not danger of death is present, he may validly and licitly absolve from any sin or censure as long as he can judge that the danger of death (not necessarily death itself) is at least probable, for if danger of death is not really present, the Church will supply jurisdiction in virtue of Canon 209. Likewise, if the confessor falsely judges that the danger of death was present when it really was not, there is no need for alarm, for the absolution was certainly valid, and, if given in good faith, also licit, in virtue of the same canon.

It is not necessary that the danger of death arise from an intrinsic cause, such as a disease, or a wound, or old age, but it suffices even if the danger arises from an extrinsic cause, such as war, a surgical operation, an aeroplane journey, etc. The Sacred Penitentiary declared on March 18, 1912, and on May 29, 1915, that soldiers mobilized for war were to be considered in danger of death even though they were not to be sent into battle immediately.[7]

The Confessor

Anyone who has been validly ordained a priest, and thereby possesses the power of orders, receives from this canon the necessary power of jurisdiction for granting absolution from any sin or censure as long as the penitent is in danger of death. Therefore, anyone

[6] Sess. XIV, *de poeniten.*, c. 7.
[7] *A. A. S.*, VII (1915), 282.

possessed of the sacramental character of priestly orders, be he apostate, heretic, or schismatic, degraded or reduced to the lay state, laboring under an irregularity, excommunication, suspension, or personal interdict, or merely one who has no jurisdiction to hear confessions, or no jurisdiction in this particular place, grants valid absolution to any penitent who is in danger of death.

In view of the wide scope given by the wording of this canon, it is the teaching of canonists and theologians that the absolution granted by any of the abovementioned priests, except an apostate, heretic or schismatic, will also be licit even in the presence of an approved priest.[8] Of course the approved priest should be preferred if there is no reason for the penitent being absolved by the unapproved priest, especially if he is laboring under a penalty. But if for any reason the penitent should prefer the unapproved priest, it is valid and licit for him to absolve. It is difficult to imagine a case in which an unapproved priest would absolve in the presence of an approved priest without any reason for so acting; but if such were the case, he would seem to commit a light sin, at any rate, by violating the order of preference demanded by natural equity.

Unless necessity urges, and another cannot be obtained, or it would be too difficult or repugnant for the penitent to confess to him who can be obtained, it is gravely illicit for a penitent to confess to an apostate, heretic, or schismatic priest even in danger of death, for this is communication *in divinis* with a heretic. But if true necessity exists, even this can be permitted as the lesser of two evils, as long as the prescriptions of the

[8] Genicot-Salsmans, *op. cit.*, II, n. 332; Cappello, *op. cit.*, II, n. 409.

natural law regarding the danger of perversion and scandal are fulfilled.[9]

The Power

The power that is granted by this canon is the jurisdiction to absolve any penitent from all sins and censures howsoever reserved. The Pontifical Commission for Interpreting the Canons of the Code has recently issued a statement to the effect that an absolution granted in virtue of the power conferred by Canon 882, is limited to the internal forum, and cannot be extended to the external forum.[10] The absolution of a censure, therefore, granted in virtue of the power received from Canon 882, has its effect only *coram Deo* and is not recognized *coram Ecclesia*.

There are no limits whatsoever to any priest's power of absolving which would affect the validity of the absolution when the penitent is in danger of death. Genicot-Salsmans would except the penalty of suspension from the confessor's faculty on this occasion, because a suspension does not impede the reception of the sacraments. He is of the opinion, therefore, that it would not be possible for a confessor to lift the suspension of a dying cleric in virtue of the jurisdiction received from Canon 882.[11] But, although it is true that the penalty of suspension does not impede the reception of the sacraments, and in no way affects the eternal salvation of the penitent's soul, yet, when the

---
[9] Lehmkuhl, II, n. 392; Genicot-Salsmans, *op. cit.*, II, nn. 130, 332.
[10] Pont. Comm. ad CC. auth. interpret., 28 dec. 1927, *A. A. S.* XX (1928), 61.
[11] Genicot-Salsmans, *op. cit.*, II, n. 332.

suspension is a censure, there does not seem to be any reason for excluding this penalty from the scope of the confessor's power in danger of death, for Canon 822 makes no distinction whatsoever, and *ubi lex non distinguit nec nos distinguere debemus*. Furthermore, the delinquent has the right to be absolved from a censure when he recedes from his contumacy, and it has always been the spirit of the Church that there be no reservations in danger of death. It would seem, therefore, that a penitent cleric has the right to be absolved by any confessor from any suspension in danger of death, so that he may go forth to meet his Judge free from any penalty which has been inflicted by the Church, even if it is merely a temporal bond. However, the lifting of the suspension by a confessor on this occasion, has its effect only *coram Deo* and is not recognized *coram Ecclesia*. Therefore, if the penitent dies and is known to have been absolved *in periculo mortis*, it may be legitimately presumed that the suspension was lifted, and *in foro externo* he may be regarded as having departed this life completely reconciled to and re-established in the Church of God. And if the penitent survives, provided no scandal will be taken, he may deport himself as absolved from the suspension unless his superiors demand that he remain under the censure *in foro externo* until he is absolved in that forum, or unless the censure was such that it is necessary for him to have recourse to a competent superior.[12]

When the suspension is a vindictive penalty, if the case is occult a confessor may suspend the obligation of observing the penalty whenever its observance will cause

[12] Canons, 2251, 2252; et Roberti in *Apollinaris*, I, (1928), 103.

scandal to others or bring ill repute to the delinquent.[13] Due to the public notice occasioned by approaching death, this condition may very easily be verified in these circumstances and there is no reason why a confessor should not therefore suspend the obligation of the further observance of the penalty imposing the things required by law. When the suspension is a vindictive penalty but the case is public and notorious, no provision is made in the Code for an emergency, most probably because of the scandal that is almost sure to accompany such a case. Therefore, in danger of death a confessor can do no more than petition the competent superior to dispense if time permits.

The Conditions

The prescriptions of the two canons cited by Canon 882 concern at most only the liceity of the confessor's action, and not the validity of his absolution. Canon 884 speaks of the liceity of the priest's action in absolving his accomplice *in peccato turpi* even in danger of death, while Canon 2252 imposes certain obligations on the penitent when he has been absolved by a simple confessor from certain censures in danger of death.

In the first case, when the penitent who is in danger of death has been the accomplice of the priest *in peccato turpi,* the canon states that it is unlawful for him to absolve that penitent even in danger of death, unless there is absolute necessity. But if he does absolve without necessity, although he commits a grave sin and incurs a severe censure,[14] yet his absolution is valid.

[13] Can. 2290.
[14] Can. 2367.

In the second case, Canon 2252 states that when the penitent is absolved by a simple confessor, in virtue of Canon 882, from a censure *ab homine,* or a censure reserved *specialissimo modo* to the Holy See, he is obliged to have recourse, within one month after he has convalesced, under pain of reincurring the censure, to the one inflicting the penalty if it is *ab homine,* or to the Sacred Penitentiary or to one having faculties over such a censure [15] if it is reserved *specialissimo modo* to the Holy See, and, having done this, he is obliged to fulfill the mandate of the superior. This obligation to have recourse, however, in no way affects the validity of the absolution.

The canon, however, directly obliges the penitent to have this recourse, without mentioning the obligation of the confessor in these circumstances. Is the confessor obliged to inform the penitent of this obligation? *Per se* it seems very probable that he is not, for the law places the obligation directly on the penitent in this canon, and if the legislator intended to place any such obligation on the priest, he would have given him the duty of imposing this burden, as he has done elsewhere.[16] *Per accidens,* however, it would seem that a confessor is obliged to inform the penitent of this obligation in most cases, for otherwise the penitent, at least if he is a layman, will never know of the obligation.

---

[15] Pont. Comm. ad CC. auth. interpret., 12 nov. 1922, ad. VIII, *A. A. S.,* XIV (1922), 663, declared that this recourse can be had only to a bishop or superior who has faculties over such censures, and not to any bishop whatsoever; the words *facultate praeditum* of Canon 2252, therefore, must be interpreted as qualifying the word *Episcopum* as well as *aliumve.*

[16] Cf. Can. 2254, § 1, and Vermeersch-Creusen, *Epit.* III, n. 452.

If the recourse is had but the penitent fails to perform the penance enjoined, some doubt that he reincurs the censure;[17] the better opinion, however, seems to be that he does, since Canon 2254 is not clear, but in the old law the censure was reincurred,[18] and therefore this discipline is to be retained until it becomes clear that the Code makes a departure from the old discipline.[19]

Although Canon 2252 does not mention any such faculty, it also seems very probable, from a comparison with Canon 2254, § 3, that a confessor absolving a penitent in danger of death from one of these censures may excuse the penitent from the obligation of having recourse to the competent superior[20] if he prudently judges that this recourse will be morally impossible for the penitent when he recuperates. This opinion is supported by the fact that the law permits a confessor to dispense from this obligation under these conditions in the urgent cases enumerated in Canon 2254; *a fortiori*, then, he should be permitted to dispense under the same conditions in the urgency of danger of death, for the same reason exists in both cases.[21] Nevertheless, in these cases a confessor must impose a congruous penance and satisfaction for the censure, which the penitent must perform within the time defined by the confessor, under pain of reincurring the censure.[22]

---

[17] Chelodi, *Jus Poenale*, n. 35; Arregui, *Summarium*, n. 617.

[18] S. C. S. Off., 30 mart. 1892, Fontes n. 1151.

[19] Cf. Can. 6, n. 4, and Vermeersch-Creusen, *op. cit.*, III, n. 452.

[20] Except the case of a dying priest who has incurred the excommunication reserved *specialissimo modo* to the Holy See, for attempting to absolve his accomplice *in peccato turpi*. Cf. Canons 2254, § 3, and 2367.

[21] Can. 20.

[22] Can. 2254, § 3.

This penance, it would seem, need not be performed until after the penitent has totally recuperated.

Finally, it also seems probable that a penitent who has been absolved while in danger of death from one of these censures and obliged to have the recourse after he has recovered, may avail himself of the privilege granted in Canon 2254, § 2, and approach a confessor having faculties over such a censure, and, having confessed the sin to which the censure is attached to this confessor, receive from him the penance for the censure, thereby dispensing with the necessity of having recourse to a superior or disregarding his mandate if the recourse were already made.[23]

ARTICLE II

The Power of Dispensing from Matrimonial Impediments

Under specified conditions, certain powers of dispensing from matrimonial impediments, and from the use of the required form of marriage, are granted to bishops and priests, by the following canons, whenever danger of death threatens one of the parties to a marriage.

Can. 1043.—Urgente mortis periculo, locorum Ordinarii, ad consulendum conscientiae et, si casus ferat, legitimationi prolis, possunt tum super forma in matrimonii celebratione servanda, tum super omnibus et singulis impedimentis juris ecclesiastici, sive publicis sive occultis, etiam multiplicibus, exceptis impedimentis provenientibus ex sacro presbyteratus

[23] Cappello, *De Censuris* n. 118.

ordine et ex affinitate in linea recta, consummato matrimonio, dispensare proprios subditos ubique commorantes et omnes in proprio territorio actu degentes, remoto scandalo, et, si dispensatio concedatur super cultus disparitate aut mixta religione, praestitis consuetis cautionibus.

Can. 1044.—In eisdem rerum adjunctis de quibus in can. 1043 et solum pro casibus in quibus ne loci quidem Ordinarius adiri possit, eadem dispensandi facultate pollet tum parochus, tum sacerdos qui matrimonio, ad normam can. 1098, n. 2, assistit, tum confessarius, sed hic pro foro interno in actu sacramentalis confessionis tantum.

Since it is the object of this book to explain the jurisdiction of the confessor only, the power of the Ordinary, pastor, and simple priest, as such, will not be included in the ensuing investigation, but the power of the confessor for the internal sacramental forum will be the sole topic of discussion. Of course it is possible that the confessor will also be the Ordinary, pastor, or priest who is about to assist at the marriage according to the norm of Canon 1098, n. 2, yet it is not as such that he will be considered here, but merely as the confessor.

This legislation, insofar as the confessor is concerned, is entirely new with the Code, the former decrees of the Holy Office on this matter granting the power exclusively to the Ordinary.[1]

The Confessor

When the danger of death is present, every priest *ipso jure* obtains jurisdiction for the internal sacra-

[1] S. C. S. Off., litt. encycl., 20 febr. 1888, Fontes n. 1109; S. C. S. Off., litt. encycl., 1 mart. 1889, Fontes n. 1113.

IN DANGER OF DEATH

mental forum,[2] and therefore is to be regarded as a confessor in this circumstance. As such, every priest enjoys all the powers of absolving and of dispensing in danger of death attributed to confessors by the Code. Therefore, every priest *ipso jure* receives the power of dispensing from these matrimonial impediments and from the required form of marriage for the internal sacramental forum, whenever a penitent is in danger of death. Accordingly, it is not necessary that the priest be a confessor (i. e., be possessed of habitual ordinary or delegated jurisdiction to hear confessions in this particular place) in order to use the power of dispensing granted to confessors by the canons cited above.

Furthermore, since every priest may hear the confession of any penitent in danger of death, so, as the confessor of Canon 1044, he may dispense any penitent from these matrimonial impediments and from the use of the required form of Matrimony, when the necessary conditions are fulfilled, regardless of whether or not the parties possess a domicile or quasi-domicile in the place of confession.

However, it must be noted that, for the priest who has not habitual jurisdiction to hear confessions in this particular place, in order that he may exercise the power of dispensing granted to him by Canon 1044, it is necessary that the penitent be the one who is in danger of death, for only in this case does he receive from Canon 882 the necessary jurisdiction for the internal sacramental forum which enables him to become the confessor required by Canon 1044.

[2] Can. 882.

102   JURISDICTION OF THE CONFESSOR

Priests who have habitual ordinary or delegated jurisdiction to hear confessions in this particular place, and who therefore may be considered as confessors, may use the power granted by Canon 1044, even when it is not the penitent but the other party to the marriage who is in danger of death, because *per se* Canon 1044 applies to cases in which either party to the marriage is in danger of death, for the law does not distinguish; and, secondly, because Matrimony is a bilateral contract in which the incapacity of one party affects the other.[3]

The Power

The power of dispensing granted by the Code to confessors as such in this circumstance seems best called delegated by law, for a confessor as such has not an office, in the strict sense of that term,[4] to which jurisdiction could be attached by the law.[5] Therefore this power does not seem to be ordinary. Nor is it delegated by an individual to a particular person, and therefore it can hardly be called *delegata ab homine*. If the confessor is at the same time the Ordinary or a pastor or one who in law is considered as coming under the name of pastor,[6] then the power of dispensing granted by these canons may be considered as ordinary, for it is attached by law to an office bearing with it ordinary jurisdiction for the internal sacramental forum. How-

---
[3] DeSmet, *De Sponsalibus et Matrimonio*, II, n. 759; Gearin, *The New Canon Law in Its Practical Aspects*, p. 151; Augustine, *A Commentary on the New Code of Canon Law*, V, p. 97.
[4] Can. 145.
[5] Wernz-Vidal, *Jus Can.*, II, n. 366.
[6] Can. 451, § 2.

ever, even in this case it would seem that the pastor and those coming under the name of pastor are forbidden to delegate this power, since the Commission for Interpreting the Code has decreed that a pastor cannot delegate the ordinary jurisdiction for the internal sacramental forum which he possesses.[7] At any rate, there is no need for delegation *ab homine* in this circumstance, since every priest *ipso jure* obtains jurisdiction for the internal sacramental forum in danger of death.

The faculty granted by the Code in this circumstance of danger of death embraces the power of dispensing from the use of the required form, and from all the impediments to Matrimony of ecclesiastical law, diriment or impeding, single or multiple, except:

1. The impediment arising from the sacred order of priesthood; and
2. The impediment arising from affinity in the direct line, in any degree, but only when the affinity arises from a consummated marriage.

It is to be noted that this faculty embraces only the impediments of ecclesiastical law, to the exclusion of impediments of the divine positive or natural law. Therefore, a confessor cannot dispense even in danger of death from the impediment of *ligamen*,[8] the impediment of consanguinity in any degree of the direct line and in the first degree of the collateral line,[9] the

[7] Pont. Comm. ad CC. auth. interpret., 16 oct. 1919, *A. A. S.*, XI (1919), 477.
[8] Con. 1069; cf. Cappello, *De Sac*, III, n. 390; Cerato, *Matrimonium a Codice Juris Canonici Desumptum*, n. 64; Chelodi, *Jus Matrimoniale*, n. 76.
[9] Can. 1076; and Cappello, *op. cit.*, III, n. 518; Vlaming, *Praelectiones*, I, n. 393; Augustine, *Com. on New Code*, V, p. 100.

impediment of impotency when it is certain [10] (but this will seldom be met in danger of death).

The confessor can use this power of dispensing in the internal sacramental forum and in the act of sacramental confession only. Therefore, the dispensation is recognized as effective only *coram Deo sed non coram Ecclesia*, and a new dispensation is required for the recognition of the validity of the marriage *coram Ecclesia*.[11]

The Code does not limit the exercise of the faculty in this circumstance to occult cases; are public cases therefore also included? Many authorities deny that public cases are included in this faculty of the confessor, and their principal reason for this position is that they hold the internal forum, by its very nature, incapable of taking cognizance of a public case.[12] However, it would seem that public cases are included in this faculty, for the internal forum, of its nature, does not exclude the exercise of jurisdiction over public cases, but, of its nature, merely excludes the act of jurisdiction from taking effect in the external forum. Therefore, in order that public cases be excluded, it would be necessary that express mention of this fact be made in the law. But no mention of this exclusion is made in these canons; on the contrary, the confessor is said to enjoy *eadem dispensandi facultate* as do the others.[13] There-

---

[10] Can. 1068.
[11] Canons 202, § 1, and 1047.
[12] Vlaming, *op. cit.*, II, n. 414; Cappello, *op. cit.*, III, n. 238; Wernz-Vidal, *op. cit.*, V, n. 428; De Smet, *De Sponsalibus*, II, n. 794; Ojetti, in *Jus Pontificium*, VI (1926), 56-61; *Il Monitore Ecclesiastico*, XXXII (1920), 62 seq.
[13] Vermeersch-Creusen, *Epitome*, II, n. 312; Chelodi, *op. cit.*, n. 44; Augustine, *op. cit.*, V, pp. 103-104; Oesterele, *Munsterisches Pastoralblatt*, LVII, 131.

IN DANGER OF DEATH

fore, in danger of death a confessor need not hesitate to dispense from any impediment of ecclesiastical law except the two mentioned above, regardless of whether the impediment is public or occult.[14]

When a dispensation from the impediment of disparity of cult or mixed religion is granted in virtue of this power, it is necessary for the confessor to obtain the customary promises. Therefore, the non-Catholic party must promise not to interfere in any way with the practice of the Catholic party's religion, and both parties must promise that the children will be baptized and reared in the Catholic religion. Although these promises regularly should be made in writing,[15] it seems quite certain that in danger of death it suffices if they are made orally.[16]

There is a much-mooted question among canonists and theologians as to whether these promises are necessary for the validity or merely for the liceity of the dispensation, and whether it is ever valid and licit to dispense from either of these impediments without obtaining these promises. Before setting forth the views of the various authors, it is necessary to note that the divine law itself prohibits such a marriage unless the danger of perversion to the Catholic party and the danger of the children being reared outside of the true faith are removed or at least rendered remote dangers. Unless this requisite of the divine law is satisfied, the Church is incapable of dispensing validly from this impediment to Matrimony. The means of satisfying

---

[14] A more complete treatment of this question is given below under the *casus perplexus*. Cf. p. 221.
[15] Can. 1061, § 2.
[16] Cf. Cerato, *op. cit.*, n. 55.

the requisites of the divine law have been established by the ecclesiastical law in the form of the customary promises, although *per se* the divine law could be fulfilled by other means.[17] Therefore, it is certain that when the divine law can be fulfilled only by obtaining the promises required by the ecclesiastical law, a dispensation granted without these promises would be invalid. It is likewise certain that the promises required by the ecclesiastical law, *per se*, are always required for the liceity of the dispensation, so that *per se* it will always be gravely sinful to grant such a dispensation without obtaining the promises. *Per accidens*, however, circumstances may mitigate or even obliterate the sinfulness of this action.

The exact point of dispute is whether a dispensation granted without obtaining these promises would ever be valid. The Church has never declared that a dispensation granted in danger of death without these promises was invalid, but she has repeatedly declared that these promises are to be sought even in danger of death.[18]

Because the Church has declared that these promises are always to be sought, and because she has never dispensed, even in the most urgent cases, without these promises, but rather has resorted to the extraordinary means of granting a *sanatio in radice,* some authors [19]

---

[17] Gasparri, *De Matrimonio*, I, n. 497.

[18] S. C. S. Off., 18 mart. 1891, Coll. n. 1750; 21 jun. 1912, *A. A. S.,* IV (1912), 442.

[19] De Smet, *op. cit.* II, n. 508 note 1, n. 591 note 4; Noldin, *Summa,* III, n. 608; Woywod, *A Practical Commentary on the Code of Canon Law,* n. 1011; and *Homiletic and Pastoral Review,* XXIII (1923), 1059; Augustine, *op. cit.*, V, p. 101; Prümmer, *Manuale Theologiae Moralis,* n. 866. Chelodi, *op. cit.*, n. 41 and Wernz-Vidal, *op. cit.*, V, n. 413, are doubtful, stating only that the dispensation is not certainly valid.

maintain that a dispensation granted without obtaining the explicit promises required by the ecclesiastical law is always invalid. On the other hand, other authors hold that, if the divine law ceases, or if the divine law can be fulfilled without using the means prescribed by the Church, such a dispensation granted without exacting the customary promises would be valid.[20] These authors maintain that although the Church has repeatedly declared that these promises are to be sought even in danger of death, and although the Church has preferred to resort to the extraordinary means of a *sanatio in radice* rather than grant a dispensation without obtaining the explicit promises required by ecclesiastical law, yet since *bonum animarum est lex suprema Ecclesiae,* the Church will not insist on the observance of her law when the obligation of the divine law has ceased, for *in extremis pereat lex.*

This opinion seems solidly probable [21] and, in virtue of Canon 209, it may be followed in practice, but the difficulty still remains of determining in a practical case when the divine law has ceased or when the requisites of the divine law have been attained without exacting the promises required by the ecclesiastical law. It would seem that the only case in which the obligation of the divine law can be said certainly to have ceased, is one

---

[20] Cappello, *De Sac,* III, 232; Genicot-Salsmans, *Instit.,* II, nn. 493, 514, 523; Cerato, *Matrimonium a Codice Jur. Can. Desump.,* n. 35; Pighi, *De Sacramento Matrimonii* n. 90; DeBecker, *De Sponsalibus et Matrimonio,* pp. 243 and 278, note 1; Petrovits, *The New Church Law on Matrimony,* nn. 160, 192; Farrugia, *De Matrimonio et Causis Matrimonialibus,* n. 83; Kubelbeck, *The Sacred Penitentiary and Its Relation to the Faculties of Ordinaries and Priests,* p. 63; *Irish Eccl. Rec.* Series IV, XXVIII (1910), 634; *Homiletic and Pastoral Review,* XXII (1922), 510.

[21] Vermeersch-Creusen, *Epitome,* II, n. 306.

in which the non-Catholic party is on the verge of death, not merely in danger of death, but in actual *articulo mortis,* death being inevitable and proximate. In this case, if the Catholic party will promise to baptize and rear the children in the Catholic faith, it seems quite certain, in virtue of Canon 209, that one could validly and, *suppositis supponendis,* even licitly grant a dispensation without exacting the customary canonical promises. In other cases it is difficult to see how the prohibition of the divine law can cease or its obligation be fulfilled without securing the canonical promises, especially if these have once been sought and been refused.

The Conditions

In order that a confessor may validly exercise the power of dispensing conferred upon him by these canons, the following conditions must be verified:

1. One of the parties to the marriage must be in danger of death. *Per se* it matters not which of the parties is in danger of death, whether it be the penitent or the other party,[22] whether it be the one directly affected by the impediment or not,[23] whether it be the one troubled in conscience or not,[24] for the canons make no distinction whatsoever. *Per accidens,* however, the confessor may be restricted in the use of this faculty to the case where it is the penitent who is in danger of

---
[22] Iidem.
[23] S. C. S. Off., 1 jul. 1891, Coll., n. 1758; Vlaming, *Praelectiones Juris Matrimonii,* II, n. 401; Chelodi, *Jus Matrimoniale,* n. 41; Wernz-Vidal, *Jus Canon.,* V, n. 413; De Smet, *op. et loc. cit.*
[24] *De Smet op. et loc. cit.;* Gearin, *op. et loc. cit.;* Augustine, *op. et loc cit.*

IN DANGER OF DEATH

death.[25] Actual *articulus mortis* need not be present, but it suffices in this case also that there be merely a prudent danger that death may follow shortly. This danger may arise either from an intrinsic or extrinsic cause, as has already been pointed out.[26]

2. The faculty can be validly used only for the cases specified in the law, viz:

- (a) For the soothing of the conscience of one of the parties; or
- (b) For the legitimization of offspring, if the case warrants it.

This is a taxative enumeration of the cases to which this faculty may be applied, so that the power cannot be validly used in any other case or for any other cause. However, it is not necessary that both causes be present in the same case, for the wording of the canon is evidently disjunctive.[27] But it is quite certain that the presence of at least one of these causes is necessary for the validity of the dispensation.[28] It hardly seems possible, however, that the condition *ad consulendum conscientiae* will not be present, or at least able to be instilled, in any case in which it is the confessor who is to dispense. Nevertheless, it must be noted that it is not necessary that absolution be granted in order to dispense from the impediment to marriage,[29] for the canon demands only that it be in the act of sacramental confession; and a sacramental confession is one made for

---
[25] Supra, p. 101.
[26] Supra, p. 91.
[27] Vlaming, *op. cit.*, II, n. 401; Augustine, *op. et loc. cit.*
[28] Genicot-Salsmans, *Instit.*, II n. 523; Cappello, *De Sac.*, III, n. 232; Motry, *Diocesan Faculties*, p. 130.
[29] Sac. Poenit, 19 maii 1834, et 4 jan. 1839.

the purpose of obtaining absolution from sin, regardless of whether or not this end is attained.[30]

If there are children to be legitimated, some further annotations are necessary. If the confessor holds an office to which the law attaches ordinary jurisdiction for the internal sacramental forum, the children are legitimated by the dispension itself, provided they are not of an adulterous or sacrilegious union, for the power granted in Canons 1043 and 1044 in this case, it would seem, is ordinary.[31] If the confessor does not hold such an office, the children are not legitimated by the dispensation itself, for the power granted by Canons 1043 and 1044 in this case seems to be only delegated by law, and Canon 1051 grants the effect of legitimizing the offspring only to a dispensation conceded from ordinary power. If the children are not yet born, this will present little practical difficulty in danger of death at any rate, for the subsequent marriage of the parents will almost always follow immediately, and this certainly legitimates the unborn child.[32] But if the children are already born, or were conceived or born of an adulterous or sacrilegious union, the confessor can do nothing but ask the penitent to reveal the condition of affairs to him outside of confession, and then petition the Holy See to grant a decree of legitimization if this is possible in the case.

Authors dispute whether or not it is possible to use the power granted by Canons 1043 and 1044 in a case in which the children are of an adulterous or sacrilegious union and the only reason for dispensing is to

[30] Noldin, *Summa Theo. Mor.*, III, n. 267.
[31] Can. 1051; cf. De Smet, *op. et loc. cit.*
[32] Can. 1116.

IN DANGER OF DEATH

legitimate the children. It is hard to conceive of the confessor being confronted with such a case, because in almost every case in which the confessor will be called upon to dispense, the condition *ad consulendum conscientiae* will be present. However, if such a case should exist, the dispensation can be granted on the authority of the affirmative opinion, because the Holy See will more easily grant a decree of legitimization to such a child if the parents are married.[33]

Finally, it is to be noted that if the impediment involved is one arising from a solemn vow of chastity, or from the order of diaconate or subdiaconate, the dispensation is valid for this marriage only, so that if the party now in danger of death recovers, marital relations will be licit; but if the party dies, the one bound by the impediment may not remarry, because the dispensation is granted primarily and principally to enable the dying person to make his peace with God.[34]

3. This power can be used validly by a confessor only in cases in which not even the local Ordinary can be approached. The impossibility of approaching the Ordinary must be taken morally, so that if he can be reached only by the use of extraordinary means,[35] or only with grave inconvenience, or with danger of violating a secret, sacramental or natural, the case can be

---

[33] Chelodi, *op. et loc. cit.*; Cappello, *op. et loc. cit.*

[34] Reiffenstuel, *Jus Canonicum Universum*, IV, Appendix, *De Dispensatione super Impedimentis Matrimonii*, nn. 12 and 13; Chelodi, *op. cit.*, n. 88.

[35] Telephone and telegraph are still considered as extraordinary means of communication and there is no obligation to use them. Cf. Pont. Comm. ad CC. auth. interpret., 12 nov. 1922, ad V, *A. A. S.*, XIV (1922), 662. In fact, the use of these means of communication is frowned upon by the Holy See. Cf. litt. encycl. Secr. Status, 10 dec. 1891, Coll. n. 1775; S. C. S. Off., 24 aug. 1892, Coll. n. 1810.

regarded as one in which the Ordinary cannot be approached. The ordinary means of approaching the Ordinary are by letter or by personal visit, so that if he cannot be approached in either of these ways without grave inconvenience, it can be considered morally impossible to approach him. It must be borne in mind, however, that the validity of the dispensation does not depend upon the actual possibility or impossibility of approaching the Ordinary, but only upon the confessor's honest and prudent judgment that such an impossibility exists, regardless of the real objective condition of affairs. Accordingly, if the confessor, judging that it is morally impossible to approach the Ordinary, grants a dispensation, this dispensation would be valid even if the Ordinary, unknown to the priest, were in the same house in which the confessor acted. There does not seem to be any obligation on the confessor to approach a delegate of the Ordinary even where this is possible, for the canon mentions only the Ordinary.[36] However, there is authority for the claim that such an obligation does exist.[37]

4. The removal of scandal is a necessary prerequisite to the *licit* use of this power. Because of the nature of the dispensation which he grants, a confessor must be especially careful that this condition is fulfilled. He must warn the parties that the dispensation which he grants, takes effect only before God, and that in the eyes of the Church and in the eyes of the community they still remain unmarried, although in the eyes of God they are really and truly married. Accordingly,

[36] Motry, *Diocesan Faculties,* p. 136.
[37] Vlaming, *Praelectiones,* II, n. 412.

IN DANGER OF DEATH

marital relations between the parties are no longer forbidden nor sinful; but because of the danger of scandal, they must be forbidden to live together publicly until a dispensation can be obtained from the bishop or the Holy See and they have renewed their consent in the external forum. This procedure is necessary at least in the case where the parties are known to have been unmarried, whatever may be said of other more or less occult cases.

In fact, in all cases in which the confessor is called upon to grant a dispensation in the internal sacramental forum, where it is at all possible it is necessary for him to make some provision to prevent the subsequent repudiation of the marriage in the external forum. What these steps will be, depends in a large measure on the nature of the impediment, the circumstances of the case, and the dispositions of the parties. If the impediment is not defamatory and there is no particular reason for keeping it secret, the penitent must be told that he is morally obliged to reveal the impediment outside of confession either to the priest assisting at the marriage, or to the confessor himself if he is to assist at the marriage, in order that a dispensation may be granted in the external forum. If the impediment is defamatory or there is a special reason for secrecy, the penitent must be asked to reveal the impediment either to the confessor outside of confession if he is to assist at the marriage, or to the priest assisting at the marriage, so that a dispensation for the internal non-sacramental forum may be granted and the dispensation registered in the secret archives of the Diocesan Curia or the Sacred Penitentiary. This procedure can be followed without betraying the secret, and at the same time providing for the recognition of the dispensation and the validity of the subsequent marriage in the external forum.[38] If the penitent refuses to submit to this reasonable mode of proceeding, the confessor, according to his prudent judgment, may dispense in the sacramental forum without making any provision for the recognition of the dispensation in the external forum, or he may refuse to dispense in the sacramental forum, for, although he has the power to do so, he is not obliged to use his power if the penitent is lacking in the proper dispositions.[39]

Dispensation from the Form

Finally, it must be noted that in danger of death a confessor also has the faculty of dispensing from the prescribed *form* of marriage (i.e., the presence of an authorized priest and two witnesses). Furthermore, there is nothing to prevent him from dispensing from both the *form* of marriage and an impediment, or several impediments, in one and the same case. However, the power of granting a *sanatio in radice* is not included in this faculty, for this is a power distinct from the faculty of dispensing and can be granted only by the Holy See or its delegate.[40] Therefore, the confessor must always advise the penitent of the necessity of renewing his consent in some manner.

In practice, therefore, if no impediment exists, and

---

[38] Can. 1047.
[39] *Nouvelle Revue Theologique,* XLVII (1920), pp. 261-274.
[40] Can. 1141 and Cappello, *op. cit.,* III, n. 232; De Smet, *De Sponsalibus,* II, n. 761; Ayrinhac, *Marriage Legislation in the New Code of Canon Law.* p. 323.

the marriage is invalid due merely to the lack of the required form, the confessor should endeavor to have the parties give their consent outside of confession, before a priest and two witnesses. If this cannot be done without scandal, or if only one witness can be obtained, the confessor may dispense from the use of the prescribed form and have the parties give their consent before him alone or merely to each other, even without the presence of any priest or witnesses. However, if the marriage is invalid because of the existence of a diriment impediment, regardless of whether or not the prescribed form was used, the confessor must inform the penitent of the necessity of renewing his consent. If the impediment was public (i.e., capable of being proven in the external forum), the consent of both parties must be renewed before a priest and two witnesses, unless the confessor sees fit to dispense from the form also. If the impediment was occult (i.e., incapable of being proven in the external forum), yet known to both parties, the consent must be renewed by both parties, but they may do this privately and in secret. If the impediment was altogether occult and known only to one party, it suffices that he alone renew his consent privately and secretly by a new act of the will, as long as the consent of the other party still perdures.[41] In these two latter cases in which the impediment was occult, it is not necessary to renew the consent in the prescribed form if the marriage already took place before an authorized priest and two witnesses. Therefore, in these cases no dispensation from the form is necessary. But if the marriage never took

[41] Can. 1135.

place before an authorized priest and two witnesses, even though an occult impediment also exists, the consent must be given in the prescribed form, or the confessor on this occasion must grant a dispensation from the form as well as from the impediment.

CHAPTER VII

IN CASES OF COMMON ERROR, DOUBT, AND INADVERTENCE

Canon 209 includes within its scope two distinct cases: the case of common error on the part of the faithful regarding the jurisdiction of the priest; and the case of doubt on the part of the priest regarding his jurisdiction. It is not necessary that both common error on the part of the faithful and doubt on the part of the priest concur, in order that the Church supply the missing jurisdiction, but it suffices that either one or the other circumstance be present. The Church is said to supply the jurisdiction, because in her common law she states that she will supply the lack of jurisdiction whenever these circumstances are present. This jurisdiction, therefore, may be called delegated by the law itself or, more properly, by the author of the law and the source of all jurisdiction, the Roman Pontiff.[1] This jurisdiction is conferred in the very act of absolution, so that before the absolution is given and after it is finished, the confessor is still devoid of this particular power of jurisdiction.[2] The deficit, supplied by the Church, may be any power of jurisdiction, but since this book is concerned only with the confessor, jurisdiction for the internal sacramental forum will be the sole topic

---
[1] Wernz-Vidal, *Jus Can.*, II, n. 379; Cappello, *De Sac.*, II, n. 486; Noldin, *Summa*, III, n. 344, n. 2.
[2] Lehmkuhl, *Theo. Mor.*, II, n. 387; Vermeersch-Creusen, *Epitome*, I, n. 284.

of discussion. Therefore, in this case the deficit supplied by the Church may be the lack of all power of jurisdiction for hearing confessions, or the lack of this power in this particular territory, or merely the lack of this power over this individual penitent, or this particular sin or censure; so that a confessor never possessed of jurisdiction at all, or never in this place, or possessed of jurisdiction but here and now lacking it over this single penitent or particular sin, confers valid absolution when the prescriptions of this canon are verified. The canon reads:

In errore communi aut in dubio positivo et probabili sive juris sive facti, jurisdictionem supplet Ecclesia pro foro tum externo tum interno.

The Church does not supply every defect in the absolution of the priest, but only those defects which she is able and is willing to supply. Some deficiencies she is unable to supply, e. g., the lack of priestly orders in a putative confessor, while others she is unwilling to supply, e. g., the lack of jurisdiction when only private or non-common error is present.[3] But the Church will supply the defect of jurisdiction in a confessor when common error on the part of the faithful is present or when a confessor finds himself the possessor of only probable jurisdiction, as long as his doubt is both positive and probable. The reason why the Church supplies the defect of jurisdiction in the former case is the common good of souls alone; and in the latter case, the good of the faithful plus the added reason that other-

[3] Reiffenstuel, II, *Jus Can. Univ.*, De Jud., n. 202 seq.

wise the confessor might become the prey of scruples and anxieties.[4]

ARTICLE I

COMMON ERROR

Error is a false subjective judgment regarding an objective reality. Philosophically it differs from ignorance, which is merely the subjective lack of knowledge regarding an object; whereas, error implies the further step of forming a judgment, and that judgment a mistaken one. The two, however, are very closely correlated, since error always implies the presence of ignorance and arises from it.[5]

Origin of the Law

The origin of the present law of the Church on this matter can be traced back to the ancient Roman Law, which had rendered slaves incapable of holding public office. According to Ulpian, one Barbarius Philippus, while he was still a slave, fled to Rome, where he sought and acquired the praetorship without disclosing the fact that he was still a slave. When his true status became known, the question arose regarding the validity of his juridical acts and judgments. Ulpian declares that none of these acts are to be considered void,

---
[4] St. Alphon., VI, n. 572; Ballerini-Palmieri, *Opus Theo. Mor.*, V, n. 396; D'Annibale, *Summula,* I, n. 79; Lehmkuhl, *op. cit.*, II, n. 387; Vermeersch-Creusen, *op. cit.*, I, n. 284; Cappello, *op. cit.*, II, n. 487, 5; Noldin, *op. cit.*, III, n. 346, *I;* Wernz-Vidal, *op. cit.*, II, n. 379.
[5] Hickey, *Summula Philosophiae Scholasticae,* I, n. 160, note 1; Clark, *Logic,* p. 419.

because of the common good, *"hoc enim humanius est: cum etiam potuit populus Romanus servo decernere hanc potestatem."*[6] Other cases of the effects of common error may also be found in the law of Justinian.[7]

In the Decree of Gratian there is a passage that is admitted generally to be the first instance of the use of this principle in Canon Law. The passage reads as follows: *"Verum, si servus, dum putaretur liber, ex delegatione sententiam dixit, quamvis postea in servitutem delapsus sit, sententia ab eo dicta rei judicatae firmitatem tenet."*[8] The Decretals of Gregory IX contain an implicit application of this principle when they state that it is necessary to re-try a case in which sentence had been passed by a judge who had been publicly excommunicated, for at that time all excommunications bore with them the deprival of jurisdiction.[9] The implication in this passage is, that if the excommunication was private and therefore unknown to the people, the sentence would be valid even after the lack of jurisdiction was discovered.[10]

No explicit statement, however, of the principle that the Church would supply jurisdiction in common error, is found either in the Decree of Gratian or in the Decretals. But because of these passages, it became an accepted axiom among canonists and theologians, that the Church would supply jurisdiction in common error. But some demanded, together with common error, that

---

[6] Corpus Juris Civilis, *Digest,* I, 14, 3.
[7] Corpus Juris Civilis, *Codex,* IV, 28, I.
[8] C. 1, C. III, q. 7.
[9] C. 24, X, *De Sententia et re judicata,* II, 27.
[10] Reiffenstuel, *op. cit.,* II, n. 197 seq.

COMMON ERROR, DOUBT AND INADVERTENCE 121

the official possess a colored title to jurisdiction (i. e., a claim to jurisdiction which had the appearance of being valid but which was vitiated by a hidden defect) before the Church would supply jurisdiction. They demanded this because in all the cases which had the official sanction of the law, a colored title was present.[11] But others denied the necessity of a colored title because, whether or not such a title was present, the reason for the principle remained as long as the faithful generally were in error.[12] The matter was still controverted until the promulgation of the new Code.

The Code raised this principle of canonists to the dignity of law, but the silence of Canon 209 regarding the necessity of a colored title is accepted by all as positive, and therefore as subversive of the necessity of such a title as long as common error is present.[13]

In the old law, when a colored title was present, little attention was directed to the actual existence of the common error, for when the colored title was present the error was presumed. The Code, however, by failing to require the presence of any real title, centers its attention on the actual existence of common error. The question to be determined therefore is: When is common error present? This is greatly disputed among canonists and theologians.

---

[11] Reiffenstuel, *op. et loc. cit*: DeAngelis, *Praelectiones Juris Canonici*, De Judiciis, IV, 23; Santi, *Praelectiones Juris Canonici*, De Iudiciis, n 14
[12] Schmalzgrueber, *Jus Eccl. Univ.*, IV, n. 180; D'Annibale, *op. cit.*, 1, n. 79; Lugo, Disp., XIX, n. 30; Suarez, V, Disp., XXVI, Sect. 6, n. 6; Diana, II, Tract. XV, n. 2.
[13] Vermeersch-Creusen, *op. cit.*, I, n. 284; Wernz-Vidal, *op. cit.*, II, n. 381; Cappello, *op. cit.*, II, n. 496; Blat, *Com. in Text. Jur. Can.*, II, n. 158; Arregui, *Sum. Theo. Mor.*, n. 608; Badii, *Inst. Jur. Can.*, I, n. 149, n. 1.

The Place of the Error

In the first place, it will be necessary to determine where the error is to exist. All agree that the error must exist in the place where the confessions are heard, even though the people of another locality might not be laboring under any misapprehension whatsoever regarding the lack of jurisdiction in this confessor.[14] But at this point concurrence of opinion ceases. Some hold that the commonness of the error is to be judged by the number of the penitents who actually approach the confessor to obtain absolution, so that the error cannot be considered common until all, or almost all, or a majority, or at least a considerable number of the faithful in a given place actually approach the putative confessor.[15] To admit this opinion would be to nullify the very reason for the law, which, all admit, is the common good of souls, for on this hypothesis it would be necessary for most of the people of a place to be invalidly absolved before the error would become common and the Church begin to supply the missing jurisdiction. Therefore, the opinion to be preferred as almost certain, is the opinion of those who teach that the basis on which the generality of the error is to be judged, is not the number who actually approach the confessor, but rather the number of people in the place where the confessions are heard.[16] The place in which the error

---

[14] *Idem.*
[15] Tanquerey, *Synopsis Theologiae Moralis,* n. 307.
[16] Lehmkuhl, *Theo. Mor.,* II, n. 389; Vermeersch-Creusen, *Epit. Jur. Can.,* I, n. 284; Cappello, *De Sac.,* II, n. 489; Wernz-Vidal, *Jus Can.,* II, n. 381; Cocchi, *Com. in Cod. Jur. Can.,* II, n. 132; *Irish Eccl. Record,* Series V, Vol. XVI-2 (1920), p. 500; *Nouvelle Revue Theologique,* L (1923), p. 172.

exists, may be any locality, community, or establishment, the people of which may be classified as a distinct unit, e. g., a diocese, a town, a parish, a church, a convent, a college, etc.[17] The people to be considered are, not all the people of a mixed community, but only the faithful, for they alone are concerned, and it is for the common good of the faithful that the Church supplies the deficient jurisdiction.

The Number in Error

The next question to be determined is: How many of the faithful of a place need be under the misapprehension before the error can be considered as common? Once again authors disagree. Some require *moral unanimity* among the people of a place, but they admit that knowledge of the confessor's deficient power on the part of one or two of the faithful would not disturb the moral unanimity.[18] A *majority* of the faithful is deemed sufficient by other authorities,[19] in order that the error be considered common. A third class of authors think that the error can be considered common when *many* of the faithful of a particular place are laboring under the misapprehension.[20] Among these, Gury-Ballerini notes judiciously that an exact number cannot be determined, for it would be absurd and like

---

[17] Vermeersch-Creusen, *op. et loc. cit.*
[18] Reiffenstuel, *Jus. Can. Univ.*, IV, n. 76; Schmalzgrueber, *Jus Eccl. Univ.*, I, n. 22; Santi, *Praelect. Jur. Can.*, De Judiciis, n. 14; Chelodi, *Jus de Personis*, n. 130; Noldin, *Summa Theo. Mor.*, III, 346; Prümmer, *Manuale Jur. Can.*, Q. 90; Woywod, *Practical Commentary on the Code of Canon Law*, I, n. 161.
[19] Gennari, *Consultations de Morale*, n. LXIX.
[20] Lehmkuhl, *Theo. Mor.*, II, n. 382; Gury-Ballerini, *Compend. Theo. Mor.*, II, n. 359; Arregui, *Sum. Theo. Mor.*, n. 602.

unto the sophists of ancient Greece to set down a definite mathematical rule.[21]

This latter opinion may be accepted as very probable and safe in practice. Therefore, the number of those in error must merely be proportionate to the number of the faithful in the place; a number which, in the moral estimation of prudent men, would be sufficient to make the error common in contradistinction to private. The error of one hundred in a community of three hundred would seem enough to make the error sufficiently common to distinguish it from private error in such a community; whereas the error of one hundred in a parish of a thousand souls, could hardly be considered common in relation to that community.

However, it must be admitted that this vague criterion for judging when an error is common and when it is not, gives rise to a serious difficulty. How is one to determine the extent of the prevailing error? How is it possible to discover how many people in a particular place actually are in error, for, as Vidal remarks,[22] many of the people of the place do not approach the confessor, and do not even think of approaching him, and many do not even know of his existence, much less of his lack of jurisdiction, and therefore cannot be said to err in judging that he possesses jurisdiction.

The Opinion of Recent Canonists

This practical difficulty has led some recent canonists to set forth the opinion that the faithful need not actu-

[21] *Op. cit.*, II, n. 359, note 9.
[22] Wernz-Vidal, *op. et loc. cit.*

ally be in error at all, as long as there is a public fact posited as a foundation from which many necessarily will be led into error.[23] An example of such a foundation would be as follows: A pastor announces to his flock on Sunday, that on a certain day a strange priest will hear confessions. The priest arrives on schedule but for some reason fails to obtain jurisdiction from the local Ordinary. These authors maintain that the announcement of the pastor is a public foundation for the error, so that the faithful, after hearing the announcement, necessarily will be led into error, and the Church will begin to supply the jurisdiction immediately.

This opinion eliminates the practical difficulty mentioned above, for, having placed the public fact from which the faithful in general might be led into error, the confessor may prudently judge that the people generally do not know that he is lacking in jurisdiction. Accordingly, the public fact becomes a very definite norm on which the confessor may base his judgment. But this theory is not without difficulties, for, in the first place, it demands the presence of something similar to the colored title of old, which the Code does not demand, and it does not provide for the case in which common error is actually present without any such public foundation. Secondly, centering its attention on the public foundation, this theory does not demand the existence of common error, for common error is not

[23] Vermeersch-Creusen, *op. cit.*, I, n. 284; Wernz-Vidal, *op. et loc. cit.* Cappello, *op. cit.*, II, n. 490; Cocchi, *op. cit.*, II, n. 132; Bucceroni, *Casus Conscientiae*, (ed. 6), II, nn. 139-5; *Nouvelle Revue Theologique*, L (1923), p. 173. *Jus Pontificium*, III (1923), 148.

actually present in these circumstances.[24] In fact, no error whatsoever seems to be present, but only a general absence of knowledge regarding the confessor's deficient power, because the notion of error implies a judgment. It seems hardly probable that the faithful, learning of the public fact, pass any judgment on the presence or absence of jurisdiction in the confessor, for even if they knew of the necessity of jurisdiction for valid absolution, it does not seem probable that they would recall it at the moment the announcement of the approach of a strange confessor is made. Therefore, the only thing that would appear to exist in the minds of the faithful is general ignorance of the lack of jurisdiction in the confessor; and it is not until each one actually approaches the putative confessor, that he can be presumed to make even an implicit judgment that he is approaching an authorized confessor, thus transporting himself from the state of ignorance into error. Then this error does not become common until many of the faithful have already approached the putative confessor.

The proponents of this opinion reject the opinion of those who hold that the Church will not supply the missing jurisdiction until the error has actually become common, because this is destructive of the very reason for the law; therefore, they hold that as soon as the public fact has been placed, the Church will supply jurisdiction immediately. None of them, however, explicitly admits that what actually exists in these circumstances is ignorance; some, admitting that there is no common error *de facto* present, prefer to call what does

[24] *Irish Eccl. Record,* Series V, Vol. XVI-2 (1920), p. 501.

exist, *error de jure* [25] or *error interpretativus.*[26] Father Jombart, however, apparently insists that common error (*error de facto*) actually is present from the beginning, for, he argues, the faithful, hearing the announcement of the pastor, immediately recall, although perhaps vaguely or subconsciously, that jurisdiction is necessary for a confessor, and then make at least a virtual judgment that the priest shall have obtained this necessary power before he arrives.[27] This, however, appears to be far fetched or at least gratuitously asserted.

But, regardless of what actually exists in these circumstances, a more fundamental question remains to be solved. Will the Church supply jurisdiction when only common ignorance exists, or the general lack of knowledge regarding the confessor's deficient power, before this general ignorance actually becomes common error and regardless of whether or not it arises from a public foundation. None of the above-mentioned authors admits that the Church will supply jurisdiction when only general ignorance exists which is not consequent upon the foundation of a public fact.

It is our opinion that the Church will supply jurisdiction when only common ignorance actually exists, even if this ignorance is not based upon the foundation of any public fact. Of course the presence of such a public foundation is an advantage, since it offers a very definite norm upon which the priest may base his judgment regarding the existence or the commonness of the ignorance, but such a foundation is not necessary either

[25] Wernz-Vidal, *op. et loc. cit.*
[26] Vermeersch-Cruesen, *op. et loc. cit.*
[27] *Nouvelle Revue Theologique, loc. cit.*

for the existence or the commonness of the ignorance. Therefore, whenever common ignorance exists or at least can be prudently thought to exist, even though it is not based upon any public foundation, in our opinion the Church will supply jurisdiction.

In this opinion there are three elements which we shall attempt to prove individually. These elements are contained in the following propositions:

I. That in common ignorance as well as in common error, the Church will supply jurisdiction;

II. That the presence of a public foundation for this ignorance is not necessary in order that the Church supply jurisdiction;

III. That not only when this common ignorance is *de facto* objectively present will the Church supply jurisdiction, but also when it is merely prudently and honestly thought to exist regardless of the objective truth of this judgment.

I. The Church will supply jurisdiction when general ignorance of the lack of jurisdiction in the confessor is present on the part of the faithful.

1. Error and ignorance differ one from the other philosophically, for error means a false judgment, whereas ignorance expresses merely an absence of knowledge. The two, however, are very closely correlated, so that error never exists without ignorance, for ignorance is the cause of the error, the *matrix erroris,* or that from which error takes its rise. It is because man lacks true knowledge of an object that he

makes a false judgment concerning it. Therefore error properly so called is *ignorance in action*.[28] Because of this close relationship between cause and effect, canonists rightly declare that, although the two are really distinct, yet juridically they have the same effects.[29] This principle receives official recognition in the fifth book of the Code, where it is stated that what has been said of ignorance applies also to inadvertence and error.[30] Therefore, if error and ignorance are to be regarded in law as equivalent, then in common ignorance as well as in common error, the Church will supply jurisdiction.

2. The very reason for the law demands that the Church supply the missing jurisdiction even when only common ignorance is present on the part of the faithful. The object of the law is to save the faithful from the dire consequences of their own ignorance when this is coupled with the inability or laxity of the priest in acquiring jurisdiction. This object could not be attained if it were necessary for most of the faithful to be actually in error before the Church would begin to supply jurisdiction, for this would necessitate many

---

[28] *Jus Pontificium*, III (1923), 150.

[29] Cappello, *op. cit.*, II, n. 529: "Ignorantiae ex communi doctrina, in Codice confirmata, aequiparantur ... error." Vermeersch-Creusen, *op. cit.*, I, n. 197: "In jure tamen aequiparantur." Wernz-Vidal, *op. cit.*, II, n. 39: "In iure tamen idem efficiunt." Proteio, *Lexicon Juris Civilis et Canonici*, verbum "error," p. 80, sic se habet: "Error esse non potest absque ignorantia. Sed ignorantia saepe est absque errore. Error procedit ad actionem dicti vel facti falsam. Ignorantia potest etiam intra animum latere nec progredi ad actionem externam. Error et ignorantia promiscue accipiuntur in jure et idem vitium in speciem significant." Cf. also Schmalzgrueber, *Jus. Eccl. Univ.*, VIII, n. 433; Maroto, *Instit. Jur. Can.*, I, n. 87-2, 402; Badii, *Instit. Jur. Can.*, I, n. 87; Suarez, Disp., IV, Sect. 8, n. 11; Ballerini-Palmieri, *Op. Theo. Mor.*, VII, n. 145.

[30] Can. 2202, § 3.

being invalidly absolved before the Church would begin to provide for *the common good.*

3. The law itself does not demand more than ignorance on the part of the faithful. This statement may appear strange at first sight, for the law uses the phrase *in errore communi* and not *in ignorantia communi,* but perhaps a glance at the history of the law will explain the use of this phrase. It has been pointed out that the principle was borrowed by early canonists from Roman Law, which declared that the law would grant stability to acts which were in themselves invalid because of a latent defect in an official which made him incapable of exercising jurisdiction.[31] This, then, was intended as a *post factum* remedy for validating acts which were already invalidly performed. It was also primarily as a *post factum* remedy that it was incorporated into the Decree of Gratian, as is evident from the words of the text.[32] At the time when the acts were being placed, nothing more than general ignorance of the defective power of the official existed among the people; but after the acts were placed, the people were rightly said to have acted *in errore communi,* since an act presupposes a judgment, and this judgment was an error because it was founded on ignorance. But this error became common only after many had placed their acts, for error is the false judgment which usually immediately precedes an action.

Canonists and theologians then extended the principle and permitted that it be used as an *ante factum* means of performing valid acts which *per se* would be invalid

---

[31] Corpus Juris Civilis, *Digest,* I, 14, 3.
[32] C. 1, C. III, q. 7.

because of the lack of jurisdiction. The axiom, however, continued to be formulated in the same words, although common error, properly so called, was present only when viewed *post factum,* and common ignorance, when viewed *ante factum.*

The Code naturally incorporated the time-honored phrase *in errore communi,* but, considering the requisites of the law *ante factum* (i. e., before putting it into use), it cannot be said to require any more than would seem ever to have been required while the acts were being placed, viz., general ignorance of the deficient power. Therefore, the present law does not demand any more than common ignorance on the part of the faithful.

To those who would maintain that this law contains an exception to the general prescriptions of law and therefore should be strictly interpreted, it can be retorted that the law rather contains a favor, granted to the faithful for the general good, and *favores ampliandi sunt.*

The next point in this opinion to be demonstrated is:

II. That the presence of a public foundation for this ignorance is not necessary in order that the Church supply jurisdiction.

1. Such a foundation is not necessary for the existence of the ignorance, for ignorance expresses merely the absence of knowledge, and it is evident that this negative quality needs no such foundation for existence.

2. Nor is a public foundation necessary for the commonness of the ignorance, for if the ignorance can exist without this foundation, its existence can be general

without such a foundation. It cannot be denied, however, that the presence of a public fact from which ignorance of the confessor's lack of jurisdiction can be deduced to be general, will be of great aid to the priest in forming his judgment regarding the commonness of the ignorance. But this is not to say that the presence of such a fact is necessary either for the existence or the commonness of the ignorance.

3. The law itself does not require the presence of any public fact, but merely states that in common error the Church will supply jurisdiction. If error and ignorance are to be considered as synonymous in law, at least insofar as concerns their effects, then in common ignorance also the Church will supply jurisdiction, for the presence of a public fact is not necessary for the existence of common ignorance. But if the Church will not supply the missing jurisdiction when only general ignorance exists, the only alternative is to wait until the ignorance becomes error and the error has become common before she will supply it. This will be only after many have been invalidly absolved.

The third point to be proved is:

III. That not only when common ignorance is *de facto* objectively present will the Church supply jurisdiction, but also when it is merely prudently and honestly thought to exist regardless of the objective truth of the judgment.

1. In support of this proposition it is necessary once again to appeal to the reason for the law. The Church has incorporated this principle into her code of law for the common good of souls, and she permits the use of

this law not only as a *post factum* remedy for acts already invalid, but also as an *ante factum* means of validating acts that would otherwise be invalid. With this in view, can the Church be said to exact actual error or ignorance which is *de facto* common before she will supply the jurisdiction that is lacking? Considering the circumstances and the human limitations within which this principle is to be used, it would be tantamount to accusing the Church of making her concession impracticable, to assert that she required such a condition. For if the validity of the absolutions were to depend on the fact that the error or ignorance was actually common, would not the use of this concession almost always be the occasion of anxieties and scruples both to the confessor and to the faithful? And would the Church be thus providing for the common good of souls? A similar case arises in the application of Canon 882. All admit that the only requisite for the validity of the absolution in this case is a prudent judgment on the part of the priest that the circumstance of danger of death exists, regardless of the objective truth of this judgment.[33] Therefore, is not Canon 209 to be interpreted in the same manner? Accordingly, it is necessary for the attainment of the end of law that the Church supply jurisdiction, not only when the ignorance of the faithful is actually common, but also whenever a confessor can prudently and honestly judge that it is common, regardless of the objective truth of his judgment.

Therefore, the only case in which the Church will

---

[33] Cappello, *De Censuris*, nn. 114 and 118; Vermeersch-Creusen, *Epit. Jur. Can.*, III, n. 452.

not supply the jurisdiction that is lacking, is when the ignorance of the confessor's deficient power is not common and the priest knows that it is not common and yet he absolves. His absolutions in this case are invalid, because no common error really exists nor is thought to exist, and the penitents who approach him either know that he is lacking in jurisdiction and that it is therefore unlawful for them to approach him, or they are among the few who do not know that the confessor is deficient in this power, and their error is private. When the confessor has a positive and probable doubt regarding the generality of the ignorance of the people, he will validly absolve, for the Church will supply the jurisdiction in virtue of the latter part of the same canon. If the priest makes no judgment whatsoever regarding the existence or the commonness of the ignorance of the faithful, but in utter indifference and laxity absolves, his absolutions will be valid or invalid according as the ignorance of the faithful is actually common or private.

To-day, in this country at least, it would appear that the faithful in general are ignorant of the necessity of jurisdiction in the confessor for the validity of his absolution, and apparently think that any priest can absolve them from their sins.[34] This condition may or may not exist, but if it does or if a confessor can

---

[34] Father Jombart (*Nouvelle Revue Theologique,* L [1923], p. 174), denies that such a condition actually exists, because the Catechism teaches that a confessor must be approved. Yet, to a casual observer it would appear that the faithful generally have no definite notion of what this approbation really means, and it would seem that many at least think that any good priest who is in good standing with his bishop, is thereby to be regarded as approved. Cf. *Irish Eccl. Record,* Series V, Vol. XXI (1923), p. 299; *Jus Pontificium,* III (1923), 151.

prudently and honestly judge that it does exist, he would seem to impart valid absolution, for if ignorance of the necessity of jurisdiction is common, *a fortiori* ignorance of the lack of it is also common.

Nor is the culpability of the ignorance any reason why the Church will not supply jurisdiction. The law does not distinguish between culpable and inculpable error as long as it is common, so also with ignorance which is the cause of error. The reason for the law likewise remains unchanged whether or not the ignorance is culpable, for a loving mother wishes to protect her children against the dire consequences of their ignorance whether or not this state of mind is due to their own negligence in seeking the truth.[35] The Church, herself, has given an indication of her mind in this regard by adopting the opinion denying the necessity of a colored title when common error is present, so that, regardless of what appearance the minister may give as to his really possessing jurisdiction, she will supply the deficit. Indeed, even if no cause whatsoever exists which would be responsible for the misapprehension of the faithful, still the Church will supply the deficient power as long as the lack of jurisdiction is generally unknown to the faithful.

One might be restrained from admitting this opinion because of the startling results which would follow upon its acceptation. For it would then be necessary to consider as valid a vast majority of the absolutions which have been given when the confessor lacked the

---

[35] The same author denies that the Church will supply jurisdiction, if this condition does exist, because the ignorance of the faithful in these circumstances is culpable in his estimation. Cf. also *Jus Pontificium, loc. cit.*

required jurisdiction. Even absolutions from reserved sins and censures, which have been imparted maliciously by confessors without the required jurisdiction, and without recourse to the prescriptions of the canons on absolution from reserved cases, would also be valid, for the penitents are in ignorance of the extent of a confessor's power, and there is no obligation on them to ascertain this fact. If these results appear to the timid to be over-liberal, let him ask himself if such is not the mind of the Church. Is not the reason for the law the common good of souls? Does not the Church wish to protect her children against the possible malice or stupidity or carelessness of the minister, and for this reason supply the deficient power of jurisdiction in common error? It would seem, therefore, that, in practice, whenever a priest can prudently and honestly judge that many of the faithful of a particular place are in ignorance of his lack of jurisdiction, or even if they are ignorant of the necessity of jurisdiction for valid absolution, if he absolves, he will absolve validly in virtue of Canon 209.

The Licit Use of This Jurisdiction

Hitherto the validity of the absolution was the only question under discussion, and nothing was said of the liceity of the action of the priest in absolving when the faithful generally were in ignorance of his lack of jurisdiction. The question now arises as to the lawfulness of the action of a priest who is wanting in jurisdiction, but who avails himself of the common ignorance of the faithful and the concession of the Church to grant absolution from sin. Since Canon 872 requires that the priest possess ordinary or delegated jurisdiction over the penitent in order that he may validly absolve him, it is entirely unlawful for a priest without this jurisdiction to avail himself of the common error of the faithful and force the Church to supply jurisdiction, unless

1. There is a grave reason for so acting, and
2. This cannot be provided for in any other way, at least without grave inconvenience.

Only when these two conditions have been fulfilled, is it lawful for a priest to absolve without jurisdiction in common error, for Canon 872 certainly imposes a grave obligation on the priest to be possessed of the power of jurisdiction before attempting to absolve from sins, and the concession of Canon 209 does not furnish him with any license to ignore this obligation, for this benignity on the part of the Church is conceded for the common good of the faithful and not for the benefit of the priest. Therefore, it seems certain that a priest commits a grave sin who absolves without the necessary jurisdiction in common error unless the above-mentioned conditions are fulfilled, for, even though his absolution is valid in virtue of Canon 209, still it is not lawful for him to avail himself of this concession without grave necessity.[36]

Noldin [37] seems to be of the opinion that it would not be sinful for a priest to avail himself of this

---

[36] Vermeersch-Creusen, *Epit. Jur. Can.*, I, n. 284; Wernz-Vidal, *Jus Can.*, II, n. 382; Maroto, *Instit. Jur. Can.*, I, n. 731; Genicot-Salsmans, *Instit. Theo. Mor.*, II, n. 331; Chelodi, *Jus de Personis*, n. 130.

[37] Noldin, *Summa Theo. Mor.*, III, n. 346, 1 *b*.

concession even without any reason, for he states that a priest who remembers that the time during which he enjoyed jurisdiction had already elapsed, need not cease hearing confessions. In view of the grave obligation imposed by Canon 872, and in view of the reason which prompts the Church to supply jurisdiction in common error, this opinion does not seem to be correct. Cappello quotes some authors as adhering to the opinion that it is only venially sinful to absolve in common error without the necessary jurisdiction and without sufficient reason for absolving.[38] Because this opinion seems probable to him, Cappello has determined to change his opinion expressed in his tract *De Censuris* [39] and free such a priest from incurring the censure inflicted by Canon 2366 on a priest who absolves without the necessary jurisdiction. Cappello, however, does not enumerate the authors proposing this opinion, and we have been unable to find them, but in view of what has already been said, this opinion also seems devoid of probability.

Furthermore, it seems quite certain that a priest absolving without the necessary jurisdiction in common error and without sufficient reason for so acting, incurs the censure of suspension *a divinis* or suspension *ab audiendis confessionibus,* according to the nature of the case, inflicted by Canon 2366. This canon inflicts the former censure on those priests who presume to hear sacramental confessions without the necessary jurisdiction, and the latter censure on those priests who presume to absolve from reserved sins without the

---
[38] *De Sacramentis,* II, n. 492.
[39] *De Censuris,* n. 542.

necessary jurisdiction. If it is gravely unlawful for a priest to absolve without the necessary jurisdiction even in common error without sufficient reason, then it follows that such a priest incurs one of these censures according to the nature of the case.

Because it does not seem certain to them that such a priest commits a grave sin, some would excuse him from incurring these censures.[40] But since the opinions holding that a priest absolving without jurisdiction in common error and without sufficient reason for so acting, commits no sin or only a light sin, appear to be devoid of probability, it seems certain that such a priest does incur these censures.

Others resort to a different mode of attack. They do not think that such a priest incurs these censures because he really does not absolve without jurisdiction, since the Church supplies this power when common error is present.[41] But this does not appear to be true, for such a priest evidently violates the grave precept expressed in Canons 872 and 893, and forces the Church to supply jurisdiction, which she does, not for the benefit of the priest, but only for the sake of the unsuspecting faithful.[42] Moreover, it is the teaching of theologians and canonists that the Church supplies this jurisdiction in the very act of absolution only, so that, before the absolution is imparted and after it is granted, the priest still remains devoid of jurisdiction.[43] Therefore, at least in the case of a priest who absolves in

[40] *Ibid., De Sacramentis*, II, n. 492.
[41] Woywod, in *Homiletic and Pastoral Review*, XXVII (1926), p. 67.
[42] Chelodi, *Jus Poenale*, n. 89; Lugo, V, Disp. XXVI, n. 3.
[43] Lehmkuhl, *Theo. Mor.*, II, n. 387; Vermeersch-Creusen, *op. cit.*, I, n. 120.

virtue of the common error of the faithful without any jurisdiction in the place where he hears the confession and without a sufficient reason for so acting, the censure of suspension *a divinis* is incurred, for Canon 2366 inflicts this censure on the priest who presumes to *hear* sacramental confessions without the necessary jurisdiction.[44]

The Cause Required in Order to Absolve Licitly

The grave cause necessary to absolve licitly without jurisdiction in virtue of the common error or common ignorance of the faithful, may be taken from among the causes enumerated by St. Alphonsus[45] as sufficient for the licit use of probable jurisdiction under the old law. These causes are:

1. If the precept of confessing urges, even if only because the penitent is in the state of mortal sin and cannot be liberated in any other way than by confessing, and an approved confessor can be obtained only with notable inconvenience;
2. If the opportunity of gaining an indulgence is at hand and the same circumstances are present;
3. If the penitent can confess to an approved priest only with the betrayal of his accomplice, but to this unapproved priest without such a betrayal;
4. If the unapproved priest has a solid reason to fear that the penitent will not make an integral confession to the priest with jurisdiction.

---

[44] Chelodi, *Jus Poenale,* n. 89; Cipollini, *De Censuris Latae Sententiae,* n. 120; Murphy, *Delinquencies and Penalties in the Administration and Reception of the Sacraments,* p. 27.
[45] St. Alphon., VI, n. 593.

This is by no means intended as an exhaustive list of the cases in which it would be licit to absolve without the necessary jurisdiction in virtue of the common error or common ignorance of the faithful, but it is merely intended to give some idea of the gravity of the cause which seems to be required for the lawful use of supplied jurisdiction in common error. Cappello is of the opinion that the desire of the penitent to communicate on a Sunday or feast day of precept or some extraordinary occasion is sufficient cause to absolve in virtue of the common error of the faithful if an approved priest cannot be obtained or can be obtained only with grave inconvenience.[46]

Finally, it must be noted that most authors are of the opinion that it is valid and licit for a penitent to approach a priest whom he knows to be lacking in jurisdiction, provided that the people of the place generally do not know this and this penitent cannot approach another confessor, or can do so only with grave inconvenience, for in this case, they argue, the sacrament will not be invalid *ex defectu dispositionis poenitentis,* nor *ex defectu jurisdictionis confessarii,* for the Church supplies jurisdiction to all in these circumstances.[47]

ARTICLE II

CASES OF DOUBT

The latter part of this canon asserts that the Church will also supply jurisdiction in positive and probable

---
[46] Cappello, *De Sac.,* II, n. 493.
[47] D'Annibale, I, n. 79, note 6; Vermeersch-Creusen, *op. cit.,* I, n. 284; Wernz-Vidal, *op. cit.,* II, n. 382; Cappello, *op. cit.,* II, n. 492.

doubt either of the law or of the fact. Doubt is defined as *a state of mind withholding assent about a proposed question,* or *a suspension of judgment between two or more contradictory propositions because of the fear of erring.*[1] An opinion is defined as *the assent of the mind given to one of two or more contradictory propositions, yet not without fear of the truth of the opposite.*[2] In the former case no choice between the opposites is made, but in the latter case a choice is made, but only timidly and without certitude.[3] Since law is concerned with actions, and actions presuppose a judgment, in law the words *doubt* and *opinion* are used synonymously.[4]

Doubt is positive when there is a grave reason supporting each of the opposing propositions. This is a case of real doubt, since there are two belligerent propositions, each supported by a grave reason, thereby making both opinions probable.

Doubt is negative when no reason or at least no grave reason exists in support of either of the two propositions. This state of mind differs from the state of ignorance only in that doubt implies that at least the question has been entertained by the intellect, whereas ignorance includes no such implication.

When one of the propositions is supported by a serious reason and the other can claim no such support, the state of mind is known as a positivo-negative doubt.[5]

---
[1] Hickey, *Summula Philosophiae Scholasticae,* I, n. 160; Maroto, *op. cit.,* I, n. 730; Vermeersch-Creusen, *op. cit.,* I, n. 284.
[2] Hickey, *op. cit.,* I, n. 161.
[3] *Ibid., op. et loc. cit.*
[4] Ferraris, *Prompta Bibliotheca,* verbum "Conscientia," n. 22 seq; Barbosa, *Tractatus Varii,* verbum "Dubium," n. XLII, in Tractatu de Dictionibus Usu Frequentioribus.
[5] *Catholic Encyclopedia,* Vol. V, p. 141, word *Doubt.*

In this circumstance the intellect is impelled to assent to the proposition supported by the grave reason, but since it does so without certitude, and only with a prudent fear of the truth of the opposite, this judgment is only an opinion, the probability of which depends on the gravity of the reason supporting it.

Doubt may concern either the law or the fact. It is a doubt of law when, for example, authors disagree as to the correct interpretation of the law; and it is a doubt of fact when, for example, it is not certain that the circumstances required by the law are present in a particular case.

Before the promulgation of the Code, many canonists denied that the Church would supply jurisdiction in cases in which the doubt was one of fact. And even when the doubt was one of law, they demanded that the opinion be supported by public probability [6] before the Church would supply jurisdiction.[7] This was called probable jurisdiction, while in the case of a doubt of fact, it was called doubtful jurisdiction.[8]

The Code abolishes these distinctions and states that the Church will supply jurisdiction in cases of doubt of law and doubt of fact as long as the doubt is positive and probable. Therefore, whenever a confessor doubts that he possesses jurisdiction, whether his doubt is a grave reason for thinking that he does possess jurisdiction, he may use Canon 209 as a reflex principle

[6] I.e., that particular interpretation of the law must have the support of approved authors.
[7] St. Alphon., VI, n. 573; Lugo, Disp. XIX, n. 29; D'Annibale, *Summula Theo. Mor.*, I, n. 80; Lehmkuhl, *Theo. Mor.*, II, n. 388.
[8] Lehmkuhl, *op. et loc. cit.*

to form a certain conscience and proceed to absolve validly and licitly without any misgivings, for the Church will supply the jurisdiction if it is really deficient.

All are agreed that in positive and probable doubt of law no cause whatsoever is required for the licit use of the supplied jurisdiction.[9] But in positive and probable doubt of fact, some require at least a slight cause in order to absolve licitly in this circumstance.[10] This is rightly denied, however, since the sacrament is not exposed to the danger of nullity, nor is the priest forcing the Church to supply jurisdiction against her will, for this concession is granted for the benefit of the priest as well as for the good of the faithful. At any rate, some slight cause will almost always be present, so that a priest with a positive doubt either of law or of fact need not hesitate to grant absolution in virtue of Canon 209.

When the doubt is only negative, the Church will not supply jurisdiction if it is lacking, for such a doubt is equivalent to no doubt whatsoever. Therefore, a confessor would act illicitly in absolving with such a doubt, since he has no serious reason for thinking that he possesses jurisdiction and is exposing the sacrament to the danger of nullity. Of course the validity or invalidity of his absolution in this case will depend on the actual presence or absence of the doubtful jurisdiction.

It is the opinion of many authors that it would be licit for a priest with a negative doubt regarding the possession of jurisdiction, to absolve conditionally when

---
[9] Wernz-Vidal, *Jus. Can.*, II, n. 382; Vermeersch-Creusen, *Epit. Jur. Can.*, I, n. 284; Cappello, *De Sac.*, II, n. 500.
[10] Cappello, *op. et loc. cit.*

the penitent is in grave necessity, for although the Church will not supply jurisdiction if it is missing, yet if it happens to be present the absolution will be valid. The grave necessity in the case makes it licit, they argue, to expose the sacrament to the danger of nullity, for *sacramenta propter homines*.[11]

ARTICLE III

INADVERTENCE

Another case of supplied jurisdiction is given in the following words of Canon 207, § 2:

Sed potestate pro foro interno concessa, actus per inadvertentiam positus, elapso tempore vel exhausto casuum numero, validus est.

This is exclusively a *post factum* remedy and is applicable only to the two cases enumerated in the law. Therefore the Church will supply jurisdiction in virtue of this canon only.

1. When a confessor who has received jurisdiction for a definite time, through inadvertence absolves after that time has elapsed; or
2. When one who has been granted faculties for a certain number of cases, through inadvertence absolves from such a case after the number for which he had faculties has been exhausted.

This is a taxative enumeration of the cases to which this canon may be applied, so that it is not possible to extend this concession to any other case. Accordingly,

[11] Genicot-Salsmans, *Instit. Theo. Mor.*, II, n. 330; Cappello, *op. cit.*, II, n. 499; Wernz-Vidal, *op. cit.*, II, n. 382; Vermeersch-Creusen, *op. et loc. cit.*

he would absolve invalidly who possessed jurisdiction over men only, if through inadvertence he absolved a woman.

Ignorance of Reservation of a Censure

The Church also supplies the missing jurisdiction and renders the absolution valid which a confessor grants, who is ignorant of the reservation of a censure, provided that the censure is not one reserved *specialissimo modo* to the Holy See, or a censure *ab homine*. This concession is made in the following words of Canon 2247, § 3:

Si confessarius, ignorans reservationem, poenitentem a censura ac peccato absolvat, absolutio censurae valet, dummodo ne sit censura ab homine aut censura specialissimo modo Sedi Apostolicae reservata.

Although the canon merely states that the absolution of the censure is valid, there can be no doubt that the absolution of the sin reserved *ratione censurae* is also valid, because once the censure is remitted, the sin to which the censure is attached is no longer reserved.[1] But if the sin is also reserved *ratione sui*,[2] then although the absolution of the censure would be valid in virtue of this canon, still the absolution of the sin would not be valid, for the sin itself has been reserved as well as the censure.[3]

[1] Can. 2246, § 3; Dargin, *Reserved Cases*, p. 80.
[2] E.g., the crime of false denunciation of an innocent confessor of the crime of solicitation in confession, made to ecclesiastical judges. Cf. Canons 894 and 2363.
[3] But if confessed along with at least one other sin, the sin reserved *ratione sui* would be indirectly remitted. Cf. Noldin, *Summa Theo. Mor.*, III, n. 224.

CHAPTER VIII

THE POWER OF ABSOLVING CARDINALS AND BISHOPS

ARTICLE I

The Confession of Cardinals

Cardinals enjoy the privilege, according to the Code, of electing a priest as a confessor for themselves and the members of their household. Such a priest *ipso jure* receives jurisdiction to absolve these penitents from all sins and censures except those reserved *specialissimo modo* to the Holy See, and those connected with the violation of a secret of the Holy Office. It is not necessary that the priest selected for this office already be possessed of habitual ordinary or delegated jurisdiction, but any priest, even unapproved, may be selected and he *ipso jure* receives jurisdiction.

This privilege is contained in the following words:

Canon 239, § 1. Praeter alia privilegia quae in hoc Codice suis in titulis enumerantur, Cardinales omnes a sua promotione in Consistorio facultate gaudent:
2° Sibi suisque familiaribus eligendi sacerdotem confessionibus excipiendis, qui, si jurisdictione careat, eam ipso jure obtinet, etiam quod spectat ad peccata et censuras, reservatas quoque, illis tantum censuris exceptis de quibus in n. 1.

The censures referred to in this canon as exceptions from the faculty enjoyed by the confessor, are the censures reserved *specialissimo modo* to the Holy See, and those attached to the violation of a secret of the Holy Office.

It must be noted that the Cardinal himself is excused from incurring any penalty inflicted by the Code, even those reserved *specialissimo modo,* unless it is expressly stated that Cardinals also are included.[1] There is only one censure in the Code which expressly includes Cardinals. This is the censure of excommunication reserved *speciali modo* to the Holy See, attached to the crime of appealing from the laws, decrees, or mandates of the Roman Pontiff to a general council.[2] However, Cardinals are also subject to the censures contained in the constitution of Pius X, *Vacante Sede Apostolica,* for crimes committed in the election of a Pope.[3] A Cardinal incurring one of these censures, or a censure attached to the violation of a secret of the Holy Office, could be absolved in virtue of Canon 2254 if the case warranted it, and recourse had to the Sacred Penitentiary. The Cardinal Major Penitentiarius would then obtain the mandate from the Holy Father himself.

The members of the Cardinal's household include all those, clerics and lay, who dwell in the same house night and day, especially the secretaries, attendants, and servants.[4] These are not excused from incurring any of the censures, but when they have incurred them, the confessor selected by the Cardinal *ipso jure* receives the power to absolve these members of the household

[1] Can. 2227, § 2.
[2] Can. 2332.
[3] Can. 2330; Pius X, const., *Vacante Sede Apostolica,* 25 dec. 1904, par. 79-86, Documentum I apud *Codicem.*
[4] Vermeersch-Creusen, *Epit. Jur. Can.,* II, n. 155; Cappello, *De Sac.,* II, n. 400.

from all censures except those reserved *specialissimo modo* to the Holy See and those annexed to the violation of a secret of the Holy Office. It must be noted that not every confessor to whom these penitents may confess, receives this power, but only he who is selected by the Cardinal as the confessor of his household.

ARTICLE II

THE CONFESSION OF BISHOPS

All bishops, both residential and titular, enjoy a similar privilege of selecting a priest as a confessor for themselves and the members of their household. The privilege is contained in Canon 349, § 1, n. 1, which reads as follows:

§ 1. Ab accepta authentica notitia peractae canonicae provisionis Episcopi sive residentiales sive titulares:
1° Praeter alia privilegia quae suis in titulis recensentur, fruuntur privilegiis de quibus in can. 239, § 1, nn. 7-12; nec non n. 2, etiam quod spectat ad casus Ordinario loci reservatos.

The extent of the power of the confessor in this case, however, is not so clear. Canon 349, § 1, n. 1, states that bishops enjoy the same privilege as Cardinals in selecting a priest as the confessor for himself and his household, and the priest so selected obtains jurisdiction *ipso jure, etiam quod spectat ad casus Ordinario loci reservatos*. Most commentators[5] interpret this to mean that the confessor receives the power to absolve from

[5] Chelodi, *Jus de Personis*, n. 195; Wernz-Vidal, *Jus Can.*, II, n. 599; Vermeersch-Creusen, *op. cit.*, I, n. 416.

all sins and censures except those reserved *specialissimo modo* to the Holy See and those annexed to the violation of a secret of the Holy Office. Accepting this interpretation, the only reason for the clause *etiam quod spectat ad casus Ordinario loci reservatos* in Canon 349, would be to emphasize the power of the confessor as regards this particular class of reservations when he is absolving the members of the bishop's household, for the bishop himself is not subject to his own reservations (if he is the Ordinary of the place where he confesses), and at any rate the confessor already has the power *ipso jure* of absolving from all sins and censures howsoever reserved, except only those reserved *specialissimo modo* to the Holy See and those annexed to the violation of a secret of the Holy Office. Therefore, the clause *etiam quod spectat ad casus Ordinario loci reservatos* of Canon 349 seems superfluous. Perhaps, then, it is the intention of the legislator to limit the extent of the power of the confessor whom the *bishop* selects, to those cases only which are reserved to the local Ordinary by the Code or by the Ordinary to himself, excluding all cases reserved to the Holy See.

Finally, it must be noted that the bishop himself is not subject to the penalties of suspension and interdict *latae sententiae* established by the Code.[6] He is subject, however, to the censures of excommunication established by the Code, and, having incurred one of these censures, he may be absolved either in virtue of this power or in virtue of Canon 2254, according as the censure is reserved and the case warrants.

[6] Can. 2227, § 2.

Title II

THE PENITENTIAL JURISDICTION GIVEN BY THE CODE TO ALL CONFESSORS IN CERTAIN CIRCUMSTANCES

Under this title, the powers of absolving and the powers of dispensing in the internal sacramental forum which the Code grants to all *confessors* in certain circumstances, will be examined. In order to avail himself of these powers, it is necessary that the priest be possessed of ordinary or delegated jurisdiction to hear confessions, for only then is he to be considered a confessor. Therefore, if the priest has not an office to which the law has attached ordinary jurisdiction for the internal sacramental forum, it is necessary that he shall have received the faculty *ad audiendas confessiones* from his competent superior before he may validly avail himself of the following powers granted by the Code. No other faculty, however, is necessary in order to use these powers, nor is a bishop, in granting faculties, able to prohibit a priest from using the powers granted to him by the Code.

This title is divided into two chapters, according to the nature of the power granted to the confessor. The first chapter concerns the power of absolving from sins and censures in certain circumstances, while the second chapter deals with the various powers of dispensing granted by the Code to the confessor.

CHAPTER IX

THE POWERS OF ABSOLVING GRANTED BY THE CODE TO ALL CONFESSORS

ARTICLE I

THE POWER OF ABSOLVING IN CERTAIN CIRCUMSTANCES FROM SINS RESERVED "RATIONE SUI"

The most frequent manner in which a confessor finds his jurisdiction restricted, is in the form of reservations of sins and censures. The reservation of these cases is merely the withholding or withdrawal of jurisdiction over them by a superior, so that the confessor, whose power has been so restricted, cannot absolve from these sins or censures. Reservation, therefore, directly affects the confessor by limiting his power to absolve and only indirectly affects the penitent.

In ordinary circumstances the simple confessor cannot absolve from such reserved cases. But in order to avoid some of the confusion and hardship often entailed by reservations, the law declares that in certain circumstances reservation ceases and the simple confessor is able to absolve from the sin; in other circumstances, although the reservation remains, certain otherwise simple confessors receive jurisdiction delegated by the common law to absolve from some of these reserved cases.

It has been pointed out that there are two classes of reserved cases:

1. Those in which the sin itself is reserved *ratione sui;*
2. Those to which a reserved censure, which impedes the reception of the sacraments, has been attached, thereby reserving the sin *ratione censurae.*

There are different sets of circumstances enumerated in the Code, in which a simple confessor may absolve from sins reserved *ratione sui,* and in which he may absolve from sins reserved *ratione censurae.* These circumstances are conditions for the validity of the absolution, and can be used only for the class of reservations for which they are enumerated. Therefore, the circumstances in which a sin reserved *ratione sui* is declared to be no longer reserved, cannot be used in the case of a sin reserved *ratione censurae* as a means of nullifying this reservation, and vice versa.

Cessation of the Reservation of a Sin Reserved "Ratione Sui"

Canon 900 sets forth the circumstances in which the reservation of a sin reserved *ratione sui* ceases. The canon reads as follows:

Quaevis reservatio omni vi caret:
1°. Cum confessionem peragunt sive aegroti qui domo egredi non valent, sive sponsi matrimonii ineundi causa;
2°. Quoties vel legitimus Superior petitam pro aliquo determinato casu absolvendi facultatem denegaverit, vel, prudenti confessarii judicio, absolvendi facultas a legitimo Superiore peti nequeat sine gravi poenitentis incommodo aut sine periculo violationis sigilli sacramentalis;

3°. Extra territorium reservantis, etiamsi dumtaxat ad absolutionem obtinendam poenitens ex eo discesserit.

This legislation is based upon an instruction of the Holy Office issued on July 13, 1916, beginning *Cum experientia*.[1] This instruction contained the words *"Quaevis Ordinariorum reservatio,"* thereby limiting the provisions of that document to those sins reserved *ratione sui* by the Ordinary. The canon of the Code, however, omits the word *Ordinariorum* and thereby institutes a change in discipline, making Canon 900 applicable to all sins reserved *ratione sui*, no matter to whom or by whom they are reserved.

The canon, however, is applicable only to sins reserved *ratione sui* and not to sins reserved *ratione censurae*. All doubt on both of these points has been dispelled by the decision of the Commission for Interpreting the Code, issued on November 10, 1925, explicitly affirming both of these contentions.[2]

1. The reservation of any sin, therefore, that has been reserved *ratione sui* ceases whenever the penitent is so sick that he is unable to leave the house. Grave illness and, *a fortiori*, danger of death is not required. Neither does absolute physical inability to leave the house seem to be required; but it would seem to suffice that because of sickness it is morally impossible for the penitent to leave the house, i. e., he can do so only with great difficulty, e. g., if the penitent were very old or a paralytic or were suffering with an injured foot.[3] Some

[1] *A. A. S.*, VIII (1916), 313.
[2] *A. A. S.*, XVII (1925), 583.
[3] Dargin, *Reserved Cases*, p. 33; Cappello, *De Sac.*, II, n. 552; Vermeersch-Creusen, *Epit. Jur. Can.*, II, n. 179.

would include under this canon those who are incarcerated in prison;[4] but since their incarceration is not due to sickness, it would seem more correct to exclude such.[5] However, it seems quite certain that this canon includes even those religious who are unable to leave the house because of sickness, even though the confessor resides in the same house.[6]

Undoubtedly all those who are about to enter into the state of Matrimony are included under the term *sponsi*, regardless of whether or not they have entered into canonical *sponsalia*. But the reservation ceases only when the confession is made as a proximate preparation for marriage, not, however, when it is merely the ordinary confession of an engaged person, whose marriage is not to take place for months or weeks.

2. The reservation of sins reserved *ratione sui* also ceases whenever the faculty to absolve has been sought from the legitimate superior for a particular case and has been denied by him even with a just cause. If, therefore, a confessor had sought the faculty to absolve from a sin reserved *ratione sui*, even from the vicar forane who had the power of delegating this faculty, and was refused for any reason whatsoever, or his petition was ignored, it would not seem to be necessary for him to make application anew to the bishop.

Such a reservation likewise ceases whenever the confessor prudently judges that he cannot seek the faculty of absolving from the legitimate superior without grave inconvenience to the penitent or without danger of violating the sacramental seal.

[4] Cappello, *op. et loc. cit.*
[5] Vermeersch, *Theo. Mor.*, III, n. 470.
[6] Vermeersch-Creusen, *Epitome*, II, n. 179.

It is to be noted that the cessation of the reservation depends only on the prudent judgment of the confessor, without any regard to the truth and reality of the inconvenience. Therefore, even if the penitent would not really suffer great inconvenience by the deferment of absolution, but the confessor falsely judged that he would at the time he presented himself for absolution, the reservation ceased and the confessor validly absolved. The inconvenience of the penitent may be inconvenience of any kind, spiritual, moral, corporeal, or economic. Such inconvenience is certainly present: when the penitent feels it a hardship to remain in mortal sin during the time necessary to procure the faculty of absolving from the superior through the ordinary channels; when the penitent cannot omit celebrating Mass or receiving Holy Communion without giving scandal or suffering loss of reputation; when it will be more than ordinarily difficult for the penitent to return to the same confessor.

In order that the reservation cease, it is not necessary that the confessor foresee that the violation of the seal of confession is certain, or even very probable, but it suffices that the confessor foresee the danger of such a violation, and immediately the reservation ceases. Therefore, whenever the confessor has a prudent fear that the superior will suspect for whom the faculty of absolving from a reserved sin is sought, the reservation ceases and the simple confessor may absolve.

3. Outside the territory of the one reserving the sin, the reservation ceases even though the penitent goes outside the territory expressly for obtaining absolution. The one sin reserved *ratione sui* by common law

RESERVED SINS

is in force everywhere, so that one can never be outside the territory of the one reserving.

But the reservations established by individual bishops are valid only for their particular territories. Therefore, a sin may be reserved in one diocese and not reserved in an adjacent diocese, and a penitent from the former diocese may go to the latter diocese and be absolved by any confessor from the sin which is reserved in the penitent's own diocese but not in the diocese in which he confesses. This follows from the principle that reservation directly affects the confessor by limiting his power of jurisdiction,[7] and from the principle that *peregrini* are absolved by virtue of jurisdiction derived from the Ordinary of the place where the confessions are heard and in penitential discipline are regarded as subjects of the Ordinary and the confessor of the place where the confessions are heard.[8]

The Commission for Interpreting the Code therefore decreed that *peregrini* are bound by the reservations in force in the diocese in which they confess.[9] Consequently, if a penitent leaves his own diocese in which his sin has been reserved by the Ordinary and confesses in another diocese in which the sin is not reserved, he can be absolved by any confessor. But if the sin is also reserved in the diocese in which he confesses, he cannot be absolved by a simple confessor of that diocese. Nor can he be absolved even if his sin is not reserved in his own diocese but is reserved in the diocese in which he

---
[7] Can. 893.
[8] Canons 874, § 1, and 881.
[9] Pont. Comm. ad CC. auth. interpret., 23 nov. 1920, *A. A. S.*, XII (1920), 575.

confesses, because a simple confessor enjoys only that jurisdiction which has not been restricted by his competent superior.

A serious difficulty, however, presents itself. A pastor, by virtue of his office, possesses ordinary jurisdiction for the internal sacramental forum over those living in the parish,[10] and those having ordinary jurisdiction may absolve their subjects everywhere.[11] Therefore, a pastor of diocese A, meeting one of his subjects in diocese B, may absolve him from those sins at least which are not reserved. May he validly absolve him from a sin which is reserved in their home diocese A but is not reserved in diocese B, which is the place of confession?

He who would affirm that the pastor could validly absolve his subject from such a sin, appeals to this third section of Canon 900 and proclaims that, outside the territory of the one reserving, all reservation ceases. Therefore, since a pastor receives his jurisdiction from the Code by virtue of his office, the reservations of his bishop restrict his jurisdiction only within his own territory, and *extra territorium reservantis, quaevis reservatio omni vi caret*.[12]

He who denies that a pastor may act thusly, declares that his jurisdiction is limited by the reservations of his own bishop, and even when he absolves his own subject in another diocese, he does so in virtue of the jurisdiction which he derives from his office in the diocese of the bishop who has restricted his jurisdiction. His

[10] Can. 873, § 1.
[11] Can. 881, § 2.
[12] *Irish Eccl. Record,* Series V, Vol. XXIII (1924), p. 628.

RESERVED SINS

power of absolving, therefore, remains restricted even outside the territory of the restricting bishop.[13]

Although both positions are fortified by strong arguments, the former seems more in keeping with the general scheme of the Code, since outside the territory of the one reserving, the reservation ceases and the pastor who receives his jurisdiction from the Code by virtue of his office, may act as if he were not restricted in the exercise of that jurisdiction.

An equally difficult question arises when a pastor of diocese A meets one of his subjects in diocese B, who confesses a sin which is not reserved in their home diocese A but is reserved in diocese B, which is the place of confession. May he validly absolve his subject from the sin not reserved in diocese A but reserved in diocese B?

Once more two contradictory opinions are expressed. One opinion states that, since the jurisdiction of the pastor is derived from his office in diocese A and limited only by the reservations of the bishop of that diocese, he may validly absolve his subject from a sin reserved in the place where the confession is heard, but not in the home diocese.[14]

The second opinion, emphasizing the description of a reservation given in Canon 893, § 1, and § 2, and the principle that *peregrini* are regarded as subjects of the Ordinary of the place where the confessions are heard, insists that the bishop of the diocese in which the confession is heard, has withdrawn the case from all inferior tribunals within his territory and summoned

[13] *Ibid.*, p. 301.
[14] *Ibid.*, p. 302.

the case to his own higher court, so that, although he is outside his diocese, the tribunal of the pastor still remains an inferior tribunal. This opinion, they argue, is supported by the fact that the Code expressly grants the faculty to the Canon Penitentiary to absolve diocesans outside the diocese from sins and censures reserved to the bishop, but is silent with regard to the exercise of this faculty by the pastor.[15]

Although not by any means certain, the former opinion would seem to be the more probable, since the pastor receives his jurisdiction from the Code by virtue of his office, and this jurisdiction would seem subject only to the restrictions of his own bishop. Therefore, it would seem that even though the sin were reserved in both dioceses, a pastor of diocese A, meeting his subject in diocese B, could absolve him from such a sin, because the reservation of the home diocese ceases outside the territory of that bishop, and the jurisdiction of the pastor is not subject to the restrictions of the bishop of the diocese in which the confession is heard.

ARTICLE II

THE POWER OF ABSOLVING FROM CENSURES AND SINS RESERVED "RATIONE CENSURAE"

PRELIMINARY REMARKS

It must be borne in mind continually that reserved cases are divided into two classes, those reserved *ratione sui* and those reserved *ratione censurae;* and the Code imposes distinct regulations according to which a simple confessor may absolve from each class of reser-

[15] *Ibid.*, p. 630.

vation. In the preceding Article the circumstances in which a simple confessor may absolve from sins reserved *ratione sui* have been explained. It now becomes our task to explain the circumstances in which the Code permits the simple confessor to absolve from reserved censures and sins reserved *ratione censurae*. The regulations governing this class of reservations are found in the second section of the fifth book of the Code, the eighth title and the first chapter, from Canon 2245 to Canon 2254.

It is not the province of this book to give an explanation of the nature of censures or the manner in which they are incurred, but it presupposes the incurrence of the censure and treats only of the requisites for absolution from it. However, some explanation of the terms to be used seems necessary.

Explanation of Terms

By reason of the manner in which it is incurred, an ecclesiastical punishment is called *latae sententiae* or *ferendae sententiae*. A punishment is *latae sententiae* if it is added to a law or precept in such a way that it is incurred *ipso facto* by the very act of committing the crime, without any further intervention of a superior. Before such a punishment produces certain canonical effects, the law sometimes requires the sentence of a judge. A sentence of this kind is called a *declaratory sentence*. This sentence does not inflict the penalty, because that being *latae sententiae* was incurred *ipso facto* at the very moment of the commission of the crime. The *declaratory sentence* merely makes the crime committed and the penalty incurred judicially manifest.

A punishment is *ferendae sententiae* when it is inflicted by a judge or a superior after the commission of a crime. Such a penalty, therefore, always requires the sentence of a judge. This sentence is called a *condemnatory sentence* and actually inflicts the penalty, which is not incurred by the delinquent until this sentence is pronounced. A penalty is always considered as *ferendae sententiae* unless it is expressly indicated that it is *latae sententiae*.[1]

By reason of the manner in which it is established, a penalty is called *a jure* or *ab homine*. A punishment is said to be *a jure* when the law itself imposes a determinate penalty for a determinate crime regardless of whether the penalty is *latae* or *ferendae sententiae*. A punishment *a jure,* therefore, must be inflicted after the manner of a true law, either universal or particular, or through a general precept.

If the punishment is imposed by a particular precept or by a *condemnatory sentence,* it is *ab homine*. If imposed by a particular precept, a penalty *ab homine* may be also *latae* or *ferendae sententiae*. In the case where a penalty *ferendae sententiae* is added to the law, the penalty is only *a jure* before the condemnatory sentence is passed; after the sentence, it is both *a jure* and *ab homine,* but is considered as *ab homine*.[2]

Finally, a distinction between censures which impede the reception of the sacraments and those which do not so impede reception, is to be noted. There are

---
[1] Can. 2217, § 2.
[2] Can. 2217, § 1, n. 3.

three species of censure: excommunication, suspension, and interdict. Of these three species, excommunication and personal interdict alone impede the reception of the sacraments, while suspension and local interdict do not bear with them this canonical effect.[3] Therefore, a penitent who is suspended or under a local interdict can be absolved from his sins if properly disposed even though he still remains under the censure. But he who incurs a censure of excommunication or personal interdict cannot be absolved from his sins until he is first absolved from the censure. The censure of excommunication may be personal or territorial, according as it is attached to a law or precept which is personal or territorial. However, it is presumed to be territorial unless it is otherwise noted.[4] A personal interdict, on the other hand, is by its very nature personal, and binds the delinquent everywhere.[5]

Reservation of Censures

A censure once incurred can be removed only by legitimate absolution.[6] This absolution may be granted by any confessor if the censure is unreserved, or by him who has the faculty to do so if the censure is reserved.[7]

All censures *ab homine,* whether *latae* or *ferendae sententiae,* are reserved to him who inflicted the censure or to him who passed the sentence or to his competent

[3] Canons 2260, § 1, and 2275, n. 2.
[4] Can. 8, § 2.
[5] Can. 2269, § 2.
[6] Can. 2248, § 1.
[7] Canons 2245, § 3, and 2253, n. 1.

superior, successor, or delegate.[8] It is not in the capacity of judge, that the censure is reserved to him who passed the sentence; rather the censure is reserved to him who established it, but exercised his judicial power either *per se vel per alios* in inflicting it.[9]

Censures *a jure et latae sententiae* are not reserved unless express mention of the reservation is made in the law itself.[10] But *latae sententiae* censures which are reserved, may be established by the Holy See or by inferior Ordinaries. The censures reserved by the Holy See are reserved either to the Holy See or to the local Ordinary. Those reserved to the Holy See are reserved *simpliciter, speciali modo,* or *specialissimo modo,* designating the kind of faculties required to absolve from the censure.[11]

Censures *a jure et ferendae sententiae* after the condemnatory sentence has been passed, are regarded as *ab homine* and therefore reserved to him who inflicted the censure or to him who passed the sentence or to his competent superior, successor, or delegate.[12]

It has already been pointed out that a censure which impedes the reception of the sacraments, *eo ipso* impedes the licit absolution of the sin to which the censure is attached, until the censure itself has been removed by absolution.[13] If this censure is one which is reserved, the sin to which the censure is attached is also reserved,

---

[8] Can. 2245, § 2.
[9] Canons 1572, § 1, and 2220, § 1; and Dargin, *Reserved Cases,* p. 66.
[10] Can. 2245, § 4.
[11] Canons 2245, § 3, and 2253, § 3.
[12] Can. 2245, § 2.
[13] Can. 2250, § 2.

so that the absolution of such a sin *per se* is not only illicit but also invalid.[14] Therefore, in this case there is really a twofold reservation, the reservation of the censure directly, and the reservation of the sin indirectly. Accordingly, such a sin is said to be reserved *ratione censurae,* in contradistinction to a sin reserved *ratione sui.*

Since the sin in this case is reserved *ratione censurae,* it follows that the reservation of the sin is dependent on the censure, so that if the censure is not incurred, or, having been incurred, is already removed by absolution, the sin to which the censure was attached is no longer reserved.[15] Therefore, if a person is excused for any reason [16] from incurring the censure which is reserved, the sin to which the censure is attached is not reserved, and any confessor may absolve from it. This rule, however, applies only to a sin which is reserved merely *ratione censurae.* If the sin, besides being reserved

[14] *Salvo praescripto* Can. 2247, § 3.
[15] Can. 2246, § 3.
[16] In order that a censure may be incurred, the crime must be: (1) external, (2) grave, (3) consummated, (4) joined with contumacy. Cf. Can. 2242, § 1, and Dargin, *Reserved Cases,* p. 46. Therefore, if the crime lacks one of these qualities, the censure is not incurred. Cf. Can. 2228. Likewise, any cause which excuses from grave imputability, also excuses the delinquent from incurring the censure. Therefore, any ignorance either of the law or of the penalty, except affected ignorance, and cras and supine ignorance, excuses one from incurring a *latae sententiae* censure. Even cras and supine ignorance excuses from the censure when the law inflicting it contains a word such as *praesumpserit,* which demands full knowledge and deliberation in order that the censure be incurred. Affected ignorance, however, never excuses. Other causes excusing from grave imputability, such as drunkenness, the omission of due diligence, weakness of mind, or impetus of passion, also excuse from incurring the censure, as long as they are of such a character as to excuse from mortal sin. Cf. Can. 2229.

ratione censurae, is also reserved *ratione sui,*[17] even though the censure was not incurred, or, having been incurred, was already removed by absolution, the sin still remains reserved *ratione sui,* and a simple confessor cannot absolve from it in ordinary circumstances.

To recapitulate: When a reserved censure has been incurred, in ordinary circumstances a simple confessor cannot absolve from the censure. If the reserved censure is one that does not impede the reception of the sacraments, the simple confessor can absolve the penitent from his sins but not from the censure, for such a censure does not import the reservation of the connected sin.[18] If the reserved censure is one that does impede the reception of the sacraments,[19] in ordinary cases the simple confessor cannot absolve the delinquent either from the censure or from his sins, for the sin to which the censure is attached is reserved *ratione censurae* to a higher tribunal, and if this sin cannot be absolved, none of the sins of the penitent can be remitted, for one mortal sin cannot be remitted without the others.[20]

However, it must be remembered that the law provides that if the confessor, ignorant of the reservation, absolves in good faith, the absolution of the censure is valid as long as it is not a censure *ab homine* or a censure reserved *specialissimo modo* to the Holy

---

[17] E.g., the crime of falsely accusing an innocent confessor of the crime of solicitation, at least when the accusation is made before ecclesiastical judges. Cf. Canons 894 and 2363.

[18] Dargin, *Reserved Cases,* p. 60.

[19] Viz., excommunication or personal interdict; cf. Canons 2260, § 1, and 2275, § 1.

[20] Noldin, *Summa Theo. Mor.,* III, n. 242.

See.[21] In this case the absolution of the sin is also valid, for the sin is no longer reserved.[22]

The Absolution of Reserved Censures in More Urgent Cases

The Code, however, provides for certain more urgent cases in which the simple confessor is granted the power of absolving from reserved censures by the law itself. These cases are enumerated in Canon 2254, and the faculties granted by this canon can be used only when the circumstances, therein specified, are verified. The faculties may be used, however, for all reserved censures, no matter to whom or by whom reserved. The canon reads as follows:

§ 1. In casibus urgentioribus, si nempe censurae latae sententiae exterius servari nequeant sine periculo gravis scandali vel infamiae, aut si durum sit poenitenti in statu gravis peccati permanere per tempus necessarium ut Superior competens provideat, tunc quilibet confessarius in foro sacramentali ab eisdem, quoquo modo reservatis, absolvere potest, injuncto onere recurrendi, sub poena reincidentiae, intra mensem saltem per epistolam et per confessarium, si id fieri possit sine gravi incommodo, reticito nomine, ad S. Poenitentiariam vel ad Episcopum aliumve Superiorem praeditum facultate et standi ejus mandatis.

§ 2. Nihil impedit quominus poenitens, etiam post acceptam, ut supra, absolutionem, facto quoque recursu ad Superiorem, alium adeat confessarium facultate praeditum, ab eoque, repetita confessione saltem delicti cum censura, consequatur absolutionem; qua obtenta, mandata ab eodem accipiat, quin

[21] Can. 2247, § 3.
[22] Cf. supra, p. 146 and Can. 2246, § 3.

teneatur postea stare aliis mandatis ex parte Superioris supervenientibus.

§ 3. Quod si in casu aliquo extraordinario hic recursus sit moraliter impossibilis, tunc ipsemet confessarius, excepto casu quo agatur de absolutione censurae de qua in can. 2367, potest absolutionem concedere sine onere de quo supra, injunctis tamen de jure injungendis, et imposita congrua poenitentia et satisfactione pro censura, ita ut poenitens, nisi intra congruum tempus a confessario praefiniendum poenitentiam egerit ac satisfactionem dederit, recidat in censuram.

Origin of the Law

This legislation is based upon a decree of the Holy Office issued June 23, 1886, and upon the subsequent replies of the same Congregation concerning this decree. The decree denied to bishops and priests the power of absolving from cases reserved to the Holy See, without having any recourse to the Sacred Congregations. But it provided that, in more urgent cases in which absolution could not be deferred without danger of grave scandal or infamy, a confessor could absolve, but must impose the burden on the penitent of having recourse to the Holy See by letter and through the confessor within one month, under pain of reincurring the censure.[23] This faculty was declared applicable to all censures reserved to the Holy See,[24] and therefore only to these, to the exclusion of censures reserved to the Ordinary.

The absolution granted in virtue of these faculties

---
[23] S. C. S. Off., 23 jun. 1886, Fontes n. 1102.
[24] S. C. S. Off., 17 jun. 1891, Fontes n. 1137.

was declared to be direct, and the privilege of obtaining a new absolution from one having faculties, instead of having recourse to the Holy See, was allowed soon after.[25] The case in which it would be difficult for the penitent to remain in mortal sin during the time necessary to obtain faculties, was then included among the more urgent cases.[26] The following year it was declared that the penitent could be excused from the obligation of having recourse, whenever it so happened that neither the confessor nor the penitent could send a letter to the Sacred Penitentiary and it would be difficult for the penitent to approach another confessor.[27] This concession later was extended to include the case in which the confessor could write the letter but the penitent could not, and it was not possible for the penitent to return to the same confessor.[28] These provisions are now included in and even extended by Canon 2254.

Extent of the Present Law

The canon embraces all censures, both those inflicted *latae sententiae* and those inflicted *ferendae sententiae*, those imposed *a jure* and those imposed *ab homine*. However, in the case in which the danger of giving scandal or the danger of destroying the reputation of the delinquent is the only reason for absolving, the power of the confessor is limited to *latae sententiae* censures, but it matters not whether they were

[25] S. C. S. Off., 19 aug. 1891, Fontes n. 1143.
[26] S. C. S. Off., 16 jun. 1897, Fontes n. 1187.
[27] S. C. S. Off., 9 nov. 1898, Fontes n. 1207.
[28] S. C. S. Off., 5 sept. 1900, Fontes n. 1247.

imposed *a jure* or *ab homine*. Therefore, in such a case a simple confessor could not absolve from a censure which was imposed *ab homine* but inflicted by a *condemnatory sentence,* yet he could absolve from a censure which was imposed *ab homine* (i. e. by a particular precept), but incurred *ipso facto* in violating the precept.[29] The simple confessor could do this even though such a censure *ab homine* by its very nature is reserved to the one who inflicted it.[30] In the case where the penitent feels it a hardship to remain in sin during the time necessary to obtain the faculty of absolving from the superior, the simple confessor may absolve from any excommunication or personal interdict (for only such censures prevent the absolution of the delinquent's sins), regardless of whether the censure was inflicted *latae* or *ferendae sententiae* or imposed *a jure* or *ab homine*.

Moreover, the faculty granted by this canon embraces all censures howsoever and to whomsoever they are reserved. The decree of 1886 included only those censures reserved to the Holy See, or the so-called Papal cases, to the exclusion of episcopal cases. The Code, however, contains no such restriction and therefore is to be interpreted as new legislation, for *ubi lex non distinguit nec nos distinguere debemus*.[31] It cannot be held, however, as some still do,[32] that this canon is applicable also to sins reserved *ratione sui,* for the position of the canon in the fifth book of the Code,

---

[29] Genicot-Salsmans, *Instit. Theo. Mor.,* II, n. 574.
[30] Can. 2245, § 2.
[31] Cappello, *De Sac.,* II, n. 579; Chelodi, *Jus Poenale,* n. 35; Cerato, *Censurae Vigentes a Cod. Jur. Can.,* n. 25.
[32] Cappello, *op. cit.,* II, n. 579; Arregui, *Sum. Theo. Mor.,* n. 614; Farrugia, *De Casuum Conscientiae Reservatione,* n. 26.

and the express wording of the law, clearly indicate that this canon applies only to censures and consequently to sins reserved *ratione censurae*. The decision of the Commission for Interpreting the Code,[33] declaring that Canon 900 can be applied only to sins reserved *ratione sui,* thereby also implies that Canon 2254 can be used only for censures and sins reserved *ratione censurae*. Therefore, it seems certain that the circumstances mentioned in these two canons are not interchangeable, and each canon may be applied to those cases only for which it is expressly intended.

The Cases

The power granted by this canon can be validly used only in the two more urgent cases specified in the law, viz.:

1. When the censure, which has been contracted *ipso facto,* cannot be observed outwardly without danger of giving scandal to others, or without danger of destroying the reputation of the one censured. This circumstance is usually present whenever the penitent is expected to receive another sacrament soon after confession, e. g., the Holy Eucharist or Matrimony; but it need not be certain that scandal or infamy will follow, for it suffices that there be danger of such an effect.[34]

2. When it will be a hardship on the penitent to remain in mortal sin during the time necessary to obtain the requisite faculty. The penitent must feel

[33] Pont. Comm. ad CC. auth. interpret., 10 nov. 1925, *A. A. S.,* XVII (1925), 583.
[34] Cappello, *op. cit.,* II, n. 578.

this hardship subjectively, but it is permitted that the confessor inculcate this sentiment.[35] It is the teaching of theologians that it may be a hardship for the penitent to remain in mortal sin even for one day.[36] The hardship required, however, need not be *valde durum* but it suffices that it *displiceat poenitenti*.[37]

Both of these circumstances need not concur in one and the same case, but it is sufficient that one of the circumstances be verified, in order that a confessor exercise this power validly.

The Recourse

When it can be done without grave inconvenience, the confessor is gravely obliged to impose the burden on the penitent of having recourse to the Sacred Penitentiary or to a bishop or other superior having faculties, within one month from the day on which absolution has been granted. The penitent must do this with the intention of fulfilling the prescriptions of the mandate of the superior. The obligation of having recourse directly affects the penitent and is to be imposed under pain of reincurring the same censure for failure to do so within the time defined. The recourse is to be had at least by letter and through the confessor. When it cannot be done in this manner, it would seem that it may be omitted [38] except in the case of a priest who has incurred the censure attached to the crime of attempting to absolve his accomplice in *peccato turpi*. This

---

[35] Vermeersch-Creusen, *Epit. Jur. Can.*, III, n. 454.
[36] St. Alphon., VI, n. 490; Genicot-Salsmans, *op. cit.*, II, n. 574.
[37] Cappello, *op. cit.*, II, n. 578.
[38] Can. 2219, § 1.

seems to be true, even though in theory the penitent would still be obliged to have recourse personally or by writing the letter personally, for it can hardly ever happen, at least in this country, that this could be done without grave inconvenience. So in ordinary cases, at any rate, whenever a confessor cannot have recourse at least by letter, it seems safe to say that the recourse may be regarded as morally impossible and may therefore be omitted except in the case mentioned in the law.

Since the recourse is usually had by letter and through the confessor, but the obligation of having recourse directly affects the penitent, it follows that the obligation of the penitent is to return to the confessor within the month. If the penitent culpably fails to return within the required time, he reincurs the censure. The time defined is *tempus utile,* so that if the penitent by any cause were prevented from acting, the time during which he was impeded would not be included within the month.[39] Therefore, if a penitent failed to return within a month because he was prevented by illness, he would not reincur the censure. But the obligation to return to the confessor within thirty unimpeded days would still remain. The censure which is reincurred is not the same censure identically, since this was removed by direct absolution, but is a new censure of the same species, which is imposed *a jure*. It follows, therefore, that it is a grave sin to fail to return to the confessor within the defined time, and this sin is reserved *ratione censurae*.

Some doubt must be admitted as to whether a

[39] Can. 35.

penitent who has recourse but fails to obey the prescriptions of the mandate of the superior, reincurs the censure. Some are of the opinion that he does not, because of the position of the phrase *et standi ejus mandatis* in the canon.[40] Chelodi seems inclined to this opinion but is not clear.[41] Vermeersch-Creusen[42] admits the probability of the opinion but adopts the opposite as more probable, because under the old law it was certain from a decree of the Holy Office[43] that such a penitent did reincur the censure, and therefore in doubt whether or not a canon of the Code makes a departure from the old law, the old law is to be retained.[44] This seems to be the true interpretation, especially since there are so many qualifying phrases in the canon that an argument from the position of such a phrase is necessarily weak.

The Commission for Interpreting the Code has issued a statement on Canon 2252, declaring that the phrase *facultate praeditum* qualified the word *Episcopum* as well as the words *aliumve superiorem*, so that recourse could not be had to, nor the mandate issued by, a bishop who had not faculties over the censure in question.[45] This interpretation evidently applies also to Canon 2254. However, since a confessor seldom knows the extent of a bishop's faculties, it is usually best for him to have recourse in every case through his own Ordinary or the Apostolic Delegate, unless special

---

[40] Arregui, *Summarium Theo. Mor.*, n. 617; Cappello, *op. cit.*, II, n. 597, § 7.
[41] *Jus Poenale*, n. 35.
[42] *Op. cit.*, III, n. 452.
[43] S. C. S. Off., 30 mart. 1892, Fontes n. 1151.
[44] Can. 6, n. 4.
[45] Pont. Comm. ad C.C. Auth. Interpret., 12 nov. 1922, *A. A. S.*, XIV (1922), 663.

circumstances persuade a different course of action.

Moreover, it must be noted that recourse cannot be had to another confessor even though he has the faculty of absolving from this censure, for the canon demands that recourse be had to the Sacred Penitentiary or a bishop or superior having the faculty.[46] However, it is permitted that the penitent confess the sin anew to another confessor who has such faculties and receive the mandate from him. This is permitted even though he has already had recourse to a superior, and in this case he may disregard the mandate of the superior when he receives it. Since he has already been absolved, he need only confess the one sin to which the censure is attached, since it is necessary for the confessor to know this sin because of the censure, but unnecessary for him to know the others because all the sins have been remitted by the former absolution. When a confessor determines that recourse is morally impossible, he may dispense from this obligation in any case, except that of a priest who has incurred the censure of excommunication attached to the crime of attempting to absolve his accomplice in *peccato turpi*.[47] The confessor may absolve such a priest but cannot dispense from the obligation of having recourse to the superior. However, there is nothing to prevent the priest censured from making use of the privilege mentioned above and confessing his sin anew to a priest having special faculties for this crime, instead of having recourse to the superior. In other cases, when the confessor prudently judges that the inconvenience

---

[46] Cf. also S. C. S. Off., 19 dec. 1900, Fontes n. 1249.
[47] Can. 2367.

attached to having recourse would be sufficiently grave to warrant a dispensation from this obligation, he must enjoin the things required by law, impose a congruous penance as satisfaction for the censure, and inform the penitent that unless this penance is performed within a time defined by the confessor, he will reincur the censure. The things which the law requires to be enjoined are:

1. That the injured party be satisfied by restitution or at least by being sued for pardon if the right of another were violated;
2. That the scandal be repaired if any were given;
3. That, together with the sacramental satisfaction, a salutary penance for the censure be imposed.[48]

In judging the moral impossibility of having recourse, the possibility or impossibility of having it within a month, is the only factor that need be taken into consideration, it would seem, because the canon refers to *hic recursus,* which seems to signify that recourse which is to be had within a month.[49] Therefore, if it is morally impossible (gravely inconvenient) for the penitent to have recourse within a month, but it would be quite possible for him to have it thereafter, he may be excused altogether from the obligation of having recourse.

Territorial Effect of the Reservation of Censures

Only those censures which are established *a jure et latae sententiae,* and reserved by an Ordinary inferior

---
[48] S. Poenit, 10 dec. 1880, apud Cappello, *De Censuris,* n. 101.
[49] Chelodi, *Jus Poenale,* n. 35; Cappello, *De Sac.,* II, n. 592.

RESERVED CENSURES

to the Roman Pontiff, are affected by the territorial limits of the Ordinary's jurisdiction. For when a censure is *ab homine,* it is reserved everywhere to him who inflicted it, or to him who passed the sentence upon the delinquent, or to his competent superior, successor, or delegate.[50] Also, when a censure is established *a jure* but is *ferendae sententiae,* the censure is not incurred until the condemnatory sentence is passed, and then it is regarded as *ab homine* and consequently is reserved everywhere.[51] And, finally, when the reserved censure is *a jure et latae sententiae* but established by the Holy See in its common law, it is not restricted by the confines of any territory, for the law is universal and established for the whole Latin Church. Such censures, therefore, are reserved everywhere, and this reservation affects the jurisdiction of every simple confessor of the Latin Church.

But when a reserved censure is established *a jure et latae sententiae* by an Ordinary inferior to the Roman Pontiff, it has no force outside of the territory over which that Ordinary exercises jurisdiction[52]. Therefore, the censure is incurred only by a violation of that law committed within the confines of the territory of that Ordinary, unless the Ordinary expressly declared that the law to which the censure is attached is personal and binds his subjects wherever they may be.[53] The consequent reservation of the sin *ratione censurae,* if the censure is an excommunication, is incurred only when the censure has been contracted. Therefore, if

---

[50] Canons 2245, § 2, and 2247, § 2.
[51] Canons 2217, n. 3, and 2245, § 2.
[52] Can. 2247, § 2.
[53] Can. 8, § 2.

178 JURISDICTION OF THE CONFESSOR

the Archbishop of Baltimore attached a reserved censure *a jure et latae sententiae* to a sin, and a resident of Baltimore committed that sin in New York, but confessed it to a simple confessor after his return to Baltimore, such a penitent could be absolved without further faculties, since he would not have incurred the censure and consequently his sin would not be reserved.[54]

The restriction of the power of inferior confessors, which constitutes the reservation of the censure, is likewise limited to the confines of the territory over which the reserving Ordinary exercises jurisdiction, so that only those confessors within his territory are unable to absolve from the reserved censure and sin. But any simple confessor outside of this territory could absolve the delinquent, even though he incurred the censure and came outside the territory of the reserving Ordinary expressly for obtaining absolution.[55] Therefore, in the case where the Archbishop of Baltimore had established a reserved excommunication *a jure et latae sententiae,* if a resident of Baltimore had incurred this penalty by committing the crime in Baltimore, but confessed it in New York, a simple confessor of the latter diocese could absolve from the sin and censure, for the reservation of the censure has no force outside of the territory of the one reserving it.

However, if the same censure was also reserved by the Archbishop of New York, a difficulty presents itself. The censure incurred in the above-mentioned case was, not the censure inflicted by the Archbishop of New York, but the censure inflicted by the Archbishop

[54] Can. 14, § 1, n. 1.
[55] Can. 2247, § 2.

of Baltimore, and outside of his territory the reservation of the censure has no force. It would seem, therefore, that a simple confessor of the Archdiocese of New York could absolve such a penitent from this censure and the sin to which it is attached, because it is the censure of the Archbishop of Baltimore which has been incurred. However, the decision of the Commission for Interpreting the Code, issued on November 24, 1920,[56] dispels all doubt. When asked, *"utrum ad normam Canon 893, §§ 1 et 2, peregrinus teneatur reservationibus loci in quo degit,"* the Commission answered, *"Affirmative."* Now Canon 893, §§ 1 and 2, refers both to the reservation of sins *ratione sui* and to the reservation of censures, since it uses the generic term *reservatio casuum*. Therefore, even though the censure incurred by the penitent was not the censure of the Ordinary of the place where he confesses, yet he cannot be absolved from this censure by a simple confessor of any place whose jurisdiction to absolve from censures of this kind has been restricted by his own Ordinary.

The effect of the reservation of censures on Orientals has already been treated.[57]

ARTICLE III

Maritime Faculties

Jurisdiction to hear confessions is granted by common law to priests who are on a sea journey in the following words:

[56] *A. A. S.*, XII (1920), 575.
[57] Supra, p. 72 seq.

Can. 883. § 1. Sacerdotes omnes maritimum iter arripientes, dummodo vel a proprio Ordinario, vel ab Ordinario portus in quo navim conscendunt, vel etiam ab Ordinario cujusvis portus interjecti per quem in itinere transeunt, facultatem rite acceperint confessiones audiendi, possunt, toto itinere, quorumlibet fidelium secum navigantium confessiones in navi excipere, quamvis navis in itinere transeat vel etiam aliquandiu consistat variis in locis diversorum Ordinariorum jurisdictioni subjectis.

§ 2. Quoties vero navis in itinere consistat, possunt confessiones excipere tum fidelium qui quavis de causa ad navim accedant, tum eorum qui ipsis ad terram obiter appellantibus confiteri petant eosque valide ac licite absolvere etiam a casibus Ordinario loci reservatis.

This faculty apparently was introduced by custom [1] and then approved and regulated by the Holy See.[2]

All priests receive this jurisdiction whenever the two conditions specified in the canon are fulfilled. Therefore it is necessary:

1. That he actually begin the sea journey, but it would seem that the journey begins for him as soon as he steps on board the boat, even though the ship has not yet left port;

2. That he shall have obtained the faculty of hearing confessions either from his own Ordinary, or from the Ordinary of the port from which the ship sails, or from the Ordinary of a port at which the ship has stopped. If the priest is a pastor, or a canon peniten-

---

[1] D'Annibale, *Summula Theo. Mor.*, III, n. 183.
[2] S. C. S. Off., 17 mart. 1869, Fontes n. 1009; 9 apr. 1900, Fontes n. 1238; 13 dec. 1901, Fontes n. 1258; 23 aug. 1905, Fontes n. 1375; 13 dec. 1906, Fontes n. 1281; S. C. de Prop. Fide, 4 febr. 1907, Coll., II, n. 2294.

tiary, he does not receive his jurisdiction for hearing confessions directly from the Ordinary, but rather from his office, to which the law has attached this power. But since he exercises this office dependently on the local Ordinary, there is no doubt that such a priest is included under Canon 883. If the priest is a religious, his proper Ordinary is the Ordinary of the place where his monastery is situated,[3] unless he is an *exempt* clerical religious. In this case, his own Major Superior would seem to constitute his proper Ordinary also, so that if he had received jurisdiction from his own *exempt* religious Superior only, it would seem sufficient for him to avail himself of the concession of this canon.[4]

It is difficult to determine exactly what is to be considered a sea journey. It is certain that it is not necessary to cross the ocean in order that one avail himself of this concession, although the expression *iter transmarinum* was used in one of the decrees which forms the foundation stone of this law,[5] and it is evident that this is the primary purpose of the law. Yet, there are other cruises which would certainly be included within the scope of the expression *iter maritimum* used by the canon, e. g., the trip from New York to Bermuda. On the other hand, it is equally certain that every excursion made in a boat, e. g., for two or three hours of recreation or fishing, is not to be considered an *iter maritimum*.[6] Therefore, it must be left to the prudent judgment of the individual priest to determine whether

[3] Vermeersch, *Theo. Mor.*, III, n. 458.
[4] Cf. Canons 198, 488, n. 8, and Cappello, *De Sac.*, II, n. 411.
[5] S. C. S. Off., 9 apr. 1900, Fontes n. 1238.
[6] Vermeersch-Creusen, *Epit. Jur. Can.*, II, n. 153.

his cruise is really a sea journey or merely an excursion of a few hours. Whenever he has a positive and probable reason to think that his cruise may be considered a sea journey, the priest may validly and licitly absolve, for if he does not receive the jurisdiction from this canon, the Church will supply the missing power in virtue of Canon 209. It is our opinion, however, that whenever several days, or one full day, or even several hours are spent in traveling on the water, e. g., over night or when it is necessary to take one's meals aboard the boat (as on the trip from New York to Albany), a true *iter maritimum* in the wide sense is present and a priest may avail himself of the faculty granted by this canon.[7]

Since the faculty is granted only for the sea journey, in virtue of this canon the priest receives no jurisdiction in the port from which the ship sails, nor in the port which is the *terminus ad quem* of the sea journey, even though he is to continue his travels farther by land.

Once the voyage has begun, however, this canon grants jurisdiction to the priest, not only over those sailing on the ship with him, but also over anyone else who approaches him, either on the boat, or while he happens to be on land *obiter*, i. e., in any place at which he might chance to stop during the journey, before he reaches the *terminus ad quem* of the voyage. The Commission for Interpreting the Code, on May 20, 1923, issued a decision on the force of the word *obiter*.[8] The Commission decreed that a priest who goes ashore

---

[7] Cf. Canons 68, 50, and Motry, *Diocesan Faculties,* pp. 25, 26.
[8] *A. A. S.,* XVI (1924), 114.

in a port at which the ship stops, could hear confessions on shore for three days, but no longer if the Ordinary could easily be approached. Nor did it matter if the priest were to sail on a different ship, as long as he was to continue on his sea journey. Cappello expresses the opinion that a priest who was forced by circumstances to remain ashore could hear confessions for many days or weeks (*per plures dies aut hebdomadas*), as long as he had the will to continue his voyage as soon as possible.[9] But the decision of the Commission seems to overrule this opinion, at least if the Ordinary can easily be approached.

The Power

The jurisdiction which is granted to the confessor in these circumstances, includes the faculty of absolving all penitents from sins and censures reserved to the Ordinary. The canon uses the generic expression *a casibus Ordinario loci reservatis,* which in itself includes both the sins and censures reserved by common law to the Ordinary, and the sins and censures which the Ordinary reserves to himself, and *ubi lex non distinguit nec nos distinguere debemus*. Therefore, even when the priest absolves on shore, he may validly and licitly absolve from both of these classes of reservation in virtue of the power granted to him by this canon. When the absolution is given at sea, evidently there is no question of the cases which an Ordinary has reserved to himself, for if the sin is reserved *ratione sui, extra territorium reservantis, quaevis reservatio omni*

[9] *De Sac.*, II, n. 412-2.

vi caret,[10] and if the sin is reserved *ratione censurae, reservatio censurae in particulari territorio vim suam extra illius territorii fines non exserit.*[11]

ARTICLE IV

THE POWER OF ABSOLVING RELIGIOUS

Preliminary Remarks

The religious state is a permanent mode of living in community life, in which the faithful undertake to observe not only the common precepts but also the evangelical counsels, by taking vows of obedience, chastity, and poverty.[1]

A religious institute is one approved by the legitimate ecclesiastical authority, in which the members take *public* vows, *perpetual* or *temporary* according to the laws of the institute, and so tend to evangelical perfection. If the vows taken are *solemn*, the institute is called an *Order*. If the vows taken are *simple*, whether *perpetual* or *temporary*, the society is called a *Congregation*.[2] A religious institute, whether an *Order* or a *Congregation*, is said to be *exempt* when it enjoys the privilege of exemption from the jurisdiction of the local Ordinary; otherwise it is called *non exempt* and is subject to the jurisdiction of the local Ordinary. A religious institute is called a *clerical religious society*,

---
[10] Can. 900, n. 3.
[11] Can. 2247, § 2.
[1] Can. 487.
[2] A vow is *public* when it is accepted by a legitimate ecclesiastical authority in the name of the Church; otherwise it is *private*. A vow is *solemn* when it is accepted as such by the Church; otherwise it is *simple*. Can. 1308.

when most of its members are raised to the dignity of the priesthood; otherwise it is a *lay religious society*.

The members of a religious institute are called *religious*. The members of an *Order* are called *regulars*. The members of a *Congregation* are called *religious of simple vows*. *Nuns,* properly so called, are religious women of an institute which by its constitution demands *solemn vows,* even though in some places, with the permission of the Holy See, only *simple vows* are taken. *Sisters* are the members of a female institute in which only *simple vows* are taken.

The *Major Superiors* of a religious institute are: *the Abbot Primate* and *the Abbot Superior of Monastic Congregations; the Abbot of a Monastery sui juris,* even though it belongs to a *Monastic Congregation; the Supreme Moderator and the Provincial Superior* of other *non-monastic* societies; and the *vicars* of all of these, provided that they enjoy the equal of provincial power.[3] These *Major Superiors* come under the title of *Ordinary,* and enjoy ordinary jurisdiction over their own subjects when their institute is an *exempt clerical religious society*.[4]

The Confessions of Religious Men

It must be noted that no special jurisdiction other than that required for hearing any confession is necessary for hearing the confessions of religious men. The priest, therefore, who possesses ordinary jurisdiction, or who is delegated by the local Ordinary, may hear the confession of any religious man within his

[3] Can. 488.
[4] Can. 198.

territory, even the confession of an *exempt religious*.[5] Any priest, either secular or religious, of the same or of a different religious society, may also receive delegated jurisdiction to hear the confessions of the subjects of an *exempt clerical religious superior* from this religious Ordinary.[6]

The subjects of an *exempt clerical religious superior*, in the matter of penitential jurisdiction, include not only the religious, the novices, and the postulants, but also any others who dwell night and day in the religious house, as servants, students, patients, or guests.[7] In order that one of these persons be considered a subject of the religious superior, it would seem to suffice that he enter the religious house with the intention of remaining at least one whole day and night. Then he would seem to become a subject immediately, and might confess to a priest having jurisdiction only from the religious superior, even though this *peregrinus* had not yet been in the house for a full day and night.[8] However, it is necessary that these persons dwell in the religious house, and not merely on the grounds in a separate dwelling.[9]

It is usual that the members of a religious society confess at stated intervals to a duly appointed *ordinary confessor*. But since it is the purpose of this book to explain only the faculties granted by the Code to the *simple confessor*, the power of the *ordinary* and *extraordinary confessor* of the religious will not be con-

[5] Can. 874, § 1.
[6] Can. 875, § 1.
[7] Can. 514, § 1.
[8] Fanfani, *De Jure Religiosorum*, n. 126; Vermeersch-Creusen, *Epit. Jur. Can.*, I, n. 581.
[9] *Iidem*.

sidered in this investigation, but the jurisdiction which is granted to every confessor in this matter will be the sole topic of consideration. The individual religious may or may not be obliged by the particular laws of his institute to confess to the duly appointed confessor at a determinate time, but without prejudice to such particular legislation he receives the right from common law to confess at any time, for the tranquillity of his conscience, to any priest having jurisdiction in the territory either from the local Ordinary or from the proper superior of the penitent religious. The only priest to whom a religious cannot confess, therefore, is one who has no jurisdiction in that territory, or one who has only jurisdiction from a religious superior of a society other than the one to which the penitent belongs. This privilege is granted in the following words of Canon 519:

Firmis constitutionibus quae confessionem statis temporibus praecipiunt vel suadent apud determinatos confessarios peragendam, si religiosus, etiam exemptus, ad suae conscientiae quietem, confessarium adeat ab Ordinario loci approbatum, etsi inter designatos non recensitum, confessio, revocato quolibet contrario privilegio, valida et licita est; et confessarius potest religiosum absolvere etiam a peccatis et censuris in religione reservatis.

This privilege was first granted on August 5, 1913, when the Sacred Congregation for Religious extended the privilege to all male religious, and the faculty to all the confessors of the world.[10]

Each and every male member of a religious society

[10] *A. A. S., V* (1913), 431.

enjoys the privilege granted by this canon, whether he be priest, cleric, or layman. Although novices are not religious properly so called, yet the privilege granted by this canon is also extended to them.[11]

It seems quite evident from the wording of the canon that this privilege is granted *per modum exceptionis* and is intended only for occasional usage. The canon certainly extends no permission to the religious to ignore or to violate the prescriptions of his particular constitution, when this prescribes or persuades confessing to the appointed confessor at definite times. Nor does this canon include the right to demand the privilege of leaving the monastery or to act in any way contrary to the rule of the house. But the canon merely permits a religious who has the opportunity, to confess to any priest approved by the Ordinary of the place where the confession is heard, even though this priest is not included among those designated to hear the confessions of religious.[12]

The canon mentions only the priest approved by the local Ordinary, because there is no doubt that a priest who has received jurisdiction from the penitent's proper *exempt religious superior* may hear one of his subjects at any time. Any priest, therefore, who has jurisdiction for hearing confessions from the local Ordinary, or who has jurisdiction to hear the confessions of the members of this particular religious society from the *exempt religious superior,* may validly and

[11] Can. 566, § 2.
[12] Genicot-Salsmans, *Instit. Theo. Mor.,* II, n. 337; Fanfani, *De Jure Religiosorum,* n. 127; Vermeersch-Creusen, *Epit. Jur. Can.,* I, n. 588; Cappello, *De Sac.,* II, n. 423.

licitly absolve any religious man of that society who approaches him. Nor is it necessary for the confessor to inquire into the motive prompting the penitent to confess, for it is the almost unanimous opinion of authors that any confession seriously made, is made for the tranquillity of the conscience of the penitent.[13] It is likewise unnecessary for the confessor to inquire whether or not the penitent has the permission of the superior to confess, for the confession is valid and licit even if it is made unknown to the superior or against his will, and the penitent is not obliged to inform the superior of his action.[14]

The Power of the Confessor

Since reservation directly affects the confessor by restricting his jurisdiction to absolve, a confessor is unable to absolve a religious penitent from any sin which he has committed, or from any censure which he has incurred, if this sin or censure has been withdrawn or withheld from the competency of his tribunal. Therefore, a confessor who has received his jurisdiction from the local Ordinary, or one who has received it from an office which he exercises under the supervision of the local Ordinary,[15] is restricted by the reservations in force in the territory in which he exercises his office. But such a confessor *ipso jure*

---
[13] Vermeersch-Creusen, *op. et loc. cit.;* Cocchi, *Com. in Cod. Jur. Can.*, II, n. 36; Fanfani, *op. et loc. cit.;* Cappello, *op. et loc. cit.;* McCormick, *Confessors of Religious*, p. 59.
[14] *Iidem.*
[15] E.g., a pastor.

receives the power of absolving from the sins and censures reserved by the religious superior, if any such exist.[16]

A *non-exempt* religious and an *exempt religious of a non-clerical institute* are subject in this matter to the jurisdiction of the local Ordinary, and the religious superior has not the power of reserving sins or censures to himself. Such a penitent, therefore, is in the same position, so far as the jurisdiction of the confessor is concerned, as is the lay penitent, and is subject to all the reservations in force in the place of confession.

An *exempt clerical religious* penitent, however, is in a slightly different position. He is not subject to the jurisdiction of the local Ordinary, and therefore is not subject directly to the sins and censures reserved by the local Ordinary. He is subject, however, to the reservations established by the Holy See and to those established by his own *exempt* clerical religious superior. The confessor having jurisdiction from the local Ordinary, *ipso jure* receives the power of absolving from the sins and censures reserved by the *exempt* clerical religious superior when the confession is made in virtue of Canon 519. Therefore, such a confessor cannot validly absolve an *exempt* clerical religious penitent from a sin or censure reserved by the Holy See; nor from a sin reserved *ratione sui* by the local Ordinary, for, although the *exempt* clerical religious is not directly subject to this latter class of reservations, yet he is indirectly subject to them inasmuch as the reservation of the sin restricts the confessor's power of

[16] Can. 519.

absolving.[17] The confessor can absolve such a penitent, however, from the sins and censures reserved by the religious superior, in virtue of the power granted to him by Canon 519, and from the sins to which the local Ordinary has attached a reserved censure which impedes the reception of the sacraments and thereby reserves the sin *ratione censurae,* because the *exempt* religious is not subject to the censure and therefore does not incur it, and when the censure is not incurred, the sin is not reserved.[18]

On the other hand, if the confessor has obtained his jurisdiction only from the *exempt* clerical religious superior of the penitent, his power of absolving is restricted by the reservations of the Holy See and by the reservations of the religious superior, but not by the reservations of the local Ordinary. Therefore, such a confessor can absolve an *exempt* clerical religious penitent from a sin or censure reserved by the local Ordinary, but not from a sin or censure reserved by the Holy See or by the *exempt* clerical religious superior, for such a confessor does not receive jurisdiction over the reservations of the religious superior from Canon 519, nor from Canon 518, § 1, unless he is a duly appointed ordinary or extraordinary confessor for a religious house of the same *exempt* society.

The Confessions of Religious Women

Until the year 1622, when Gregory XV issued his constitution *Inscrutabili,* nuns who were subject to the

[17] *Commentarium pro Religiosis,* III (1922), pp. 69-77.
[18] Cf. Canons 2226, § 1, and 2246, § 3.

local Ordinary were obliged to confess to a priest who had obtained approbation from that Ordinary. Such a priest also received his jurisdiction from the local Ordinary unless he had already obtained his jurisdiction from the Holy See. But the confessor of nuns, who were subject to an *exempt* regular superior of a masculine Order, received his approbation and jurisdiction from the *exempt* religious superior. Gregory, however, changed this discipline, and declared that henceforth all confessors of nuns, regardless of whether the priest or the nuns enjoyed the privilege of exemption, must obtain their approbation from the local Ordinary.[19]

In 1670 Clement X declared that priests, both secular and religious, who had received approbation for hearing the confessions of secular people, were not thereby to be regarded as approved also for nuns, but for hearing the confessions of these, special approbation was required.[20]

Leo XIII, in his constitution *Conditae a Christo*,[21] and the Sacred Congregation for Religious, in the decree *Cum de Sacramentalibus*,[22] extended this regulation of Clement X to all religious women, whether nuns with solemn vows or merely religious women with simple vows.

Abolishing the necessity of approbation, the Code requires special jurisdiction to hear the confession of any religious woman, and this jurisdiction is obtain-

---

[19] Gregorius XV, const., *Inscrutabili*, 5 febr. 1622; Fontes n. 199.
[20] Clemens X, const., *Superna*, 21 jun. 1670, § 4; Fontes n. 246.
[21] Collectanea, n. 2097.
[22] *A. A. S.*, V (1913), 62.

able only from the local Ordinary of the place where the religious house is situated. These prescriptions are contained in Canon 876, which reads as follows:

§ 1. Revocata qualibet contraria particulari lege seu privilegio, sacerdotes tum saeculares tum religiosi, cujusvis gradus aut officii, ad confessiones quarumcumque religiosarum ac novitiarum valide et licite recipiendas peculiari jurisdictione indigent, salvo praescripto can. 239 § 1, n. 1, 522, 523.

§ 2. Hanc jurisdictionem confert loci Ordinarius, ubi religiosarum domus sita est, ad normam can. 525.

This special jurisdiction is granted when the local Ordinary states expressly or equivalently that he is granting the faculty *ad audiendas confessiones religiosarum ac novitiarum.*[23] This jurisdiction may be granted generally for all religious women, or merely for one particular institute or house. If the jurisdiction is restricted to a particular institute or convent, it cannot be exercised validly beyond the limits of the delegation.[24] Likewise, even when the jurisdiction is delegated for all religious women, it cannot be exercised validly outside the territory of the delegating bishop.

The Code itself, however, grants this special jurisdiction to any confessor who has received jurisdiction to hear the confessions of secular women, provided certain conditions are fulfilled. The first case, in which such a confessor receives this special jurisdiction

[23] Augustine, *Commentary on the Code of Canon Law*, IV, p. 269.
[24] Clemens X, const., *Superna*, 21 jun. 1670, § 4; Fontes n. 246; cf. also Cappello, *De Sac.*, II, n. 440.

JURISDICTION OF THE CONFESSOR

ipso jure, is contained in Canon 522, which reads as follows:

Si, non obstante praescripto can. 520, 521, aliqua religiosa, ad suae conscientiae tranquillitatem, confessarium adeat ab Ordinario loci pro mulieribus approbatum, confessio in qualibet ecclesia vel oratorio etiam semi-publico peracta, valida et licita est, revocato quolibet contrario privilegio; neque Antistita id prohibere potest aut de ea re inquirere, ne indirecte quidem; et religiosae nihil Antistitae referre tenentur.

Origin and Development of This Law

The Sacred Congregation of Bishops and Regulars, on August 27, 1852, granted permission to nuns who, while retaining their habit, were outside of their convent for any reason, to confess to a priest who was approved for the confessions of secular women only.[25] Such a confessor thereby *ipso jure* received the special approbation necessary for hearing the confessions of nuns. Later some of the conditions were modified and the privilege was extended to include other religious women.[26]

This same privilege was contained in the *Normae* of 1901,[27] and the decree *Cum de Sacramentalibus*[28] allowed the use of the privilege not only in churches but also in public and semi-public oratories. The Code has re-enacted the decree of 1913 with some further alterations.

---
[25] Fontes n. 1964.
[26] S. C. Ep. et Reg., 22 apr. 1872, § 3; Fontes n. 2000.
[27] S. C. Ep. et. Reg., 28 jun. 1901, § 149.
[28] S. C. de Religiosis, 3 febr. 1913, § 14, *A. A. S.,* V (1913), 64.

CONFESSIONS OF RELIGIOUS

Conditions for the Valid and Licit Use of This Power

In order that a confessor, who ordinarily has not the special jurisdiction required to hear the confession of a religious woman, may validly and licitly absolve such a penitent in virtue of this canon, it is necessary:

1. That the confession be made for the tranquillity of the conscience of the penitent;
2. That the penitent approach the confessor for this purpose;
3. That the confessor be possessed of jurisdiction to hear the confessions of secular women in the place where the confession is to be heard;
4. That the confession be made in a church, a public or semi-public oratory, or a place legitimately designated to hear the confessions of women.

Because of the many and varying interpretations given by authors to these conditions it will be necessary to examine them individually.

1. *Tranquillity of Conscience*

The confession must be made for the tranquillity of the conscience of the penitent. Almost every recent author of note declares that every confession seriously made, is made for the tranquillity of the conscience of the penitent, and therefore in this canon nothing more is required by this phrase than is required in every confession.[29] For any confession that is not made seriously, is both invalid and illicit because of the lack of the necessary dispositions on the part of the penitent. Therefore the phrase *ad suae conscientiae tranquillitatem* seems to be used in this canon to denote the exceptional and occasional nature of such a confession, rather than to express any special condition necessary on the part of the penitent.

This view is supported by the prescription of Canon 520, § 2, giving the right to a special confessor permanently if the religious so desires. Therefore, a confessor who finds a religious woman confessing to him habitually, should urge her prudently but firmly to desist or to petition the Ordinary to grant him the necessary special jurisdiction to be her particular confessor according to the norm of Canon 520, § 2.[30] He need have no hesitancy, however, in absolving one who approaches him occasionally, provided the remaining conditions are fulfilled.

2. *The Approach to the Confessor*

The penitent must approach the confessor for the purpose of confessing. This is a condition necessary for the validity of the absolution, since upon the ful-

---

[29] Vermeersch-Creusen, *Epit. Jur. Can.*, I, nn. 588, 595; Chelodi, *Jus de Personis*, n. 256; Fanfani, *De Jure Religiosorum*, n. 127; Cappello, *op. cit.*, II, n. 442; Cocchi, *Com. in Cod. Jur. Can.*, II, n. 42; Choupin, *Nature et Obligations de l'Etat Religieux*, p. 228; Leitner, *Handbuch des kathol. Kirchenr.*, p. 358; Augustine, *Commentary on the New Code*, IV, p. 269; McCormick, *Confessors of Religious*, p. 183; *Am. Eccl. Rev.*, LXI (1920), 446; *Commentarium pro Religiosis*, II (1921), 16; *Linzer Quartalschrift*, LXXVI (1923), 3.

[30] Genicot-Salsmans, *Instit. Theo. Mor.*, II, n. 339; Vermeersch, *Theo. Mor.*, III, n. 485; Cappello, *op. cit.*, II, n. 453.

fillment of the conditions specified in this canon, depends the obtaining of the special jurisdiction required for the valid absolution of a religious woman. However, the elements which constitute an *approach* have been the subject of varying interpretations. Until recently many authors were of the opinion that the word *adeat* excluded the summoning of the priest for the purpose of confessing.[31] Others argued that as long as the initiative was taken by the religious woman in seeking to confess, such action constituted an *approach,* no matter what means were used.[32] The Pontifical Commission for Interpreting the Code has recently decided in favor of this latter opinion, stating that the word *adeat* of Canon 522 must not be so understood that the confessor cannot be called by the religious woman to the place legitimately designated for the confessions of women, even of religious women.[33] It must be noted, however, that the canon gives the religious woman no right to demand the summoning of such a confessor by the superior,[34] thereby differing from Canon 523; but if she succeeds in summoning him *vel per se vel per alios,* the Commission has decided that such an action constitutes an *approach,* and fulfills the condition prescribed in Canon 522.

[31] Prümmer, *Manuale J. C.,* p. 297; Biederlack-Fuehrich, *De Religiosis Cod. J. C.,* n. 49; McCormick, *Confessors of Religious,* p. 193; *Commentarium pro Religiosis,* II (1921), 19; *Linzer Quartalschrift,* LXXVI (1923), 3; *Irish Eccl. Record,* Series V, XXII (1923), 642.

[32] Vermeersch-Creusen, *Epitome,* I, n. 595; Choupin, *op. cit.,* p. 228; Motry, *Diocesan Faculties,* p. 96.

[33] Pont. Comm. ad CC. auth. interpret., 28 dec. 1927, *A. A. S.,* XX (1928), 61.

[34] S. C. de Religiosis, 1 dec. 1921, apud Hilling, *Codicis Juris Canonici Interpretatio,* p. 39.

3. The Jurisdiction Required in the Confessor

The priest must be possessed of jurisdiction to hear the confessions of women, either secular or religious, in the place where the confession is to be heard. This condition also is necessary for the validity of the absolution granted in virtue of Canon 522. Therefore one who had no jurisdiction to hear confessions, or no jurisdiction within this territory, or jurisdiction to hear the confessions of men only, could not validly absolve a religious woman in virtue of this canon. This is more practically applicable in places where there is the custom of approving young priests to hear the confessions of men only. It is to be noted, however, that the priest must be possessed of jurisdiction in the territory in which the confession is to be heard. But if the place of confession is an *exempt* religious house, it suffices that the priest have jurisdiction over secular women in the diocese in which the religious house is situated, for the privilege of exemption is rather personal than territorial, and is enjoyed only by the male religious in this matter. A priest having maritime faculties according to the norm of Canon 883, could also absolve a religious woman who approached him, it would seem, provided the other conditions prescribed by Canon 522 were fulfilled.

4. The Place of Confession

The confession must be made in a church, a public or semi-public oratory, or a place designated for hearing the confessions of women. The Commission for Interpreting the Code was asked, "whether the words of Canon 522, *confessio in qualibet ecclesia vel oratorio etiam semi-publico peracta valida et licita est*, must be so understood that a confession made outside of these places would be not only illicit but also invalid." On November 24, 1920, the Commission issued the following reply: "Canon 522 must be so understood that the confessions, which a religious woman makes for the tranquillity of her conscience to a confessor approved by the local Ordinary for women, are valid and licit, as long as (*dummodo*) they are made in a church or oratory, even semi-public, or a place legitimately designated for hearing the confessions of women." [35]

Interpreting the interpretation of the Commission, authors disputed whether or not the clause concerning the place where the confessions were to be heard, imposed a condition necessary for the validity of the absolution. Some were of the opinion that a confession heard, in virtue of Canon 522, outside of one of the places enumerated, would be invalid as well as illicit.[36] These authors appealed to the use of the word *dummodo* in the reply of the Commission, introducing the clause designating the place where the confession could be heard validly and licitly. This word is enumerated in Canon 39 as one of the particles which introduce a condition necessary for the validity of a

[35] *A. A. S.*, XII (1920), 575.
[36] Fanfani, *De Jure Religiosorum*, n. 137; Blat, *Com. in Text. Jur. Can.*, II, pars II, n. 585; *Il Monitore Ecclesiastico*, XXXIII (1921), 160.

rescript.[37] Accordingly, these authors argued, it was used designedly in the reply of the Commission.

Others, on the contrary, denied that a confession heard in virtue of Canon 522, outside of one of the places enumerated, would be invalid, although, they admitted, it would be illicit.[38] The supporters of this opinion pointed out that the Commission was asked the question at issue directly, and in their reply, which could have been given in a simple affirmative or negative, they chose to be deliberately ambiguous, thereby manifesting their unwillingness to answer the question.

The Commission has recently issued a second reply to this question, upholding the former opinion. The Commission now states unequivocally that the confession of a religious woman heard, in virtue of Canon 522, outside of one of the places designated in Canon 522 and in the first reply of the Commission on November 4, 1920, would be not only illicit but also invalid.[39]

Another dispute has centered around the phrase, *in loco ad audiendas confessiones mulierum legitime destinato,* used in the first reply of the Commission. Some thought that this phrase was to be understood to mean only a place where the confessions of secular women could be heard, to the exclusion of the place

---

[37] Can. 39. "Conditiones in rescriptis tunc tantum essentiales pro eorundem validitate censentur, cum per particulas *si, dummodo,* vel aliam ejusdem significationis exprimuntur."

[38] Chelodi, *Jus de Personis,* n. 258; Prümmer, *Manuale J. C.,* n. 190; Choupin, *L'Etat Religieux,* p. 230; Leitner, *Handbuch,* p. 336; Aertnys-Damen, *Theo. Mor.,* II, n. 378; *Commentarium pro Religiosis,* II (1921), 21; *Nouvelle Revue Theologique,* XLVIII (1921), p. 55.

[39] Pont. Comm. ad CC. auth. interpret., 28 dec. 1927, *A. A. S.,* XX (1928), 61.

where religious women alone confess.[40] The reasons offered in support of this opinion were: first, that Canon 522 used the phrase *pro mulieribus* to mean secular women, when speaking of the approbation of the priest, and therefore the phrase should be understood to mean secular women in the reply of the Commission; secondly, that unless Canon 522 is so limited, the necessity of the special jurisdiction required by Canon 876 is destroyed.

Other authorities denied that the phrase was to be so understood, and permitted the confession of a religious woman, made according to the prescriptions of Canon 522, to take place in any place legitimately designated for hearing the confessions of women, including the confessional in a religious house.[41] The reasons adduced for this opinion were of far greater weight. They were: first, that the phrase *pro mulieribus* used in Canon 522, primarily means approved for secular women, but it is used in contradistinction to approved for men only, and therefore it by no means excludes the confessor who is approved for the confessions of religious women only, for such a confessor is approved for women; consequently, the phrase *pro mulieribus* designating the place of confession in the reply of the Commission is to receive the same wide interpretation; secondly, that it appears to be the intention of the legislator to permit the use of this privilege

---

[40] Fanfani, *op. cit.*, n. 137; Gury-Ferreres, *Casus Conscientiae*, II, n. 573; Chelodi, *Jus de Personis*, n. 258; Cocchi, *Com. in Cod. J. C.*, II, n. 42; *Commentarium pro Religiosis*, II (1921), 36.

[41] Vermeersch-Creusen, *Epitome*, I, n. 595; Genicot-Salsmans, *Instit. Theo. Mor.*, II, n. 339; Cappello, *De Sac.*, II, n. 448; McCormick, *Confessors of Religious*, p. 202; *Il Monitore Ecclesiastico*, XXXIII (1921), 162.

even in the religious house itself, for the phrase *extra proprium domum* used in the decree *Cum de Sacramentalibus* [42] is omitted in Canon 522; thirdly, that a decree of the Sacred Congregation of the Holy Office has declared that the confessional in a religious house, which ordinarily is used only for the confessions of religious women, could also be used for the confessions of secular women; [43] fourthly, that Canon 909, in speaking of the place where the confessions of women are to be heard, uses the word *mulierum* to include both secular and religious women.

The question is no longer disputable, for the Commission, in the recent reply already quoted, has dispelled all doubt by asserting that the religious woman may summon the priest *ad loca confessionibus mulierum vel religiosarum legitime destinata.*[44]

The proper place for hearing any sacramental confessions is a church or a public or semi-public oratory.[45] The confessional used for hearing the confessions of women, whether secular or religious, should always be located in an open and conspicuous place, and generally in a church or public or semi-public oratory destined for women.[46] The confessional should have a fixed screen, containing small perforations, between the penitent and the confessor.[47] The confessional of *nuns* should be so situated that the confessor is outside of the cloister, while the *nun* remains within.[48] The con-

[42] S. C. de Rel., 3 febr. 1913, *A. A. S.,* V (1913), 62.
[43] S. C. S. Off., 25 nov. 1874, Fontes n. 1033.
[44] Pont. Comm. ad CC. auth. interpret., 28 dec. 1927, *A. A. S.,* XX (1928), 61.
[45] Can. 908.
[46] Can. 909, § 1.
[47] Can. 909, § 2.
[48] S. C. de Religiosis, 6 febr. 1924, *A. A. S.,* XVI (1924), 95.

fessions of any women should not be heard outside of the confessional except in cases of sickness or some other true necessity, and then those precautions should be used which the Ordinary judges opportune.[49] These regulations, however, *per se* merely affect the liceity of the priest's action, and not the validity of the absolution, i. e., they do not affect the validity of the absolution if it is a religious woman, when the priest is habitually possessed of the special jurisdiction required for hearing the confessions of religious women validly.

When the confessor does not habitually possess this special jurisdiction, but hears the confession merely in virtue of the jurisdiction granted by Canon 522, these regulations regarding the place of confession do affect the validity of the absolution, because it is only upon the actual fulfillment of the conditions laid down in the law, that Canon 522 grants the special jurisdiction required for the valid absolution of a religious woman. Such a confessor, therefore, can validly absolve a religious woman only in the confessional located in a church, oratory, or other open and conspicuous place, or, if not in a confessional, in some other place which has been *legitimately designated for hearing the confessions of women*. The local Ordinary is the one to designate the place for hearing the confessions of women. He may do this either by diocesan statute, general decree, or on the occasion of his canonical visit. No embarrassment or inconvenience, however great it may be, can excuse a priest, hearing the confession of a religious woman in virtue of the

[49] Can. 910, § 1.

jurisdiction granted by Canon 522, from hearing that confession in a place legitimately designated for the confessions of women. If he does hear the confession outside of such a place, e.g., in a parlor, the absolution thus granted is both invalid and illicit.

However, since it is now certain that the religious may use this privilege within the religious house itself, a confessor need not hesitate to absolve such a penitent even within the religious house, as long as the confession is made in the proper place.

Conclusion

In conclusion it may be noted that the conditions now certainly necessary for the validity of the absolution granted in virtue of Canon 522, are:

1. That the religious women take the intiative in approaching the confessor;
2. That the priest be possessed of jurisdiction to hear the confessions of women, either secular or religious, in the place where the confession is to be heard;
3. That the confession be heard in a Church, public or semi-public oratory, or a place legitimately designated for hearing the confessions of women.

The remaining condition, regarding the motive of the penitent in approaching the confessor, need give no concern as long as the penitent seriously wishes to confess.

Absolution of a Sick Religious Woman

The second instance in which the Code *ipso jure* grants to the confessor the special jurisdiction required for hearing the confessions of religious women, is in the case of grave sickness. The constitution *Pastoralis Curae* of Benedict XIV, gave to nuns who were in danger of death, the right to request a special confessor from the bishop or religious superior to whom they were subject.[50] This concession was repeated in the decree of the Sacred Congregation of Bishops and Regulars, issued on June 28, 1901, regulating the confessions of religious.[51]

The decree *Cum de Sacramentalibus* extended the concession to all religious women, both nuns and those of simple vows, and permitted the use of it, not only in danger of death, but even in a grave sickness. The religious now need not apply to the bishop or religious superior for such a priest, but might call any approved confessor directly.[52]

The Code incorporates these provisions in Canon 523, which reads as follows:

Religiosae omnes, cum graviter aegrotant, licet mortis periculum absit, quemlibet sacerdotem ad mulierum confessiones excipiendas approbatum, etsi non destinatum religiosis, arcessere possunt eique, perdurante gravi infirmitate, quoties voluerint, confiteri, nec Antistita potest eas sive directe sive indirecte prohibere.

---

[50] Benedictus XIV, constit. *Pastoralis Curae*, 5 aug. 1748, § 58, Fontes n. 388.
[51] S. C. Ep. et Reg., 28 jun. 1901.
[52] S. C. de Rel., 3 febr. 1913, § 15, *A. A. S.*, V (1913), 64.

A religious woman, therefore, who is gravely ill may be absolved validly and licitly by any confessor who has jurisdiction for hearing the confessions of women, as often as the penitent wishes to confess during her illness. The special jurisdiction required for the valid absolution of a religious woman is *ipso jure* granted to the priest by this canon.

Conditions for the Validity of the Absolution

In order that this special jurisdiction be conceded and therefore in order that the absolution of the priest be valid, the fulfillment of two conditions is necessary:

1. That the penitent be gravely ill;
2. That the priest be approved for the confessions of women.

The determining of the gravity or non-gravity of the ailment is left to the prudent judgment of the priest. It is explicitly declared in the law itself that it is not necessary that the danger of death be present. The illness, however, must be grave; hence, a slight indisposition such as an ordinary cold or a slight attack of indigestion or a sprained muscle would not be considered grave illness. A grave illness would be an ailment which might induce danger of death in the proximate future, or one which would have a weakening effect on the patient for some time to come; in other words, an ailment which is liable, in view of the circumstances, to become fatal. In deciding upon the gravity of the illness, the condition of the individual patient must receive the greatest consideration, for what would be grave illness for one in view of her age, physical health, etc., would not be such for another. Under ordinary circumstances, the presence of an abnormal temperature may always be regarded as an indication of the presence of a sufficiently grave illness.[53]

In doubt whether or not an ailment is to be considered grave, a priest may always validly and licitly absolve as long as the doubt is positive and probable, for the Church will supply the necessary jurisdiction if it happens to be deficient. The validity of the absolution does not depend on the actual presence of grave illness, but merely on the priest's honest and prudent judgment that such an illness is present. Therefore, if it later becomes clear that the illness of the penitent was not grave, the validity of the absolution would not be affected by the discovery.[54]

The priest must be possessed of jurisdiction for hearing the confessions of women. But is it necessary that he be possessed of this jurisdiction in the place where the confession is heard? In other words, must he have obtained this jurisdiction from the local Ordinary of the place where the confession is to be heard or is it sufficient that he be approved for hearing the confessions of women by any local Ordinary?

It is not clear, for the law merely states that he must be approved for hearing the confessions of women. On the one hand, it would seem that this jurisdiction must be obtained from the local Ordinary of the place where the confession is to be heard, for this is the general rule expressed in Canons 874 and

---

[53] Cappello, *De Sac.*, II, n. 454; Vermeersch-Creusen, *Epit. Jur. Can.*, I, n. 595; Fanfani, *De Jure Religiosorum*, n. 137; McCormick, *Confessors of Religious*, p. 221.

[54] Can. 209.

876.[55] Whenever the legislator has departed from this rule, he has stated so very explicitly as, for example, in the case of jurisdiction for hearing confessions while on a sea voyage.[56]

On the other hand, it must be noted that it is not in virtue of the jurisdiction received from the local Ordinary that the priest absolves the sick religious woman, but in virtue of the special jurisdiction, required for absolving religious women validly, which is conferred *ipso jure* by Canon 523. When the legislator wishes to confer this jurisdiction only on priests approved for the confessions of women in the place where the confession of the religious woman is to be heard, he states this expressly, as in Canon 522. Therefore, it also seems probable that the phrase *ab Ordinario loci* was intentionally omitted and, as a consequence, any priest having jurisdiction for hearing the confessions of women from any Ordinary, may validly and licitly absolve in virtue of Canon 523, even though he has no jurisdiction in the place where the confession is to be heard.[57]

Since both opinions appear to be probable, a doubt of law exists, and in practice a priest can follow the milder view until the matter is decided officially.[58]

It seems certain that a priest having jurisdiction for hearing the confessions of religious women only, may also validly and licitly absolve in virtue of this canon, for surely he is included among those approved for the confessions of women.

[55] Papi, *Religious in Church Law*, p. 59.
[56] Can. 883.
[57] *Am. Eccl. Review*, LXXIV (1926), 39; McCormick, *Confessors of Religious*, p. 225.
[58] Can. 209.

A priest called upon to hear the confession of a sick nun in virtue of Canon 523, *ipso facto* obtains the right to enter the cloister, and may hear the confession of the sick nun in the infirmary or the nun's room.[59] This he may do as often as the nun wishes to confess while her grave illness perdures.

The religious woman is not restricted to calling upon only one priest in virtue of Canon 523, but may call upon different priests at different times.

The superior is gravely prohibited in any case from interfering in any way, directly or indirectly, with the sick woman's wishes.

[59] Can. 600, and S. C. de Rel., 6 febr. 1924, *Instructio de Clausura*, III, 2, g, A. A. S., XVI (1924), 99.

CHAPTER X

THE POWERS OF DISPENSING GRANTED BY THE CODE TO ALL CONFESSORS

ARTICLE I

The Power of Dispensing from the Eucharistic Fast

It has been the law of the Church for centuries that the faithful could receive the sacrament of the Holy Eucharist only when they had observed the natural fast from the preceding midnight.[1] This law, however, has always admitted of two exceptions, viz.:

1. When the danger of death was present; and
2. When it was necessary to consume the Holy Eucharist to avoid irreverence toward the Sacrament.[2]

The Code maintains this discipline[3] but adds a concession of more recent origin. This concession is contained in Canon 858, § 2, and reads as follows:

Infirmi tamen qui jam a mense decumbunt sine certa spe ut cito convalescant, de prudenti confessarii consilio sanctissimam Eucharistiam sumere possunt semel aut bis in hebdomada, etsi aliquam medicinam vel aliquid per modum potus antea sumpserint.

---

[1] Cf. C. 54, D. II, de cons.; Martinus V (in Conc. Constantien.), const., *In eminentis,* 22 febr. 1418, Fontes n. 44, et apud Denzinger n. 626.
[2] *Ibid.*
[3] Can. 858, § 1.

Although particular grants of a similar nature were given at various times to bishops because of peculiar circumstances,[4] still no general faculty in this matter was granted until 1906. At this time the faculty was granted whereby those who had already been sick for a month, could receive Holy Communion after taking some liquid nourishment; but this could be done only twice in a month, unless the patient dwelt in a house where the Blessed Sacrament was reserved or Mass was able to be celebrated. In this case it was permitted that the patient use the privilege twice in a week.[5]

The Code now extends the privilege of receiving Holy Communion twice in a week after taking some liquid nourishment, or even a solid as medicine, to all those who have been sick for a month and have no certain hope of becoming well in a short time.

Strictly speaking, it is the Code itself which dispenses such persons from the law of the Eucharistic fast, but the intervention of a confessor is necessary so as to verify the presence of the required conditions. Therefore, the confessor does not dispense, but he merely decides whether or not the necessary conditions are present and permits the use of the privilege granted by the Code.

Conditions

The conditions necessary for the licit use of the privilege are:

[4] Benedictus XIV, ep. *Quadam*, 24 mart. 1756, §§ 3, 9, Fontes n. 439; S. C. S. Off., 7 sept. 1897, Fontes n. 1192.
[5] S. C. C., 7 dec. 1906, Collect. n. 2244.

1. That the penitent be really sick, i.e., be incapacitated by a disease or weakness or old age or some other cause which would confine him to bed or at least prevent him from following his ordinary occupation;[6] but it is not necessary that the sickness be dangerous or even grave, and some are of the opinion that this privilege could be used by such a penitent even when he is able to come to a nearby church to receive Holy Communion;[7]
2. That the incapacity of the penitent already have perdured for a month; in law, the word *month* is taken to mean the space of thirty days, or one calendar month;[8] therefore, it is not permissible to anticipate an illness lasting for this length of time nor to shorten the period even by a few days, as some do;[9]
3. That there be no certain hope of the patient's rehabilitation within a few days, a certain hope being one giving some moral certitude;[10]
4. That the nourishment taken, be only liquid; if it is medicine, however, it may be in the form of a solid, for the phrase in the canon *per modum potus,* strictly interpreted, may be considered as not modifying the phrase *aliquam medicinam.*[11]

These conditions being verified, a confessor may

[6] S. C. C., 6 mart. 1907.
[7] Cappello, *De Sac.,* I, n. 506; Noldin, *Summa Theo. Mor.* III, n. 157.
[8] Can. 32, § 2.
[9] Cappello, *op. et loc. cit.*
[10] Vermeersch-Creusen, *Epitome,* II, n. 124.
[11] Cf. S. C. S. Off., 4 jun. 1893; 7 sept. 1897, Collect. n. 1983; Genicot-Salsmans, *Instit. Theo. Mor.,* II, n. 202.

permit the use of this privilege to such a penitent, but only once or twice in a week.

ARTICLE II

THE POWER OF DISPENSING FROM MATRIMONIAL IMPEDIMENTS IN URGENT CASES

Under conditions similar to those required in danger of death, a confessor is granted the faculty of dispensing from the same matrimonial impediments in certain urgent cases. Although in many details this faculty and the conditions required for its use are the same as in the circumstance of danger of death, yet there is sufficient divergence between the two cases to warrant a separate and distinct treatment of the case of urgency, even at the cost of repeating some of the statements already made.

This power is granted to the confessor in the following words of Canon 1045:

§ 1. Possunt Ordinarii locorum, sub clausulis in fine can. 1043 statutis, dispensationem concedere super omnibus impedimentis de quibus in cit. can. 1043, quoties impedimentum detegatur, cum jam omnia sunt parata ad nuptias, nec matrimonium, sine probabili gravis mali periculo, differri possit usque dum a Sancta Sede dispensatio obtineatur.

§ 2. Haec facultas valeat quoque pro convalidatione matrimonii jam contracti, si idem periculum sit in mora nec tempus suppetat recurrendi ad Sanctam Sedem.

§ 3. In iisdem rerum adjunctis, eadem facultate gaudeant omnes de quibus in can. 1044, sed solum pro casibus occultis in quibus ne loci quidem Ordinarius adiri possit, vel nonnisi cum periculo violationis secreti.

This legislation is entirely new with the Code, at least insofar as concerns the confessor, which is the sole aspect under which this power will be treated.

The Confessor

Unlike the faculty granted in danger of death, the power of dispensing in the internal sacramental forum in this case is not granted to every priest, but only to the confessor who has habitual ordinary or delegated jurisdiction to hear confessions in this place. However, the confessor may exercise this power over any penitent who approaches him, regardless of whether or not he has a domicile or quasi-domicile within his territory, and regardless of where the subsequent marriage is to take place.[1] Nor is it necessary that it be the penitent who is laboring under the impediment directly, but the confessor may dispense from an impediment which affects the other party to the marriage directly, and the penitent only indirectly, for the power of dispensing is given for the marriage.

The Power

The power of dispensing conceded to confessors by this canon, *per se* seems to be delegated by law, for the office of confessor as such is not an ecclesiastical office in the strict sense of that term,[2] to which ordinary

[1] Canons 881 and 1043.
[2] Can. 145.

jurisdiction could be attached by law.[3] *Per accidens*, however, the power may be considered as ordinary if the confessor is also a pastor or one holding an office to which ordinary jurisdiction for the internal sacramental forum is attached by law.[4] But even though his power is ordinary, the pastor seems to be forbidden to delegate it, at least for use in the internal sacramental forum.[5]

The faculty granted on this occasion is the power of dispensing from all the matrimonial impediments of ecclesiastical law except:

1. The impediment arising from the sacred order of priesthood; and
2. The impediment of affinity in the direct line, arising from a consummated marriage.

It must be noted that only impediments of the ecclesiastical law are included in this faculty, to the exclusion of all impediments of the divine positive or natural law. Therefore, the impediment of *ligamen*,[6] the impediment of *consanguinity* in any degree of the direct line,[7] and the impediment of *impotency* when it is certain, antecedent, and perpetual,[8] are also excluded from the sphere of this faculty.

---

[3] Can. 197, § 1.
[4] Canons 873 and 451.
[5] Pont. Comm. ad CC. auth. interpret., 16 oct. 1919, *A. A. S.*, XI (1919), 477.
[6] Can. 1069; cf. also Cappello, *De Sac.*, III, n. 390; Chelodi, *Jus Matrimoniale*, n. 76; Cerato, *Matrimonium a Codice Juris Canonici Desump.*, n. 64.
[7] Can. 1076; even if only doubtfully (dubio juris vel dubio facti) an impediment of the divine law; therefore also consanguinity in the first degree of the collateral line. Cf. Cappello, *op. cit.*, III, n. 224; Vlaming, *Praelect. Jur. Matr.*, I, n. 393.
[8] Can. 1068.

Although some are of the opinion that the power of dispensing from the required form of marriage is also included in this faculty,[9] still it seems quite certain that it is not, for Canon 1043 draws a clear distinction between the form and the impediments of Matrimony, and Canon 1045, in granting the power of dispensing in urgent cases, expressly mentions only the impediments.[10]

The law expressly states that this power of dispensing in these urgent cases may be used either to validate a marriage that is about to take place or to convalidate a marriage already contracted, as long as there is the same danger in delay and there is not sufficient time to recur even to the Ordinary. But the power of granting a *sanatio in radice* is not included in this faculty. Therefore, whenever the confessor dispenses from an impediment for the convalidation of a marriage already contracted invalidly, it is necessary for him to warn the penitent that he must renew his consent by a new act of the will. If the impediment dispensed was public (i. e., capable of being proven in the external forum) the consent must be renewed by both parties in the form prescribed by law. If the impediment was occult (i. e., incapable of being proven in the external forum) but known to both parties to the marriage, it suffices that the consent be renewed by both parties privately and secretly. If the impediment was occult and known

---

[9] De Smet, *De Sponsal.*, II, n. 764, note 2, who still regards the form as an impediment. Vermeersch, *Theo. Mor.* (ed. 1923), III, n. 755, *2d,* and 758 *c,* although he seems to have changed his opinion in the *Epitome Juris Canonici* (ed. 1925), II, n. 309.

[10] Blat, *Com. in Text. J. C., III,* pars 1, n. 437; Chelodi, *Jus Matrimoniale,* nn. 41-3; Wernz-Vidal, *Jus. Can.,* V, n. 413; Cappello, *op. cit.,* III, n. 233; Petrovits, *The New Church Law on Matrimony,* n. 164.

only to one of the parties to the marriage, the consent need be renewed by that party alone privately and secretly, as long as the consent of the other party still perdures.

The Conditions

In order that a confessor may validly and licitly dispense from these impediments to marriage in these urgent cases, the following conditions must be verified:

1. The dispensation must be granted for the internal sacramental forum and in the act of sacramental confession only;
2. The case must be urgent, i. e., all things must be prepared for the wedding, which cannot be deferred until a dispensation can be obtained from the local Ordinary without probable danger of grave evil;
3. The case must be occult;
4. It must be impossible to approach even the local Ordinary;
5. If the impediment to be dispensed is the impediment of disparity of cult or mixed religion, the canonical promises must be obtained in order that the dispensation be valid;
6. All scandal must be removed, at least in order that the granting of the dispensation be licit.

Because of the varied explanations of these conditions given by authors, it is deemed advisable to treat each separately.

1. *The Forum*

It seems certain that a confessor can use this power of dispensing for the internal forum in the act of sacramental confession only.[11] However, at least one author is of the opinion that this power may also be used in the internal non-sacramental forum.[12] But this opinion seems to lack all foundation, for Canon 1045, in granting the faculty, states that *omnes de quibus in can. 1044 gaudeant eadem facultate* and Canon 1044 expressly restricts the exercise of the power of dispensing by the confessor to the internal forum *in actu sacramentalis confessionis tantum*. It must be noted, therefore, that the dispensation granted by the confessor is recognized as effective only *coram Deo sed non coram Ecclesia,* and a new dispensation is required in order that the validity of the marriage be recognized *coram Ecclesia.*[13]

2. *The Urgency*

The law itself determines what cases are to be considered urgent, viz., as often as an impediment is detected when all things are prepared for the marriage and the marriage cannot be deferred until a dispensation is obtained without probable danger of grave evil. The preparations spoken of here are regarded by some as the canonical preparations only,[14] but others more

---
[11] Vermeersch-Creusen, *Epitome*, II, n. 312; Cappello, *op. cit.*, III, n. 238; De Smet, *op. cit.*, II, n. 794; Farrugia, *De Matrimonio et Causis Matrimonialibus*, n. 89 *b*.
[12] Leitner, *Lehrbuch des katholischen Eherechts*, p. 336.
[13] Canons 202, § 1, and 1047.
[14] Cappello, *op. cit.*, III, n. 233; Augustine, *Commentary on New Code*, V, p. 107.

properly interpret this phrase to mean any preparations, canonical, civil, or even social.[15] But insofar as the confessor is concerned, it seems the phrase may be interpreted to mean the confession made as an immediate preparation for marriage, for only in this case will there be insufficient time to approach the Ordinary. The evil that might be entailed by deferring the marriage must be a grave evil, but an evil of any kind suffices, be it spiritual, corporeal, economic, or social.[16] It is not necessary that it be certain that the evil will follow, nor is it necessary that there be a certain danger that the evil will follow, but it suffices if there is even a probable danger that a grave evil may be entailed.

Is it necessary that some preparations for the marriage be actually made, or will it suffice if the marriage is to take place immediately although no preparations have actually been made for it but serious evil will be entailed by the delay involved in obtaining the necessary dispensation? For example, in a case in which illicit relationship has taken place between persons bound by an impediment, the man, perhaps home on a vacation, is willing to marry just now, but if the present opportunity is not availed of, he is more than likely to depart and marry another. Although there are no preparations made for the wedding, no date set, no friends invited, etc., yet very serious evil most probably will be entailed by delay.

Some authors seem to be of the opinion that it is

---

[15] Chelodi, *Jus Matrimoniale*, n. 41; Petrovits, *The New Church Law on Matrimony*, n. 164; Reiffenstuel, *Jus Canonicum*, IV, Appendix, *De Dispensatione super Impedimentis Matrimonii*, n. 63.

[16] Blat, *op. cit.*, III, pars 1, n. 437; Farrugia, *op. cit.*, n. 84.

necessary that both conditions be present in a case before a confessor, pastor, or Ordinary can dispense in virtue of the power granted by Canon 1045.[17] However, a milder opinion has been proposed which would permit the use of this faculty when the marriage is to take place immediately and there is grave evil to be feared in delay, although no preparations in the strict sense have been made for the marriage.[18] The supporters of this opinion maintain that the legislator intends to provide for all urgent cases in this canon and does not mean to restrict the use of it to the one case where all the preparations for the wedding have been made. This phrase *cum omnia parata ad nuptias,* they argue, is merely a stereotyped expression used by authors before the Code as an example of an urgent case, whereas the older authors expressed the condition of urgency in much more general terms.[19] This interpretation seems very probable, since it is evidently the lack of time and the grave evil that might be entailed by delay which prompted the legislator to grant this faculty.

Finally, it is to be noted that it is not necessary that the impediment should have been entirely unknown up to the time it is revealed, but it suffices that only at this

---

[17] Vermeersch-Creusen, *op. cit.,* II, n. 308; De Smet, *op. cit.,* II, n. 764.

[18] *Il Monitore Ecclesiastico,* XXXVII (1925), 297-301. *Irish Eccl. Record,* Series V, Vol. XVI (1920), 408, quotes a private reply of the S. Cong. de Sacramentis given to Cardinal Logue on Sept. 12, 1919, stating that he *utatur jure suo* in dispensing in the above-mentioned case.

[19] Sanchez, *De Sancto Matrimonii Sacramento,* II, disp. XL, n. 7; Reiffenstuel, *Jus Canonicum,* Appendix, *De Dispensatione super Impedimentis Matrimonii,* n. 62; Benedict. XIV, *De Synodo Dioecesana,* lib. IX, c. II, n. 2; DeBecker, *De Sponsalibus et Matrimonio,* p. 305; Gasparri, *De Matrimonio,* I, n. 442.

late hour it has come to the knowledge of the confessor.[20] Nor does it matter if the parties had concealed it in bad faith until immediately before the marriage,[21] although Wernz-Vidal would not permit this, because it seems to him to be putting a premium on fraud.[22]

3. *Occult Cases*

Canon 1045 restricts the confessor's power of dispensing in these circumstances to occult cases, but the meaning of the phrase *pro casibus occultis* until recently has been the source of much controversy among authors. Some considered the phrase as equivalent to *occult impediments,* and therefore to be interpreted according to Canon 1037 to mean those impediments which could not be proven in the external forum.[23] This interpretation would render the faculty granted by Canon 1045 useless, except for occasional cases of crime and consanguinity, for all the diriment impediments under the Code, with the exception of some cases of crime and blood relationship resulting from the carnal lapse of one or other of the parents, are by their nature public (i. e., capable of being proven in the external forum).

Other authors argued, therefore, that the phrase

[20] Pont. Comm. ad CC. auth. interpret., 1 mart. 1921, ad IV, *A. A. S.,* XIII (1921), 178.
[21] Gasparri, *op. cit.,* I, n. 319; Cappello, *De Sac.,* III, n. 233; Pighi, *De Sacramento Matrimonii,* n. 92; Petrovits, *The New Church Law on Matrimony,* n. 165; Augustine, *Commentary on New Code,* V, p. 107.
[22] Wernz-Vidal, *Jus Can.,* V, n. 413, note 59.
[23] Ojetti in *Jus Pontificium,* An. VI (1926), 56-61; Wernz-Vidal, *op. cit.,* V, n. 428; Pighi, *op. cit.,* n. 90, *3a;* Augustine, *op. cit.,* V, p. 108.

pro casibus occultis had a wider extension than the phrase *pro impedimentis occultis* and that consequently the faculty included within its scope any impediment which was actually occult (i. e., actually unknown to the public or known only to a few, e. g., five or six discreet and prudent persons in a town who were not likely to broadcast their knowledge), even though the impediment of its nature was public (i. e., capable of being proven in the external forum).[24] This opinion was supported by the fact that Canon 1971, § 1, n. 2, retained the distinction between impediments *natura sua* public or occult, and those *de facto* public or occult, which prevailed before the Code.

The Pontifical Commission has recently decided the controversy in favor of this latter opinion, stating that the words *pro casibus occultis* of Canon 1045 must be so understood that they include not only impediments *"natura sua et facto occultis"* but also impediments *"natura sua publicis et facto occultis."* [25]

However, as regards the confessor, a further difficulty arises. Because of the nature of the internal sacramental forum in which alone he may dispense, not a few authorities maintain that a confessor is unable

[24] Chelodi, *Jus Matrimoniale*, nn. 40, 44; Blat, *Commentarium*, lib. III, pars 1, n. 437; Cappello, *op. cit.*, III, n. 236d; Fanfani, *De Jure Parochorum*, n. 306c, Dub. III; Cerato, *Matrimonium a Codice J. C. Desump.*, n. 38; Genicot-Salsmans, *Institutiones Theo. Mor.*, II, n. 523, 3, note 2; also *Casus Conscientiae*, casus 1074, 1075, 1076; Vermeersch, *Theo. Mor.*, n. 758c; Petrovits, *op. cit.*, nn. 166, 167; Motry, *Diocesan Faculties*, p. 139; *Il Monitore Ecclesiastico*, XXXII (1920), 62; *Nouvelle Revue Theologique*, XLVII (1920), 261-274; *Irish Eccl. Record*, Series V, Vol. XVI (1920), 404-408; Arendt, in *Jus Pontificium*, An. VI (1926), 145-158.

[25] Pont. Comm. ad CC. auth. interpret., 28 dec. 1927, *A. A. S.* XX (1928), 61.

to dispense from impediments which are naturally public, even though in a particular case they are actually occult.[26] Such impediments, they argue, of their nature need to be removed in the external forum and this the confessor is incapable of doing. Moreover, if the confessor should dispense in the internal sacramental forum, the door would be thrown open to abuses of all kinds against the law, for it would be necessary to condemn marriages as invalid in the external forum which were valid in the sight of God. The limitation of the confessor's powers, therefore, arises not so much from the wording of the law as from the very nature of the impediment and of the confessor's office.

The reasons adduced for this opinion prove only the inadvisability of dispensing in the internal sacramental forum, but cannot be said to prove the incapability of the confessor to dispense from such impediments. For, granting that a naturally public but actually occult impediment needs to be removed in the external as well as in the internal forum, yet there is nothing in the nature of the impediment to prevent its being removed in the internal forum while it still remains in the external forum, for the public nature of the impediment *per se* does not prevent its being removed in the sight of God, so that marital relations between the parties would be licit and further sinfulness on that score be averted. Furthermore, there is nothing in the

---

[26] Ojetti, in *Jus Pontificium* An. VI (1926), 56-61; Hilling, in *Archiv für katholisches Kirchenrecht*, CII (1922), 1-13; Editor of *Il Monitore Ecclesiastico*, XXXII (1920), 62-68; Vermeersch-Creusen, *Epitome*, II, nn. 312-3; De Smet, *De Sponsal.* II, n. 466; Farrugia, *De Matrimonio et Causis Matrimonialibus*, nn. 87-89; Cappello, *De Sac.*, III, n. 238; Wernz-Vidal, *Jus Can.*, V, n. 428.

nature of the internal sacramental forum which would render it incapable of dispensing from a naturally public but actually occult impediment, for from its very definition the internal forum differs from the external only in the extent in which their respective effects are recognized; the exercise of jurisdiction in the internal forum having its effect recognized only *coram Deo,* while the exercise of jurisdiction in the external forum has its effect recognized also *coram Ecclesia.*[27] This is clearly implied in Canon 202. Moreover, the Code explicitly recognizes the capability of the internal forum to act in public cases of a kindred matter, for in Canon 2251 it speaks of the absolution granted in the internal forum from censures incurred in the external. Therefore, if the confessor is not restricted by the public nature of the impediment nor by the nature of the internal forum, he can dispense from naturally public but actually occult impediments unless the law restricts his power. But the law does not restrict his power; on the contrary, in the third section of the canon, the confessor is granted the same power which is conferred upon Ordinaries in the first section, except that the confessor may use it only for occult cases. But an impediment naturally public and actually occult is to be considered as an occult case, as has been shown. This is further confirmed by the fact that the same third section of Canon 1045 gives, as one of the circumstances in which the confessor enjoys this faculty, the case in which it is impossible to approach the Ordinary without danger of violating a secret. This circumstance, however, may be present in the case of

[27] Cf. supra, p. 6.

a naturally public impediment which is actually occult, as well as in the case of an impediment naturally and actually occult. Finally, if naturally public but actually occult impediments were to be excluded from the confessor's faculty, it would render the grant made in Canon 1045 almost useless, for, as has been pointed out, almost all the diriment impediments to Matrimony under the Code are *natura sua publica.* This opinion certainly can claim intrinsic probability at least, and is supported by sufficient extrinsic authority [28] to render it safe in practice in virtue of Canon 209.

However, the indiscriminate use of this power by a confessor, although it cannot be said to be illicit, would be imprudent and inadvisable because of the dangerous consequences of such a dispensation. Therefore, whenever a confessor discovers an impediment to a marriage, if at all possible he should take some steps to prevent the subsequent repudiation of the marriage in the external forum. If the impediment is actually public (i. e., known to many in the place, or the circumstances are such that it will soon become public knowledge), then a confessor cannot dispense, whether the impediment is naturally public or occult, and the penitent must be referred to the pastor or some priest who will approach the Ordinary. But if the impediment is actually occult (i. e., unknown to the people of the place or known only to a few discreet and prudent

---

[28] Chelodi, *Jus Matrimoniale,* n. 44; Cerato, *Matrimonium a Codice Juris Canonici Desump,* n. 38, 1 and 2; Genicot-Salsmans, *Instit. Theo. Mor.,* II, n. 523, *3,* note 4; "Socius," in *Il Monitore Ecclesiastico,* XXXII (1920), 59-62; Arendt, in *Nouvelle Revue Theologique,* XLVII (1920), 261-274; and in *Jus Pontificium,* An. VI (1926), 145-158; *Irish Eccl. Record,* Series V, Vol. XVI (1920), 404-408.

persons who are not likely to divulge the secret), the confessor can dispense, whether the impediment is naturally public or occult, but should do so only as a last resort. If this actually occult impediment is in no way defamatory and there is no special reason for keeping it secret, the penitent should be told that he is morally obliged to reveal it to the pastor or the priest to assist at the marriage, who may dispense in the external forum, or to the confessor himself outside of confession if there is time for him to approach the Ordinary. If the impediment is defamatory or there is special reason for secrecy, the confessor may dispense for the internal sacramental forum, thereby safeguarding the penitent's conscience, but arrange to have the penitent disclose the impediment to the confessor himself outside of confession. The erstwhile confessor can then obtain another dispensation for the external forum from the Ordinary or for the internal non-sacramental forum from the Sacred Penitentiary, according as the secrecy of the case demands, and have the parties renew their consent before him after this dispensation has been obtained. If it will not be possible for the parties to renew their consent afterward, a *sanatio in radice* may be obtained from the superior instead of a dispensation. If it is not possible or the penitent is unwilling to reveal the impediment to the confessor outside of confession or to another priest, the confessor may dispense or may refuse to dispense in the internal sacramental forum (according to his prudent judgment of the dispositions of the penitent and the circumstances of the case), without making any provision for the recognition of the marriage in the external forum. It would seem that it is the mind of the Church to grant this power to the confessor for just such an exceptional and urgent case, in order that her children may be protected from the greatest of all evils—mortal sin—nor is she deterred from granting her benign concession by the possibility of its abuse by the unworthy.

4. The Approach to the Ordinary

The fourth condition necessary for the validity of the dispensation granted by the confessor in virtue of Canon 1045, is that it be impossible to approach the Ordinary or that he can be approached only with danger of violating a secret. The impossibility of approaching the Ordinary need not be physical, but it suffices if it is morally impossible to approach him, i. e., it can be done only by using extraordinary means,[29] or only with grave inconvenience, or with danger of violating a secret. The secret need not be a sacramental secret, but it suffices if it is a natural secret which is in danger of being violated by approaching the Ordinary.[30] It must be remembered that the validity of the dispensation does not depend on the actual possibility or impossibility of approaching the Ordinary, but only on the confessor's honest and prudent judgment that it is impossible to do so.

---

[29] Telephone and telegraph are still considered as extraordinary means of communication and there is no obligation to use them. Cf. Pont. Comm. ad CC. auth. interpret., 12 nov. 1922, ad V, A. A. S. XIV (1922), 662. In fact, the use of these means of communication is frowned upon by the Holy See. Cf. litt. encycl. Secr. Status, 10 dec. 1891, Coll. n. 1775; S. C. S. Off., 24 aug. 1892, Coll. n. 1810.

[30] Vermeersch-Creusen, *op. cit.*, II, n. 311; Cerato, *op. cit.*, n. 38.

Finally, there does not seem to be any obligation to approach a delegate of the Ordinary even if that is possible,[31] for the canon mentions only the Ordinary; however, at least one author maintains that there is such an obligation.[32]

5. *The Promises in Dispensing from the Impediments of Disparity of Cult and Mixed Religion*

As it has already been pointed out, the divine law prohibits the marriage of a Catholic with one of another religion unless the danger of perversion to the Catholic party and the danger of the children being baptized and reared outside of the true faith are removed or at least rendered remote. Unless this condition is fulfilled, the Church is incapable of dispensing from the impediments of disparity of cult or mixed religion. The means of fulfilling this requisite condition of the divine law have been established by the Church in the form of the customary canonical promises whereby the non-Catholic party promises not to interfere in any way with the practice of the Catholic party's religion, and both parties promise that the children will be baptized and educated in the Catholic religion. These promises regularly should be made in writing,[33] but in a case of urgency such as this, it seems that it will suffice if they are made orally. Before granting a dispensation from either of these impediments, the confessor must obtain these promises in order that he may dispense validly and licitly.

---

[31] Motry, *Diocesan Faculties*, p. 136.
[32] Vlaming, *Praelectiones Jur. Matr.*, II, n. 412.
[33] Canons 1061, § 1, n. 2, and 1071.

Are these promises necessary for the validity of the dispensation or merely for the liceity of the priest's action in dispensing? In ordinary cases there is no doubt that these promises, as the means of fulfilling the requirements of the divine law, are necessary for the validity of the dispensation.[34] But when the prohibition of the divine law has ceased or its conditions have been fulfilled by other means, are the canonical promises required by the ecclesiastical law still necessary for the validity of the dispensation? Many authorities insist that they are,[35] while others deny their necessity for validity in such circumstances.[36] However, almost all admit that such a case is possible only in the extreme urgency of danger of death, outside of which it is not possible to conceive of a case in which the prohibition of the divine law shall have ceased or its prescriptions shall have been fulfilled by other means than the canonical promises.[37] Therefore, for all practical purposes it will suffice to say that a confessor can

---

[34] Almost all commentators.
[35] De Smet, *op. cit.*, II, n. 508, note 1, n. 591, note 4; Noldin, *Summa Theo. Mor.*, III, n. 608; Woywod, *Practical Commentary on the Code of Canon Law*, n. 1011; and in the *Homiletic and Pastoral Review*, XXIII (1923), 1059; Augustine, *Commentary*, V, p. 101; Prümmer, *Manuale Theologiae Moralis*, n. 866; Chelodi, *Jus Matrimoniale*, n. 41, and Wernz-Vidal, *Jus Can*, V, n. 413, are doubtful, stating only that the dispensation is not certainly valid.
[36] Cappello, *De Sac.*, III, n. 232; Genicot-Salsmans, *Instit. Theo. Mor.*, II, nn. 493, 514, 523; Cerato, *Matrimonium a Cod. Jur. Can. Desump.*, n. 35; Pighi, *De Sacramento Matrimonii*, n. 90; De Becker, *De Sponsalibus et Matrimonio*, pp. 243 and 278, note 1; Petrovits, *The New Church Law on Matrimony*, nn. 160, 192; Farrugia, *De Matrimonio et Causis Matrimonialibus*, n. 83; *Irish Eccl. Record*, XXVII (1926), 634; *Homiletic and Pastoral Review*, XXII (1922), 510.
[37] Cappello, *op. cit.*, III, n. 233.

never validly and licitly grant a dispensation from the impediment of disparity of cult or mixed religion, in virtue of the power granted to him by Canon 1045, without first obtaining the canonical promises. The opinion of those who hold that even in the circumstances mentioned in Canon 1045 the canonical promises are necessary only for the liceity of the priest's action and not for the validity of the dispensation,[38] seems devoid of all probability and unsafe in practice. The supporters of this opinion maintain that the just cause required for the validity of a dispensation by law,[39] is present in these circumstances in the form of the evil which may be caused by the delay in dispensing, while the ablative absolute (used in Canon 1043, to which Canon 1045 refers) imposing the obligation of obtaining the canonical promises, does not certainly imply a condition necessary for validity.[40] But this argument can hardly be considered valid, since Canon 1061, as the law for this particular dispensation, requires for the validity of the dispensation, not only a just cause, but also the obtaining of the canonical promises as the means of fulfilling the requisite of the divine law. So, only when the prohibition of the divine law has ceased or when its condition has been fulfilled by other means than the canonical promises, can the Church be considered as willing to release from her obligation, and this circumstance cannot exist outside of the extreme urgency of danger of death.

[38] Cerato, *op.cit.*, n. 37; Pighi, *op. et loc. cit.*
[39] Can. 84, § 1.
[40] Can. 39; cf. also Maroto, *Instit. Jur. Can.*, I, n. 284, and Vermeersch-Creusen, *Epitome*, I, n. 130.

6. *The Removal of Scandal*

Finally, a confessor must admonish the penitent to take whatever steps are necessary to remove any scandal which may have been occasioned in the past, and to prevent further scandal in the future as a result of the marriage. The means of attaining these ends will differ in individual cases, so that the determining of the means to be employed must be left to the prudent judgment of the individual confessor. It is to be noted, however, that this condition concerning the removal of scandal of its very nature is only a prerequisite for the licit use of the power of dispensing, and in no way affects the validity of the dispensation. Nevertheless a confessor, because of the nature of the dispensation which he grants, must be particularly solicitous about this condition.

ARTICLE III

THE POWER OF DISPENSING FROM IRREGULARITIES ARISING FROM AN OCCULT CRIME

An irregularity is a perpetual canonical impediment which *per se* and primarily prohibits the licit reception of Orders, and secondarily prohibits the licit exercise of Orders received. An irregularity may be contracted either *ex defectu* or *ex delicto*. An irregularity *ex defectu* arises from the privation of a quality, which privation, even though not sinful, renders one unfit for the sacred ministry. An irregularity *ex delicto* arises from a grave and external crime even though occult, which renders the delinquent unfit for the sacred ministry.[1]

This latter species of irregularity arises from the following crimes:

1. The crime of apostasy from the faith, heresy, or schism;
2. The crime of permitting baptism to be conferred on oneself by a non-Catholic, outside of the case of extreme necessity;
3. The crime of attempting marriage, even by a merely civil ceremony, while either of the parties is bound by the bond of valid marriage, or religious vows even simple and temporary, or while the man is in Sacred Orders;
4. The crime of perpetrating voluntary homicide, or procuring the abortion of a human fetus, the effect following, or even co-operating in these crimes;[2]
5. The crime of mutilating oneself or another, or attempting to take one's own life;
6. The crime, committed by a cleric, of practicing the forbidden profession of medicine or surgery, when a death follows;
7. The crime of exercising an order reserved to clerics in major orders, by one lacking the necessary order or prohibited from exercising it by a canonical penalty, whether personal or local, medicinal or vindictive.[3]

---

[1] Can. 968, and Vermeersch-Creusen, *op. cit.*, II, n. 252; Noldin, *Summa Theo. Mor.*, III, n. 479.
[2] Motry, *Diocesan Faculties*, p. 152.
[3] Can. 985.

IRREGULARITIES

The crime is called *public,* when it has already become public knowledge, or when it was committed in such circumstances or has since fallen into such circumstances, that it can and must be prudently thought that it will easily become known. The crime is otherwise called *occult.*[4]

In Canon 990, the Code grants the faculty of dispensing from an irregularity arising from an occult crime in the following words:

§ 1. Licet Ordinariis per se vel alium suos subditos dispensare ab irregularitatibus omnibus ex delicto occulto provenientibus, ea excepta de qua in can. 985, n. 4 aliave deducta ad forum judiciale.

§ 2. Eadem facultas competit cuilibet confessario in casibus occultis urgentioribus in quibus Ordinarius adiri nequeat et periculum immineat gravis damni vel infamiae, sed ad hoc dumtaxat ut poenitens ordines jam susceptos exercere licite valeat.

Since this book concerns only the jurisdiction of the confessor, only his power of dispensing in the internal sacramental forum will be examined.

This faculty was first granted in 1909, even in somewhat broader scope than in the present canon.[5] In this canon, the Code grants, to all confessors who are possessed either of ordinary or delegated jurisdiction for the internal sacramental forum, the power of dispensing from all irregularities arising from an occult crime,[6] except those arising from the crime of perpetrating or co-operating in the perpetration of voluntary homicide, or from the crime of procuring or co-operating in the procuration of an abortion, when the effect

[4] Can. 2197.   [5] S. C. S. Off., 6 sept. 1909, Fontes n. 1288.
[6] Hickey, *Irregularities and Simple Impediments,* p. 87.

has followed, or from any other crime when the case has already been brought to the judicial forum, ecclesiastical or civil. The confessor, however, can use this power only in a more urgent case in which the Ordinary cannot be approached and there is danger of grave loss or evil repute coming upon the delinquent. And even in this case he can dispense only for the licit exercise of orders already received, but not for the further reception of other orders. In this latter case the reception of the orders must be deferred until a dispensation can be obtained from the Ordinary. It must be noted, however, that when a confessor dispenses, it is not necessary to have any further recourse, even when it is possible to have recourse without grave inconvenience.

ARTICLE IV

THE POWER OF DISPENSING FROM VINDICTIVE PENALTIES

Vindictive penalties are those which tend directly toward the expiation of a crime and therefore have as their primary end the good of the community. Accordingly, they are inflicted perpetually, or for a definite time, and the remission of the penalty is not contingent upon the repentance of the delinquent.[1] Therefore, amendment of life gives the offender no right to be released from the penalty. In all of these characteristics vindictive penalties are unlike censures.[2]

[1] Can. 2286.
[2] Cf. Canons 2241, 2242, 2248, 2250.

VINDICTIVE PENALTIES

The Code does not attempt to enumerate all the vindictive penalties that may be imposed, but a list of the principal vindictive penalties is given in Canon 2291. Vindictive penalties, like others, may be *latae* or *ferendae sententiae,* according as they are incurred *ipso facto* or only by the *condemnatory sentence* of a judge.[3]

After a vindictive penalty has been incurred, it can be removed only upon the expiration of the time for which it was inflicted, or by a dispensation granted by the proper authority.[4] The proper authority for dispensing from the penalty in ordinary cases is he who inflicted it, or his competent superior, successor, or delegate.[5] The judge who passed sentence upon the delinquent, merely as a judge has not the authority to dispense from the observance of the penalty.[6] But in imposing certain vindictive penalties by a condemnatory sentence, under certain conditions, a judge may suspend the execution of the sentence, pending the good behavior of the delinquent.[7]

For more urgent occult cases in which the delinquent cannot observe a vindictive penalty inflicted *latae sententiae* without bringing infamy to himself or giving scandal to others, the Code grants to any confessor the power of suspending the obligation of observing the penalty, but he must impose the burden of having recourse to, and accepting the mandate of, the Sacred Penitentiary or a bishop having faculties. This recourse must be had within a month, under pain of

---
[3] Can. 2217, § 1, n. 2.
[4] Can. 2289.
[5] Can. 2236, § 1.
[6] Can. 2236, § 3.
[7] Can. 2288.

reincurring the penalty. When the recourse is morally impossible or gravely inconvenient, however, the confessor has the power of dispensing even from this obligation, according to the norm set down in Canon 2254. This power, which can be exercised only in the internal sacramental forum, is contained in Canon 2290, which is as follows:

§ 1. In casibus occultis urgentioribus, si ex observatione poenae vindicativae latae sententiae, reus seipsum proderet cum infamia et scandalo, quilibet confessarius potest in foro sacramentali obligationem servandae poenae suspendere, injuncto onere recurrendi saltem intra mensem per epistolam et per confessarium, si id fieri possit sine gravi incommodo, reticito nomine, ad S. Poenitentiariam vel ad Episcopum facultate praeditum et standi ejus mandatis.

§ 2. Et si aliquo casu extraordinario hic recursus sit impossibilis, tunc ipsemet confessarius potest dispensationem concedere ad normam Can. 2254, § 3.

Therefore, a confessor can use the faculty validly, only when the following conditions are verified:

1. The crime is occult;
2. The case is urgent, i. e., the penalty cannot be observed without revealing the secret sin and causing scandal or bringing loss of reputation on the delinquent;
3. The penalty was inflicted *latae sententiae*.

The recourse is to be had in the same manner and under the same conditions as set down in Canon 2254. Dispensation from the recourse may also be granted under the same conditions as prescribed in Canon 2254.[8]

[8] Cf. supra, p. 172 seq.

It seems probable that the concession made in Canon 2254, § 2, because of the analogous circumstances may also be used by one laboring under a vindictive penalty as well as by one under censure. Therefore, it would seem possible for a penitent who had incurred a vindictive penalty, the observance of which was suspended by a confessor in virtue of Canon 2290, to approach a privileged confessor who had faculties to dispense from the vindictive penalty, and receive the mandate from him, instead of having recourse to the prescribed superior or awaiting his mandate.

CHAPTER XI

OTHER POWERS GRANTED BY THE CODE TO ALL CONFESSORS

ARTICLE I

The Power of Extending the Paschal Time

Canon 859 § 1. Omnis utriusque sexus fidelis, postquam ad annos discretionis, idest ad rationis usum, pervenerit, debet semel in anno, saltem in Paschate, Eucharistiae sacramentum recipere, nisi forte de consilio proprii sacerdotis, ob aliquam rationabilem causam, ad tempus ab ejus perceptione duxerit abstinendum.

In Canon 859, § 1, every confessor is granted the faculty of extending the time set for the fulfilling of the Paschal precept for his penitents individually for any reasonable cause. Although individual grants of this character had been given earlier,[1] yet the first

[1] Cf. S. C. S. Off., 23 mart. 1656. Fontes, n. 730.

general concession of this kind is found in the encyclical letter of Benedict XIV beginning *Inter omnigenas*.[2] In this concession the priest was able to extend the time only within the period between the beginning of Lent and the feast of Pentecost, and he could do this only when it was impossible for the people, because of circumstances, to fulfill the precept during the two weeks then defined by law.

The confessor now may extend the time for fulfilling the Easter duty indefinitely and do this for any reasonable cause. When the fulfillment of the precept is impossible, of course, the prescriptions of the positive law of the Church cease as long as the impossibility perdures. In this case no dispensation is necessary. But when it is not impossible nor even gravely inconvenient to fulfill the precept, but for some reason it would be for the betterment of the penitent to postpone the fulfilling of the obligation, a dispensation is necessary and can be obtained from any confessor. To postpone the making of the Easter duty without such a dispensation would be gravely sinful.[3]

ARTICLE II

The Power of Commuting the Conditions for Gaining an Indulgence

For those who are hindered by a legitimate impediment from fulfilling the conditions required for gaining

---

[2] 2 febr. 1744, § 21, Fontes n. 339.
[3] Vermeersch-Creusen, *Epitome,* II, n. 126.

an indulgence, the faculty is granted by Canon 935 to all confessors to commute the works enjoined into others. The canon reads as follows:

Pia opera ad lucrandas indulgentias injuncta, confessarii possunt in alia commutare pro iis qui, legitimo detenti impedimento, eadem praestare nequeant.

This faculty was first granted by Benedict XIV among the faculties given to confessors for the jubilee year [1] and was later extended to include other indulgences.[2]

This faculty is applicable to all indulgences, most probably even to the Portiuncula indulgence.[3] In order that the commutation be valid, it is necessary that an impediment actually exist. If the confessor is doubtful of the sufficiency of the cause on account of which the commutation is sought, he may validly and licitly grant the commutation.[4] But if he is doubtful of the existence of a cause, he cannot grant the commutation in virtue of Canon 84, yet there does not seem to be any reason for excluding the use of Canon 209. The works into which the conditions are commuted should be in proportion to the gravity of the conditions from which he dispenses and the gravity of the impediment on account of which the commutation is sought. The object of the indulgence, however, must be substantially

---

[1] Ep. encycl. *Inter praeteritos,* 3 dec. 1749, §§ 52-55, Fontes n. 404.
[2] S. C. de Prop. Fide, 19 sept. 1773, Collect. n. 499. S. C. Indulg., *Urbis et Orbis,* 18 sept. 1862, Collect. n. 1231.
[3] Vermeersch-Creusen, *op. cit.,* II, n. 221; Cappello, *De Sac.,* II, n. 975.
[4] Can. 84.

preserved, and only the conditions enjoined for gaining it are to be changed, e. g., when an indulgence is granted for frequent Communion, it necessarily supposes this, although the other conditions such as the prayers, etc., may be commuted.[5]

[5] Vermeersch, *Theo. Mor.*, III, n. 633.

Title III

THE PENITENTIAL JURISDICTION GRANTED BY THE CODE TO PASTORS AND MISSIONARIES

In addition to the powers already mentioned, the Code grants some special powers of absolving and of dispensing to confessors who are at the same time pastors or missionaries. Those mentioned in a foregoing chapter of this book,[1] who are included under the name of pastor in law, also enjoy these special powers of absolving and of dispensing which the Code grants to pastors. Other confessors, however, do not enjoy these powers *ipso jure,* although they may be delegated to them among the faculties granted by their individual bishops. It must be noted also, that pastors are unable to delegate these special powers to other priests, at least for use in the internal sacramental forum.[2]

In the first chapter of this title, the power of absolving granted to pastors in certain circumstances, and the power of absolving granted to missionaries during the time of a mission, will be the subjects of investigation. In the second chapter, the power of dispensing from the laws of festal observance, fast and abstinence, which the Code grants exclusively to Ordinaries, pastors, and those coming under the name of pastor in law, will be the topic of discussion.

[1] Supra, p. 46 and Can. 451.
[2] Cf. Pont. Comm. ad CC. auth. interpret., 16 oct. 1919, *A. A. S.,* XI (1919), 477.

CHAPTER XII

THE POWER OF ABSOLVING FROM SINS RESERVED "RATIONE SUI"

Pastors

During the time in which the Paschal precept is to be fulfilled, *pastors,* and those who are considered in law as coming under the name of pastors,[1] enjoy by the prescriptions of common law [2] the faculty of absolving from sins reserved *ratione sui* by the local Ordinary. This power of absolving seems ordinary since it is annexed by law to an office bearing with it ordinary jurisdiction for the internal sacramental forum. During this time, it must be noted, the reservation does not cease, and therefore not every confessor can absolve from the sin; but the reservation remains, and by common law *pastors,* and those who in law are included under the name of pastors, are granted the power to absolve from it.

Canon 899 § 3. Ipso jure a casibus, quos quoquo modo sibi Ordinarii reservaverint, absolvere possunt tum parochi, aliive qui parochorum nomine in jure censentur, toto tempore ad praeceptum paschale adimplendum utili, tum singuli missionarii quo tempore missiones ad populum haberi contingat.

The time for fulfilling the Paschal precept by common law extends only from Palm Sunday until Low

[1] Supra, p. 46, and Can. 451, § 2.
[2] Can. 899, § 3.

Sunday.[3] In this country, by virtue of a special indult the time may be begun as early as the first Sunday in Lent.[4] Since Canon 899, § 3, grants this special faculty of absolving from reserved sins to pastors for the whole time during which the Paschal precept is to be fulfilled, there is little reason for doubting that the pastors of this country enjoy this faculty from the first Sunday of Lent to Trinity Sunday. Although this faculty evidently is granted to facilitate the fulfillment of the Paschal precept, yet there is nothing in the law that would restrict the use of it during this time to that confession only which is made to fulfill the Paschal precept. Therefore, it seems quite certain that during this time the confession need not be made for the purpose of fulfilling the Paschal precept.[5]

Canon 859, § 1, grants to priests the faculty of extending this time beyond the limits set by the Ordinary, for individual persons, during which they may fulfill the Paschal precept. When a person enjoying such an extension confesses, a pastor and those included under the name of pastor, still enjoy the faculty granted in Canon 899, § 3, even outside of the time defined by the Ordinary, as long as the confession is made to fulfill the Paschal precept. Likewise, when a penitent has been unable to fulfill this precept during the defined time, the above-mentioned confessors may exercise this faculty as long as the confession is made for the

---

[3] Can. 859, § 2.
[4] Cf. S. C. de Prop. Fide, 16 oct. 1830, apud *Concilia Provincialia Baltimorae habita*, p. 86; etiam *Acta et Decreta Concilii Plenarii Baltimorensis II*, 257.
[5] Cappello, *De Sac.*, II, n. 559; Vermeersch-Creusen, *Epitome*, II, n. 180; Genicot-Salsmans, *Instit. Theo. Mor.*, II n. 346.

purpose of fulfilling this precept, for Canon 899, § 3, states expressly that the time is *tempus utile*.[6]

Missionaries

Missionaries enjoy this same power of absolving from sins reserved *ratione sui* by the bishop, during the time they are engaged in giving a mission.[7] Because of the similarity of their activities, retreat masters are also usually included under this canon when they are giving retreats to many collectively. It seems probable that they would also enjoy this faculty when they are giving a retreat even to one person individually.[8]

Cappello is of the opinion that during the time of a mission, not only the missionaries, but also other priests who are deputed to hear confessions enjoy this faculty.[9] But this would seem to be an unlawful extension of the power, for the canon grants the faculty to missionaries personally, and not to priests who hear confessions during the time of a mission. The concession, therefore, is personal, and it is the missionary who is privileged, and not the time of the mission.

[6] Can. 35.
[7] Can. 899, § 3.
[8] Cappello, *op. cit.*, II, n. 559.
[9] *Op. cit.*, II, n. 559, § 3.

CHAPTER XIII

THE POWER OF DISPENSING FROM THE LAWS OF FESTAL OBSERVANCE, FAST AND ABSTINENCE GRANTED PASTORS

Law of Festal Observance

The general law of the Church prescribes the assistance of all the faithful who have reached their seventh birthday [1] at the Holy Sacrifice of the Mass, and their abstinence from servile works and forensic acts on feast days of precept. Unless legitimate customs or particular indults permit different behavior, the law likewise prescribes the abstinence of the faithful from public marketing, trading, and other forms of buying and selling on these days.[2]

The feast days of precept for the whole Church, according to the Code, are as follows:

1. Every Sunday of the year;
2. The feasts of the Nativity of Our Lord, the Circumcision, the Epiphany, the Ascension, and Corpus Christi;
3. The feasts of the Immaculate Conception, and the Assumption of Our Blessed Lady;
4. The feast of St. Joseph, the feast of Sts. Peter and Paul, and the feast of All Saints.[3]

---

[1] Can. 12.
[2] Can. 1248.
[3] Can. 1247, § 1.

By a particular indult for the United States, the feasts of the Epiphany, Corpus Christi, St. Joseph, and Sts. Peter and Paul are not days of precept in this country.[4]

Law of Abstinence

The law of abstinence forbids the use of meat and juice from meats on days of abstinence.[5] Every Friday of the year unless it happens to be a feast day of precept outside of Lent,[6] is a day of abstinence but not a day of fast.[7] All who have completed their seventh year of age are obliged by the law of abstinence.[8]

Contrary to the general notion existing today, there is no general indult for working men in this country. This was sought and denied by the Sacred Congregation de Propaganda Fide in a letter to His Eminence the late Cardinal Gibbons on March 15, 1895.[9] The Congregation, however, granted to the individual Ordinaries of this country the faculty of permitting the use of meat on days of abstinence to working men and their families whenever the observance of the common law of the Church was especially difficult. This faculty was granted for ten years and has since been continually renewed.[10] The faculty explicitly states

---
[4] *Conc. Baltimorensis III*, n. 111; Epist. S. C. S. Off., 31 dec. 1885, apud *Acta et decreta Conc. Baltimor. III*, p. CV; also Can. 1253.
[5] Can. 1250.
[6] Can. 1252, § 4.
[7] Can. 1252, § 1.
[8] Can. 1254, § 1.
[9] Apud *Amer. Eccles. Review*, XII (1894), 425.
[10] Cf. *ibid*, XXXVI (1909), 304; *Boston Pilot*, Febr. 13, 1926; Woywod, *Practical Commentary on the Code of Canon Law*, Supplement, Roman Documents Affecting the Laws of the Code issued up to December, 1926."

PASTOR'S POWER OF DISPENSING 247

that the permission to dispense does not extend to the following days of abstinence: all Fridays, Ash Wednesday, any day of Holy Week, and Christmas Eve. The difference between the faculty of dispensing and a general indult is that the former requires the individual Ordinaries to make an explicit statement permitting the use of the privilege whenever conditions are such that, in their prudent judgment, the use of the privilege is necessary; whereas a general indult requires no such execution on the part of the Ordinaries.

Law of Fasting

The law of fasting prescribes that only one meal be taken in a day, but it does not forbid a slight collation in the morning and in the evening according to the custom in force in individual localities.[11] Every day of the Lenten season is a day of fast but not a day of abstinence.[12] The days on which both the law of abstinence and the law of fasting must be observed, are the following:

1. Ash Wednesday;
2. The Fridays and Saturdays of Lent (except the afternoon of Holy Saturday);[13]
3. The Ember Days;
4. The vigils of the feasts of Pentecost, the Assumption of Our Blessed Lady, All Saints, and the Nativity of Our Lord.[14]

[11] Can. 1251, § 1.
[12] Can. 1252, § 3.
[13] Can. 1252, § 4.
[14] Can. 1252, § 2.

All who have completed their twenty-first year and have not yet completed their fifty-ninth year of age are obliged by the law of fasting.[15]

The Ordinaries of the United States have also obtained the privilege of transferring the observance of the law of abstinence on the Saturdays of Lent to Wednesdays.[16]

Those who are obliged to fast but who may be included under the privilege granted to working men and their families, where this privilege is in use, may eat meat once in the day on the days for which the privilege is granted. This is evident from the wording of the letter mentioned above.

The Code grants no power of dispensing from these laws to confessors as such, but any confessor may authentically declare whether or not his penitent is obliged by these laws, or whether or not he may avail himself of the privilege granted to working men and their families.

Power of Dispensing

The Code, however, does grant to *pastors* the power of dispensing their own subjects even outside their territory, and *peregrini* within their territory as individuals or as families, in single instances, from the law of festive observance, or from the laws of fast and

---

[15] Can. 1254, § 2.
[16] S. C. C., 4 jun. 1920, apud Woywod, *op. cit.,* Supplement: "This privilege together with the faculty of dispensing working men and their families expired in 1925 and was renewed by cablegram to His Eminence Cardinal O'Connell, informing him of this fact and that rescripts were being forwarded to the individual bishops. *Boston Pilot,* Feb. 13, 1926."

PASTOR'S POWER OF DISPENSING

abstinence, or from the law of fast or of abstinence. This faculty is granted in the following words of Canon 1245, § 1:

Non solum Ordinarii locorum, sed etiam parochi, in casibus singularibus justaque de causa possunt subjectos sibi singulos fideles singulasve familias, etiam extra territorium, atque in suo territorio etiam peregrinos, a lege communi de observantia festorum itemque de observantia abstinentiae et jejunii vel etiam utriusque dispensare.

This faculty formerly was obtained only by the local Ordinary in his quinquennial faculties and subsequently delegated by him.[17] Now it is obtained *ipso jure,* not only by local Ordinaries, but also by *pastors.* It is to be noted, however, that the power given to pastors is the power of dispensing, and not the power of commuting the obligation of these laws into other works. Therefore, a pastor can only relax the obligation of the laws, but cannot convert the obligation into other works, for this would be paramount to making a new law, and this requires legislative power which the pastor lacks.[18]

This power of dispensing may be exercised either in the external or in the internal forum,[19] but as this book is concerned solely with the jurisdiction of the confessor, it is merely with the exercise of this power in the internal sacramental forum that it need be concerned.

Since a *pastor* enjoys ordinary jurisdiction for the

---
[17] Cf. Benedictus XIV, ep. encycl., *Libentissime,* 10 jun. 1745, § 22, Fontes n. 358; S. C. S. Off., 17 mart. 1883, Fontes n. 1081.
[18] Vermeersch-Creusen, *Epitome,* II, n. 553.
[19] Can. 202, § 3.

internal sacramental forum,[20] it appears that this power of dispensing must also be classified as ordinary. However, since this is jurisdiction to be exercised in hearing confessions, it would also seem that a *pastor* is prohibited from delegating this power at least for use in the internal sacramental forum.[21]

It must be borne in mind that when the observance of these laws becomes morally impossible, the obligation of the law *ipso facto* ceases.[22] Therefore, it is not necessary that the fulfillment of the law be morally impossible in order that a dispensation be sought or granted. It suffices that a just cause be present, which in itself is not sufficient to excuse from the observance of the law, but which renders the seeking of a dispensation reasonable. It is necessary for the validity as well as the liceity of the dispensation, however, that such a cause really exist. In doubt about the sufficiency of a cause, it is certain that a dispensation may be validly and licitly granted;[23] and in doubt about the existence of a cause, although it can hardly ever occur, it would seem to be valid and licit to grant a dispensation in virtue of Canon 209.

Finally, it is to be noted that this dispensation is personal unless it is declared to be otherwise, and therefore the one dispensed may avail himself of his privilege everywhere.[24]

---

[20] Can. 873, § 1.
[21] Cf. Pont. Comm. ad CC. auth. interpret., 16 oct. 1919, *A. A. S.* XI (1919), 477.
[22] Maroto, I, n. 232.
[23] Can. 84, § 2.
[24] Can. 74, and Vermeersch-Creusen, *op. cit.,* II, n. 554.

BIBLIOGRAPHY

Sources

Acta Apostolicae Sedis (Romae, 1909—).
Acta Sanctae Sedis, 41 vols. (Romae, 1865-1908).
Acta et Decreta Concilii Plenarii Baltimorensis II (Baltimorae, 1868).
Acta et Decreta Concilii Plenarii Baltimorensis III (Baltimorae, 1886).
Codex Juris Canonici (Romae, 1918).
Collectanea S. C. de Propaganda Fide, 2 ed., 2 vols. (Romae, 1907).
Concilia Provincialia Baltimorae habita (Baltimorae, 1842).
Concilii Tridentini Canones et Decreta (Parisiis, 1910).
Corpus Juris Civilis (Berlin, 1886).
Corpus Juris Canonici, ed. Richter-Friedberg, 2 vols. (Lipsiae, 1922).
Fontes Codicis Juris Canonici, 4 vols. (Romae, 1923-1926).

References

Aertnys-Damen, *Theologia Moralis*, 10 ed., 2 vols. (Buscoduci, 1921).
Alphonsus Liguori, St., *Theologia Moralis*, 2 vols. (Turonis, 1879).
Arregui, Antonius M., *Summarium Theologiae Moralis* (Bilbao, 1923).
Augustine, Charles, *A Commentary on the New Code of Canon Law*, 3d ed., 9 vols., (New York—St. Louis, 1921-1924).
Ayrinhac, H. A., *Marriage Legislation in the New Code of Canon Law* (New York, 1918).
Ayrinhac, H. A., *Legislation on the Sacraments in the New Code of Canon Law* (New York, 1928).
Badii, Caesar, *Institutiones Juris Canonici*, 2 vols (Florentiae, 1921).
Ballerini-Palmieri, *Opus Theologicum Morale* (Prati, 1889).
Barbosa, Augustinus, *Tractatus Varii* (Lugduni, 1660).
Barbosa, Augustinus, *De Officiis et Potestate Episcopi et Parochi* (Romae, 1658).
Batiffol, Pierre, *Etudes d'Histoire et Theologie Positive* (Paris, 1902).
Bargilliat, M., *Praelectiones Juris Canonici*, 37 ed. (Parisiis, 1923-1924).
Benedictus XIV, (Prosper Lambertini), *De Synodo Dioecesana* (Romae, 1806).

Biederlack-Fuehrich, *De Religiosis Codicis Juris Canonici* (Oeniponte, 1919).
Billot, Ludovicus, *De Ecclesiae Sacramentis,* Vol. VII, 2 ed. (Romae, 1897).
Bizzari, Andreas, *Collectanea in Usum Secretariae Sacrae Congregationis Episcoporum et Regularium* (Romae, 1885).
Blat, Albertus, *Commentarium in Textum Juris Canonici,* 5 vols. (Romae, 1921).
Bonaventura St., *Opera Omnia,* tom. IV (Quaracchi ad Claras Aquas, 1892-1898).
Boudinhon, Augustus, "Sur l'Histoire de la Penitence a propos d'un Ouvrage Recent," in *Revue d'Histoire et de Litterature Religieuses* (Paris, 1897).
Brandys, Maximillian, *Kirchliches Rechtsbuch* (Paderborn, 1920).
Bucceroni, Januarius, *Casus Conscientiae,* 6 ed., 2 vols. (Romae, 1918).
Cappello Felix, M., *De Censuris,* 2 ed. (Turin, 1925).
Cappello, Felix, M., *De Sacramentis,* Vol. I (1921), Vol. II (1926), Vol. III (1923, Turin).
Casey, P. H., *Notes on a History of Auricular Confession* (Philadelphia, 1899).
Catholic Encyclopedia, Vols. VIII, XI (New York, 1907-1912).
Cerato, Prosdocimus, *Censurae Vigentes a Codice Juris Canonici,* 2 ed. (Patavii, 1921).
Cerato, Prosdocimus, *Matrimonium a Codice Juris Canonici Desumptum,* 3 ed. (Patavii, 1920).
Chelodi, Joannes, *Jus Matrimoniale,* 3 ed. (Tridenti, 1921).
Chelodi, Joannes, *Jus de Personis* (Tridenti, 1925).
Chelodi, Joannes, *Jus Poenale* (Tridenti, 1920).
Chokier, Erasmus, *Tractatus de Jurisdictione Ordinarii in Exemptos* (Coloniae-Agrippinae, 1629).
Choupin, Lucien, S. J., *Nature et Obligations de l'Etat Religieux* (Paris, 1923).
Cicognani, Hamletus, *Commentarium in Codicem Juris Canonici* (Romae, 1925).
Cipollini, Albertus, D., *De Censuris Latae Sententiae* (Taurini, 1925).
Clark, J., *Logic* (New York, 1916).
Cocchi, Guidus, *Commentarium in Codicem Juris Canonici,* 2 ed. (Turin, 1925).
Dargin, Edward V., *Reserved Cases* (Washington, 1924).
De Angelis, Philippus, *Praelectiones Juris Canonici* (Romae, 1877).
D'Annibale, Josephus, *Summula Theologiae Moralis* (Mediolani, 1881).
DeBecker, Julius, *De Sponsalibus et Matrimonio* (Louvain, 1903).
DeLugo, J., S. J., *Disputationes Scholasticae et Morales* (Parisiis, 1868).
Denzinger, Henricus, et Bannwart, Clemens, *Enchiridion Symbolorum et Definitionum,* quam paravit, J. B. Umberg, S.J., 14 and 15 ed. (Friburgi Brisgoviae, 1922).

BIBLIOGRAPHY

DeSmet, Aloysius, *De Sponsalibus et Matrimonio*, 4 ed. (Brugis, 1923).
Devoti, Joannes, *Institutionum Canonicarum*, Lib. IV (Leodii, 1860).
Diana, Antonius, *Coordinati Opera Omnia* (Venetiis, 1728).
Duchesne, Louis, *Liber Pontificalis* (Parisiis, 1886).
Fagnanus, Prosperus, *Commentarium in Libros Decretalium* (Venetiis, 1729).
Fanfani, P. Ludovicus, *De Jure Parochorum* (Turin, 1924).
Fanfani, P. Ludovicus, *De Jure Religiosorum* (Turin, 1925).
Farrugia, Nicolaus, *De Casuum Conscientiae Reservatione*, 2 ed. (Romae, 1922).
Farrugia, Nicolaus, *De Matrimonio et Causis Matrimonialibus* (Taurini-Romae, 1924).
Ferraris, Lucius, F., *Prompta Bibliotheca Canonica* (Parisiis, 1865).
Führich, Maximillian, *De Religiosis* (Oeniponte, 1919).
Gasparri, Petrus, *De Matrimonio* (Parisiis, 1904).
Gearin, J., *The New Canon Law in Its Practical Aspects* (Philadelphia, 1918).
Genicot-Salsmans, *Institutiones Theologiae Moralis*, 10 ed. (Bruxellis, 1922).
Genicot-Salsmans, *Casus Conscientiae*, 5 ed. (Bruxellis, 1925).
Gennari, Casimirus, *Consultations de Morale, de droit Canonique et de Liturgie* (Paris, 1907-1910).
Gury-Ballerini, *Compendium Theologiae Moralis*, 7 ed. (Romae, 1882).
Gury-Ferreres, *Casus Conscientiae*, 4 ed. (Barcelona, 1920-1921).
Hickey, John, *Irregularities and Simple Impediments* (Washington, 1920).
Hickey, J. S., *Summula Philosophiae Scholasticae* (Dublin, 1919).
Hilling, Nicolaus, *Codicis Juris Canonici Interpretatio* (Friburgi Brisgoviae, 1925).
Honore, Leon, S.J., *Le Secret de la Confession* (Paris, 1924).
King, James, *Administration of the Sacraments to Dying Non-Catholics* (Washington, 1924).
Kubelbeck, Wm. J., *The Sacred Penitentiary and Its Relation to the Faculties of Ordinaries and Priests* (Washington, 1918).
Kurtscheid, Bertrand, *Das Beichtssiegel in Seiner Geschichtlichen Entwuhlung* (Freiburg, 1912).
La Croix, Claudius, *Theologia Moralis* (Venetiis, 1756).
Lea, Henry, C., *A History of Auricular Confession and Indulgences* (Philadelphia, 1896).
Lega, Michael, *Praelectiones in Textum Juris Canonici*, 2 ed. (Romae, 1910).
Lehmkuhl, Augustinus, *Theologia Moralis*, 2 vols. (Friburgi Brisgoviae, 1888).
Leitner, Martin, *Handbuch des katholischen Kirchenrechts*, 2 ed. (Regensburg, 1922).
Leitner, Martin, *Lehrbuch des katholischen Eherechts*, 3 ed. (Paderborn, 1920).

Mansi, J. D., *Sacrorum Conciliorum Nova et Amplissima Collectio,* 51 vols. (Venetiis, 1759-1798).

Maroto, Philippus, *Institutiones Juris Canonici,* 3 ed. (Romae, 1921).

McCormick, Robert, *Confessors of Religious* (Washington, 1926).

Melo, Antonio, O.F.M., *De Exemptione Regularium* (Washington, 1921).

Migne, P. J., *Patrologia Latina* (Parisiis, 1847-1851).

Migne, P. J., *Patrologiae Graecae Cursus Completus* (Parisiis, 1858-1864).

Morinus, Joannes, *Commentarius Historicus de Disciplina in Administratione Sacramenti Poenitentiae* (Venetiis, 1702).

Motry, Hubert, *Diocesan Faculties* (Washington, 1922).

Murphy, George L., *Delinquencies and Penalties in the Administration and the Reception of the Sacraments* (Washington, 1923).

Noldin, H., S.J., *Summa Theologiae Moralis* (Oeniponte, 1921, 1922).

Oberhauser, Benedictus, *Van Espen Jus Ecclesiasticum in Epitome Redactum* tom. 1 (Bassani, 1784).

Papi, Hector, S.J., *Religious in Church Law* (New York, 1924).

Pesch, Christian, S.J., *Praelectiones Dogmaticae,* Vol. VII, *De Sacramento Poenitentiae,* ed. 4 and 5 (Freiburg, 1920).

Petavius, Dionysius, S.J., *Dogmata Theologica,* tom. V and VIII (Parisiis, 1866).

Petrovits, Joseph, *The New Church Law on Matrimony,* 2 ed. (Philadelphia, 1926).

Pighi, J. B., *De Sacramento Matrimonii* (Veronae, 1919).

Pignatoro, Felice, *De Disciplina Poenitentiali Priorum Ecclesiae Saeculorum Commentarius* (Romae, 1904).

Proteio, P., *Lexicon Juris Civilis et Canonici,* sive potius, *Thesaurus de Verborum, quae ad Jus pertinent, Significatione* (Lugduni, 1567).

Prümmer, Dominicus, O. P., *Manuale Juris Canonici,* 3 ed. (Friburgi Brisgoviae, 1922).

Prümmer, Dominicus, S.J., *Manuale Theologiae Moralis,* 3 ed. (Friburgi Brisgoviae, 1923).

Rauschen, Gerhard, *Eucharist and Penance in the First Six Centuries of the Church* (St. Louis, 1913).

Reiffenstuel, Anacletus, *Jus Canonicum Universum* (Venetiis, 1785).

Roelker, Edward, G., *Principles of Privilege* (Washington, 1926).

Sabetti-Barrett, *Compendium Theologiae Moralis,* 27 ed. (New York, 1919).

Sanchez, Thomas, *De Sancto Matrimonii Sacramento* (Antverpiae, 1626).

Santi, Franciscus, *Praelectiones Juris Canonici* (Ratisbonae, 1886).

Schmalzgrueber, Franciscus, *Jus Ecclesiasticum Universum* (Romae, 1843).

Suarez, Franciscus, *Opera Omnia* (Parisiis, 1861).

Tanquerey, Adrianus, *Synopsis Theologiae Dogmaticae* (Romae, 1921).

Tanquerey, Adrianus, *Synopsis Theologiae Moralis et Pastoralis* (Romae, 1921).
Thomassinus, Ludovicus, *Vetus et Nova Ecclesiae Disciplina*, editio Latina prima post duas Gallicanas (Parisiis, 1688).
Thomas Aquinas, St., *Summa Theologica* (Taurini, 1917).
Van Espen, Z. B., *Operum Juris Ecclesiastici Universi* (Louvain, 1732).
Vermeersch, Arthurus, S. J., *Theologia Moralis*, tom. III (Romae, 1923).
Vermeersch-Creusen, *Epitome Juris Canonici* (Mechliniae-Romae, Vol. I, 1924, Vols. II, III, 1925).
Vicentia, Gabriel, *De Privilegiis Regularium* (Venetiis, 1768).
Vlaming, Th. M. *Praelectiones Juris Matrimonii*, 3 ed. (Bussum in Hollandia, 1919).
Watkins, Oscar, D., *A History of Penance* (London-New York, 1920).
Wernz, Franciscus, *Jus Decretalium* (Prati, 1915).
Wernz-Vidal, *Jus Canonicum*, Vol. II (1923); Vol. V (1925, Romae).
Woywod, Stanislaus, *A Practical Commentary on the Code of Canon Law* (New York, 1925).

Periodicals

American Ecclesiastical Review (Philadelphia, 1889——).
Apollinaris (Romae, 1928——).
Archiv für katholisches Kirchenrecht (Mainz, 1857——).
Commentarium pro Religiosis (Romae, 1920——).
Homiletic and Pastoral Review (New York, 1900).
Il Monitore Ecclesiastico (Romae, 1888——).
Irish Ecclesiastical Record, (Dublin, Fourth Series, 1897-1912; Fifth Series, 1913——).
Jus Pontificium (Romae, 1920——).
Linzer theologisch-praktische Quartalschrift (Linz, 1832——).
Münsterisches Pastoralblat (Munster, 1868——).
Nouvelle Revue Theologique (Paris, 1856——).

FORMULARY

The following petitions may be of use to the confessor in dealing with reserved cases. If the case is reserved to the Holy See, it may be sent directly to the Sacred Penitentiary, addressed

>All' Eminenza Cardinale Penitenziere Maggiore,
>>Palazzo del Sant' Ufficio,
>>>Roma,
>>>>Italia.

or through the
>Apostolic Delegation,
>>1811 Biltmore Street,
>>>Washington, D. C.

or through the Diocesan Chancery Office.

I.

PETITION FOR FACULTY TO ABSOLVE FROM A SIN RESERVED RATIONE SUI

To be addressed to the Bishop, Vicar General, or Chancery Office of the Diocese.

>>>*Locus—dies—mensis—annus.*

Reverendissime Domine:

Titius (Titia) peccatum reservatum in hac dioecesi commisit scilicet.......................... (*mention the sin*).

Nunc autem poenitens et rite dispositus, humiliter absolutionem petit. Deinde reverenter supplico, ut mihi infrascripto confessario facultas concedatur, pro hac vice a praedicto casu reservato absolvendi.

Omni qua par est reverentia subscribit,

>>*N. N.*
>>(*Domicilium*)

FORMULARY

The only sin reserved *ratione sui* to the Holy See, is the sin of false denunciation of an innocent priest, of the crime of solicitation in confession, made before ecclesiastical judges (Canon 894). This sin is also reserved *ratione censurae* (Canon 2363). The following petition may be used to obtain the faculty of absolving one guilty of that crime.

To be addressed to the Bishop or Chancery Office of the Diocese, or to the Apostolic Delegation, 1811 Biltmore St., Washington, D. C., and to be forwarded by them, or directly to the Sacred Penitentiary as follows:

All' Eminenza Cardinale Penitenziere Maggiore,

    Palazzo del Sant' Ufficio,
      Roma,
        Italia.

Locus—dies—mensis—annus.

Eminentissime et Reverendissime Domine:
Titius (Titia) peccatum reservatum Sanctae Sedi falsae delationis apud judices ecclesiasticos commisit, qua sacerdos innocens *N. N.* de crimine sollicitationis accusatus est. Insuper excommunicationem speciali modo Sedi Apostolicae reservatam de qua in Canone 2363 incurrit. **(If such is the case.)**

Jam poenitens, falsa denunciatione formaliter retractata damnaque reparata, alioquin rite dispositus (disposita), absolutionem humiliter petit.

Dignetur Eminentia Vestra mihi infrascripto confessario a peccato (et censura) in praedicto casu, absolvendi facultatem concedere.

Summa qua par est devotione permaneo, Eminentiae Vestrae humillimus et obsequentissimus,

N. N.
(*Domicilium*)

II.

PETITION FOR FACULTY TO ABSOLVE FROM A RESERVED CENSURE AND (IF SUCH IS THE CASE) FROM A SIN RESERVED "RATIONE CENSURAE"

I.

If the censure is reserved by the Ordinary or to the Ordinary or if it is reserved "simpliciter" to the Holy See and the case is occult (Can. 2237, § 2), the petition is to be addressed to the Bishop, Vicar General, or Chancery Office of the Diocese.

Locus—dies—mensis—annus.

Reverendissime Domine:

Titius (Titia) contraxit censuram { excommunicationis / suspensionis / interdicti personalis } reservatam

{ Ordinario / Sedi Apostolicae simpliciter in casu occulto, }

propter............................(*mention the crime*).

Nunc vero hujus delicti sincere poenitens, humiliter absolutionem petit. Quapropter Reverendissimus Dominus absolvendi ab hac censura facultatem mihi pro ista vice impertiri dignetur.

Omni qua par est reverentia subscribit,

N. N.
(*Domicilium*)

II.

If the censure is reserved to the Holy See "specialissimo modo," "speciali modo," or merely "simpliciter" but the case is public, the petition is to be addressed to the Sacred Penitentiary either directly or through the Apostolic Delegation or the Diocesan Chancery Office.

Locus—dies—mensis—annus.

Eminentissime et Reverendissime Domine:

Titius (Titia) contraxit censuram $\begin{cases} \text{excommunicationis} \\ \text{suspensionis} \\ \text{interdicti personalis} \end{cases}$ reservatam Sedi Apostolicae $\begin{cases} \text{specialissimo modo} \\ \text{speciali modo} \\ \text{simpliciter in casu publico} \end{cases}$ propter

.................................*(mention the crime)*.

Nunc vero hujus delicti sincere poenitens, absolutionem humiliter petit. Quapropter Eminentia Vestra absolvendi ab hac censura facultatem mihi infrascripto confessario pro ista vice impertiri dignetur.

Summa qua par est devotione permaneo Eminentiae Vestrae humillimus et obsequentissimus,

N. N.
(*Domicilium*)

III.

MANNER OF HAVING RECOURSE AFTER A RESERVED CENSURE HAS BEEN REMITTED BY ABSOLUTION IN AN URGENT CASE.

I.

If the censure was reserved by the Ordinary or to the Ordinary or if it was reserved "simpliciter" to the Holy See and the case was occult (Can. 2237, § 2), the petition is to be sent to the Bishop, Vicar General, or Chancery Office of the Diocese.

Locus—dies—mensis—annus.

Reverendissime Domine:

Titius (Titia) contraxit

censuram { excommunicationis / suspensionis / interdicti personalis } reservatam

{ Ordinario / Sedi Apostolicae simpliciter in casu occulto, }

propter............................(*mention the crime*).

Ab hac delicto et adnexa censura Titius (Titia) absolutus(a) fuit ad normam Canonis 2254, cum aliunde esset rite dispositus(a). Nunc vero ad hoc Tribunal recurrit, ut mandata recipiat, ea fideliter exsecuturus(a). Dignetur Reverendissimus Dominus rescriptum mittere ad confessarium infrascriptum.

Omni qua par est reverentia subscribit,

N. N.
(*Domicilium*)

II.

If the censure was reserved to the Holy See "specialissimo modo," "speciali modo," or merely "simpliciter" but the case was public, the petition is to be addressed to the Sacred Penitentiary either directly or through the Apostolic Delegation, or the Diocesan Chancery Office.

Locus—dies—mensis—annus.

Eminentissime et Reverendissime Domine:

Titius (Titia) contraxit censuram { excommunicationis, suspensionis, interdicti personalis } reservatam

Sedi Apostolicae { specialissimo modo, speciali modo, simpliciter in casu publico } propter

.... *(mention the crime).*

Ab hac delicto et adnexa censura Titius (Titia) absolutus(a) fuit ad normam Can. { 882, 2252, 2254 } cum aliunde rite dispositus(a). Nunc vero ad hoc Tribunal recurrit, ut mandata recipiat, ea fideliter exsecuturus(a). Dignetur Eminentia Vestra rescriptum mittere ad confessarium infrascriptum.

Summa qua par est devotione permaneo Eminentiae Vestrae humillimus et obsequentissimus,

N. N.
(Domicilium)

IV.

MANNER OF HAVING RECOURSE AFTER THE OBSERVANCE OF A VINDICTIVE PENALTY HAS BEEN SUSPENDED BY A CONFESSOR IN AN OCCULT AND URGENT CASE

To be addressed to the Sacred Penitentiary or to the Apostolic Delegation, or to the Bishop, Vicar General or Chancery Office of the Diocese according to the nature of the penalty.

Locus—dies—mensis—annus.

Eminentissime et Reverendissime Domine:
(If it is to be sent to the Holy See)

Reverendissime Domine:
(If it is to be sent to the Bishop)

Titius incurrit poenam vindicativam latae sententiae .... (*mention the penalty*, e. g., suspensionis a divinis pro anno), propter........................ (*mention the crime*).

Cum sine infamia (vel scandalo) Titius poenam istam observare non posset, cumque casus occultus et urgentior esset, infrascriptus confessarius ad normam Canonis 2290 obligationem servandae poenae suspendit.

Nunc vero ad hoc Tribunal recurrit, ut mandata recipiat, ea fideliter exsecuturus.

Dignetur { Eminentia Vestra / Reverendissimus Dominus } rescriptum mittere ad confessarium infrascriptum.

Omni qua par est reverentia subscribit,

N. N.
(*Domicilium*)

INDEX

A

Abbots, as Ordinaries, 43; penitential jurisdiction of, 51, 185

Abortion, irregularity arising from the procuration of, 232

Absolutio complicis, in danger of death, 96

Absolution, in early Church, 17 seqq.; of Orientals, 72 seqq.; in danger of death, 90 seqq.; in common error, 117 seqq.; in cases of doubt and inadvertence, 141 seqq.; of Cardinals and members of their households, 147 seq.; of bishops and members of their households, 149 seq.; of reserved sins in urgent cases, 152 seqq.; of reserved censures in urgent cases, 160 seqq.; of voyagers, 179 seqq.; of religious men, 185 seqq.; of religious women, 191 seqq.

Abstinence, law of, 246; faculty of dispensing from, 248

Accomplice, *in peccato turpi,* absolution of, in danger of death, 96

Accusation, false, of an innocent confessor, 72

Actor (accuser) in confession, 7

Administrators, diocesan, 43; parochial, 47

Aeroplane journey, and danger of death, 92

Affinity, impediment of, 103, 215

Age, for abstaining, 246; for fasting, 248

Ahyto, Bishop of Basil, and confession to one's proper pastor, 28

Alexander VII and the privileges of religious confessors, 61

Alphonsus, St., and confession during Paschal time, 33

Annual confession, in the early Church, 29; under the law of Trent, 33; under the law of the Code, 237 seq.; 242 seq.

Apostasy, irregularity arising from, 232

Apostate priest, absolution by, in danger of death, 93

Apostolicae Sedis, Constitution of Pius IX, 61

Approaching—Ordinary in matrimonial dispensations, 111 seq., 227;—confessor by a religious woman, 196

Approbation, the necessity of, under the old law, 34; under the law of the Code, 40

Articulo mortis, in, definition of, 91

Assistants, the penitential, jurisdiction of, 47 seqq.

INDEX

Aurelius and the penitential discipline, 22 (note 17)

Auricular confession, use of, 12 seqq.

B

Baptism by non-Catholic, irregularity arising from the reception of, 232

Basil, St., and private confession, 13

Benedict XI and the privileges of religious confessors, 31

Benefice, parochial, jurisdiction attached by law to, 34, 36, 81

Bigamy, attempted, irregularity arising from, 232

Bishop, acquiring jurisdiction immediately from God, 5 (note 2); as minister of reconciliation, 17 seqq.; position under law of Trent, 36; under the law of the Code, 40; jurisdiction of, 42; jurisdiction for hearing confession of, 149 seq.

Bonaventure, St., and jurisdiction of confessor, 10

Boniface VIII, on privilege of choosing one's confessor, 29; on privileges of religious confessors, 31

British Isles, early penitential discipline in, 27

C

Canon Penitentiary, in the early Church, 13; jurisdiction of, under Code, 50

Canones Hippolyti and the form of ordination, 22

Cardinals, jurisdiction of, 42; jurisdiction for hearing the confessions of, 147 seqq.

Carthage, Second Council of, on penitential discipline, 22 (note 17)

Celtic system of confession, 16, 27

Censures, in the early Church, 25; involving loss of ecclesiastical office, 51 seq.; privileges of religious priests in absolving from, 59 seq.; affecting Orientals, 72 seq.; absolution from, in danger of death, 90 seqq.; kinds of, 161 seq.; reservation of, 163 seq.; absolution from, in more urgent cases, 167 seq.

Cessation, of ordinary jurisdiction, 51; of delegated jurisdiction, 57; of reserved sins, 153 seq.

Chastity, solemn vow of, dispensing from matrimonial impediment of, 111

Clausura and confession of nuns, 202; and confession of sick nun, 209

Clement VIII and the privileges of religious confessors, 61

Clement X and approbation of regulars, 37

Clerical religious society, definition of, 184

Code of Canon Law, Canons of:
    4, 62 (note)
    207, 145

INDEX

Code of Canon Law—(*Cont.*)
  209, 62 (note); 118
  239, 147
  349, 149
  519, 187
  522, 194
  523, 205
  613, 63
  858, 210
  859, 237
  872, 11
  873, 42
  874, 53
  876, 193
  882, 91
  883, 180
  893, 66
  899, 242
  900, 153
  935, 239
  990, 233
  1043, 99
  1044, 100
  1045, 213
  1245, 249
  2254, 167
  2290, 236

Colored title, in cases of common error, 121

Common error and jurisdiction, 117 seqq.

Commutation, of pious works for gaining an indulgence, 238

Condemnatory sentence, 162

Confession, annual, prescribed in early Church, 29; under the law of Trent, 33; under the law of the Code, 237 seq.; 242 seq.

Confessional for women, regulations concerning the, 202

Congregation, Religious, defined, 184; members of, 185

Congregations, Roman, jurisdiction of, 6

Consanguinity, impediment of, 103, 215

Conscience, soothing of, 109; *See also* Tranquillity of conscience

Contumacy, necessary for incurring censure, 165 (note 16)

Cum experientia, Instruction of Holy Office, 154

Custom of regarding pastors as approved for whole diocese, 38

Cyprian, St., on private confession, 14; on penitential discipline, 18, 20, 23

D

Danger of death, power of absolving from sins and censures in, 90 seqq.; power of dispensing from matrimonial impediments in, 99 seqq.

Declaratory sentence, 161

Decretals of Gregory IX and common error, 120

Degraded priest, absolution by, in danger of death, 93

Delegated jurisdiction, definition of, 7; under the law of Trent, 33 seqq.; under the law of the Code, 52 seqq.

Deprivation of office, 51

Diaconate, order of, matrimonial impediment of, 111, 215

Diriment impediments, dispensing from, 103

Disease and danger of death, 92

Disparity of cult, the matrimonial impediment of, 105 seqq.; 228 seqq.

Dispensation, from matrimonial impediments in danger of death, 99 seq.; from Eucharistic fast, 210 seqq.; from matrimonial impediments in occult and urgent cases, 213 seqq.; from irregularities, 231 seqq.; from vindictive penalties, 234 seqq.

Doubt, positive and probable, powers granted to all priests in, 141 seqq.

Dying, absolution of. *See* Danger of death

E

Easter duty, in early Church, 29; under the law of Trent, 33; under the law of the Code, 237 seq., 242 seq.

Eastern Church, private confession in, 15; minister of Penance in, 19 seq.; disappearance of public penance in, 26. *See also* Oriental Catholics.

Ecclesiastical offices, 81, 86; ordinary jurisdiction attached by law to, 42 seq.; loss of, 51 seq.

Error, common, power granted to all priests in, 119 seqq.; origin of law, 119; place of, 122 seq.; number involved in, 123 seq.; opinion of recent canonists regarding, 124 seqq.; conditions for the licit use of supplied jurisdiction in, 136 seq.; causes required for absolving licitly in, 140 seqq.

Eucharistic fast, power of dispensing from, 210; conditions required, 211

Excommunicated priest, absolution by, in danger of death, 93

Excommunication, involving loss of office, 51 seq.; kinds of, 161 seq.; reservation of, 163 seq.; absolution from, in more urgent cases, 167 seq.

Exempt clerical religious superiors, penitential jurisdiction of, 50 seq.

Exempt Religious Order or Congregation, 184; the power of absolving a member of, 190

Exomologesis, 17 seqq.

Extension of Paschal time, 237

External forum, jurisdiction for, 6; in early Church, 25; excluded from power granted by Code, in danger of death, 94

Extra-sacramental jurisdiction, defined, 6

F

Faculties, definition of, 53; maritime, 179 seqq.

Fasting, law of, 247; power of dispensing from, 248; before Communion, dispensation for sick, 210 seq.

INDEX

Ferendae sententiae, defined, 161

Festal observance, law of, 245; power of dispensing from, 248

Form of Matrimony, power of dispensing from, 103, 114 seq.

G

Greek-Ruthenian Catholics in the U. S., government of, 74 seqq.; regulation regarding the absolution of, 76. *See also* Oriental Catholics

Gregory IX, bull of, granting penitential jurisdiction to religious, 30; Decretals of, on common error, 120

Gregory XV and approbation, 37

Gregory of Nyssa, St., and penitential discipline, 21

Guests of exempt religious houses, penitential jurisdiction over, 51

H

Heretical priest, absolution by, in danger of death, 93

Hippo, Council of, and penitential jurisdiction, 23

Holy days of obligation, 245

Holy Orders, matrimonial impediment of, 103, 215

Holy Saturday and fast, 247

Homicide, voluntary, irregularity arising from, 232

Households of Cardinals and bishops, power of absolving members of, 147, 149

I

Ignorance, effect on reservation, 69 seq.; philosophical difference from error, 119; juridically same as error, 128 seq.

Illegitimate children, legitimized by dispensation, 110

Impediments, matrimonial, dispensation from, in danger of death, 99 seqq.; in occult and urgent cases, 213 seqq.

Impeding impediments, dispensing from, 103

Impotency, impediment of, 104, 215

Inadvertence, absolution through, 145

Indulgence, power of commuting conditions for, 238 seqq.

"Indult," for working men regarding abstinence, 246

Innocent I, Pope, and penitential discipline, 21

Institution, canonical, in an ecclesiastical office, 81

Inter cunctas, Constitution of Benedict XI, 31

Interdict, personal and local, 163 seq.

Interdicted priest, absolution by, in danger of death, 93

Internal forum, jurisdiction for, 6 seq.; in early Church, 25; power granted by Code, in danger of death, only for, 94

Interpretive error, 125 seq.
Irregular priest, absolution by, in danger of death, 93
Irregularities, power of dispensing from, 231 seqq.

J

Judicial jurisdiction, definition of, 7
Jurisdiction, power of, distinct from orders, 3 seq.; definition of, 4 seq.; kinds of, 5 seq.; necessity of, 8 seq.; absolving without, 117, 136

L

Lapse of time, and loss of office, 51; and delegated jurisdiction, 57
Lapsi, in the early Church, 18, 20, 23
Latae sententiae, defined, 161
Lateran, Council of, and annual confession, 29
Latins, confessions of, to Greek-Ruthenian priest, 75
Lay religious society as distinct from clerical religious, 185
Legitimatization of offspring, 110 seq.
Leo the Great, Pope St., and private confession, 13
Leo X and confession to proper pastor, 32; and jurisdiction of regulars, 34
Liceity and validity of an act compared, 86
License, for hearing confessions in early Church, 22 seqq.; under the law of Trent, 34 seqq.
Ligamen, impediment of, 103, 215
Limitation of jurisdiction, 56 seq.
Loss of ecclesiastical offices, 51 seq.

M

Major Superiors as Ordinaries, 43, 185
Marcellus, Pope, and *titles,* 14, 21
Marriage, attempted after civil divorce, and excommunication, 50; attempted when either party is already married, or under religious vows, or man is in Sacred Orders, irregularity arising from, 232
Martin IV and confession to proper pastor, 32
Matrimonial impediments, power of dispensing from, in danger of death, 99 seq.; in occult and urgent cases (*casus perplexus*), 213 seq.
Medicine, profession of, irregularity arising from, 232
Minister of Penance, in first four centuries, 17 seq.; in the fifth and sixth centuries, 26; from the seventh century to the Council of Trent, 27 seq.; from the Council of Trent to the Code, 33 seq.; under the law of the Code, 40 seqq.

INDEX

Missionaries, powers granted to, by the Code, while giving missions, 244

Mixed religion, impediment of, 105 seqq.; 228 seqq.

Mobilization of soldiers and danger of death, 92

N

Namur, Synod of, and jurisdiction of pastors, 38

Necessity of jurisdiction, for hearing confessions, 8 seq.

Nicæa, Council of, and absolution in danger of death, 91

Non-exempt religious, confessions of, 190

Novices, of exempt clerical religious institute, jurisdiction over, 51, 186; of female religious institute, 193 seq.

Nun, defined, 185

O

Occult cases and power of dispensing from matrimonial impediments, 104, 221 seqq.; from irregularities, 231 seq.; from vindictive penalties, 233 seq.

Occult crime defined, 233

Offices, ecclesiastical, 81, 86; ordinary jurisdiction attached by law to, 42 seq.; loss of, 51 seq.

Old age and danger of death, 92

Operation, surgical, and danger of death, 92

Oratory, public and semi-public, as place for confession of religious woman, 198 seq.

Order, defined, 184; members of, 185

Ordinarius loci, defined, 43

Ordinary jurisdiction, defined, 6; under the former discipline, 24, 25, 27; under the Code, 42 seqq.; cessation of, 51 seqq.

Oriental Catholics, absolution of, 45; effect of reservation on, 72 seqq.; government of, in the U. S., 74 seqq. *See also* Greek-Ruthenian

Origen and private confession, 14; on the minister of Penance, 19 seq.

P

Paris, Sixth Synod of, on religious confessors, 30

Parish priest, the, early jurisdiction of, 27 seqq.; under Trent, 33 seqq.; under the Code, 42. *See also* Pastor

Particular jurisdiction defined, 6

Paschal precept, 32; powers granted to confessor for extending time of, 237 seq.; power of pastors to absolve from sins reserved by the Ordinary during Paschal time, 242 seq.

Pastors, the early jurisdiction of, 27 seqq.; under Trent, 33 seq.; under the Code, 42 seq.; power of absolving from sins

INDEX

reserved by Ordinary during Paschal time, 242 seqq.; power of dispensing from laws of festal observance, fast and abstinence, 245 seq.

Paul V, and privileges of religious, 60

Paulinus and private confession, 13

Peccato turpi, in, absolution of accomplice in danger of death, 96

Penalty, for hearing confession without jurisdiction, 138 seq.

Penance, sacrament of, a judicial act, 8; institution of, 9; history of, in the early Church, 12 seqq.; prescribed annually, 29

Penitent, obligation of, regarding recourse, 172 seq.

Peregrini, absolution of, in the early Church, 28; under the law of Trent, 38 seq.; under the law of the Code, 44 seq.; with regard to reservations, 157 seq.

Periculo mortis, in, definition of, 91. *See also* Danger of death

Petitions, forms of, for faculties for reserved cases, 256 seqq.

Pius IX and Censures, 61

Place, for confessions of women, 202 seq.; of religious women, 198 seq.; 209.

Pope, the, jurisdiction of, 6, 42

Portiuncula indulgence and commutation, 239

Postulants, of exempt clerical religious institute, jurisdiction over, 51

Potestas jurisdictionis, distinct from orders, 3 seq.; definition of, 4 seq.; kind of, 5 seq.; necessity of, 8 seq.; absolving without, 117, 136

Potestas ordinis, distinct from jurisdiction, 3 seq.

Precept of annual confession, in the early Church, 29; under the law of Trent, 33; under the law of the Code, 237 seq., 242 seq.

Prefects Apostolic as Ordinaries, 43

Prelates *nullius* as Ordinaries, 43

Presumption of jurisdiction, 55

Priesthood, Order of, matrimonial impediment of, 103, 215

Privileges of religious confessors, beginning of, 30; under Trent, 35; under the Code, 58 seqq.

Promises, the, and dispensing from matrimonial impediments of disparity of cult and mixed religion, 105 seq., 228 seq.

Provincial Superior, of exempt clerical religious society, penitential jurisdiction of, 51, 185

Public cases and dispensing, from matrimonial impediments, 110 seq., 221 seq.; from irregularities, 231 seq.; from vindictive penalties, 233 seq.

Public crime defined, 233

Public penance in early Church, 17 seqq.

Q

Quasi-parochi, jurisdiction of, 46

R

Reconciliation, minister of, 17 seqq.
Recourse after absolution in danger of death, 97 seq.; after absolution from a censure in an urgent case, 172 seqq.; after the suspension of a vindictive penalty in an urgent case, 235 seq.; forms of petitions for recourse, 260 seq.
Regulars, defined, 185; and Papal privileges under the old law, 30 seq.; under the Code, 58 seqq.
Religious, as confessors, in early Church, 26, 28 seqq.; restriction of, 35; under the Code, 58 seqq.; definition of, 185; confessions of religious men, 185 seqq.; confessions of religious women, 191 seqq.; confessions of sick religious women, 205 seqq.
Removal from office, 51
Reservation, and privileges of religious, 59 seqq.; nature of, 66 seq.; purpose of, 67 seq.; effect of ignorance on, 69 seq.; divisions of, 70 seq.; effect of, on Orientals, 72 seq.; of sins *ratione sui,* 152; cessation of, 153 seqq.; of censures, 163 seq.; territorial effect of the reservation of censures, 176 seq.
Resignation from office, 51
Retreat masters, and faculties of missionaries, 244
Reus (accused) in confession, 7
Roman Law and error, 119 seq.
Rural deans. *See* Vicars forane
Ruthenians. *See* Greek-Ruthenian

S

Sacramental jurisdiction defined, 6
Sanatio in radice, 114, 216
Scandal, removal of, and dispensing in danger of death, 106 seq.; in occult and urgent cases, 231
Schismatic priest, and absolution in danger of death, 93
Scholasticism and jurisdiction, 24
Sea journey, powers granted to confessors on, 179 seqq.
Secret, violation of,—of Holy Office, 148, 150;—as a reason for dispensing from matrimonial impediments, 227
Secret confession. *See* Auricular confession.
Seculars, acquisition of jurisdiction for confessions by, in the early Church, 22 seq., 27 seq.; under the law of Trent, 33 seq.; under the Code, 40 seqq.

Self-mutilation, irregularity arising from, 232

Servants of exempt religious superiors, jurisdiction over, 51

Shipboard faculties, 179 seq.

Sick religious woman, confession of, 205; dispensation from Eucharistic fast for, 210

Simple confessor, definition of, 81

Sister, defined, 185

Sixtus IV and confession to parish priest, 32

Socrates and private confession, 14, 20

Soldiers mobilized for war, and danger of death, 92

Strangers. See *Peregrini*

Students of exempt religious houses, jurisdiction over, 51

Subdiaconate, order of, matrimonial impediment of, 111, 215

Subjects of exempt religious superiors, 51, 186

Suicide, attempted, irregularity arising from, 232

Super Cathedram, Constitution of Boniface VIII, 31

Superiors, local, jurisdiction of, 51; major, jurisdiction of, 51; delegation by, 54; definition of, 185

Supplied jurisdiction, 117 seqq.

Supreme Moderator of non-monastic religious institutes, penitential jurisdiction of, 185

Surgery, profession of, irregularity arising from, 232

Suspended priest, absolution by, in danger of death, 93

Suspension, censure of, and its effects, 51, 163; lifting of, by confessor during danger of death, 94 seq.; as a vindictive penalty, 235

T

Telegraph, notification of jurisdiction by, 56; extraordinary means of communication, 111 (note 35); 227 (note 29).

Telephone, notification of jurisdiction by, 56; extraordinary means of communication, 111 (note 35), 227 (note 29).

Tertullian on Penance, 17

Title, colored, and common error, 121 seq.

Titles, priests of, in early Church, 14, 21, 25

Tranquillity of conscience, 189, 195

Transfer, and loss of office, 51

Travelers, on sea, absolution of, 179

Trent, Council of, on institution of sacrament of Penance, 9; on jurisdiction of confessor, 9; on mode of confessing, 12; and the Paschal confessor, 33; on reservations, 33; on jurisdiction of seculars, 34; and the Code compared, 40; on absolution in danger of death, 90

Trullo, Council of, and religious confessors, 26

INDEX

U

Unborn children, legitimization of, 110
Universal jurisdiction defined, 6
Urban VIII and approbation, 37
Urgent cases, absolution of reserved censures in, 167 seqq.; dispensation from matrimonial impediments in, 213 seqq.; dispensation from irregularities in, 231 seqq.; suspension of vindictive penalties in, 234 seqq.

V

Vagi, absolution of, 44 seq.
Validity, and liceity of an act compared, 86
Vicarius adjutor, 47, 49
Vicarius cooperator, 47 seq.
Vicarius curatus, 47
Vicarius delegatus as Ordinary, 43
Vicarius oeconomus, 47
Vicarius substitutus, 47
Vicars Apostolic as Ordinaries, 43
Vicars Capitular as Ordinaries, 43
Vicars forane, 155
Vicars General as Ordinaries, 43
Vicars, parochial, jurisdiction of, 46 seq.
Vindictive penalties, power of dispensing from, 234 seqq.
Vows, 184

W

War, and danger of death, 92
Withdrawal of jurisdiction, 57
Working man's "indult" regarding abstinence, 246
Works for gaining indulgence, commutation of, 238
Wounds and danger of death, 92

BOOKS OF DOCTRINE, INSTRUCTION, DEVOTION, MEDITATION, BIOGRAPHY, NOVELS, JUVENILES, ETC.

PUBLISHED BY
BENZIGER BROTHERS

NEW YORK
36-38 BARCLAY ST.

CINCINNATI
429 MAIN ST.

CHICAGO
205-207 W. WASHINGTON ST.

Books not marked *net* will be sent postpaid on receipt of the advertised price. Where books are marked *net*, ten per cent. must be added for postage. Thus a book advertised at *net* $1.00 will be sent postpaid on receipt of $1.10.

I. INSTRUCTION, DOCTRINE, APOLOGETICS, CONTROVERSY, EDUCATIONAL.

ANECDOTES AND EXAMPLES ILLUSTRATING THE CATHOLIC CATECHISM. SPIRAGO. *net*, $3.00.
BOY GUIDANCE. KILIAN, O.M. Cap. *net*, $2.00.
CATECHISM EXPLAINED, THE. SPIRAGO-CLARKE. *net*, $3.75.
CATECHISM OF THE VOWS FOR THE USE OF RELIGIOUS. COTEL, S.J. *net*, $0.75.
CATECHIST AND THE CATECHUMEN, THE. WEIGAND. *net*, $1.80.
CATHOLIC BELIEF. FAÀ DI BRUNO. Paper, $0.35; cloth, *net*, $1.00.
CATHOLIC CEREMONIES AND EXPLANATION OF THE ECCLESIASTICAL YEAR. DURAND. Paper, $0.35; cloth, *net*, $1.00.
CATHOLIC CUSTOMS AND SYMBOLS. HENRY, Litt.D. *net*, $2.00.
CATHOLIC NURSERY RHYMES. SISTER MARY GERTRUDE. Retail, $0.25.
CATHOLIC'S READY ANSWER, THE. HILL, S.J. *net*, $2.00.
CATHOLIC TEACHER'S COMPANION, THE. KIRSCH, O.M. Cap. Imitation leather, *net*, $3.00; real leather, $4.50.
CATHOLIC TEACHING FOR YOUNG AND OLD. WRAY. Paper, $0.35.
CEREMONIAL FOR ALTAR BOYS. BRITT, O.S.B. *net*, $1.00.
CHILD PREPARED FOR FIRST COMMUNION. ZULUETA. Paper, *$0.25.
CHRISTIAN APOLOGETICS. DEVIVIER-MESSMER. *net*, $2.50.
CORRECT THING FOR CATHOLICS. BUGG. *net*, $1.25.
DIVINE GRACE. WIRTH. *net*, $0.40.
EXPLANATION OF THE BALTIMORE CATECHISM. KINKEAD. *net*, ¶$1.60.
EXPLANATION OF THE APOSTLES' CREED. ROLFUS. *net*, $1.00.
EXPLANATION OF THE COMMANDMENTS. ROLFUS. *net*, $1.00.
EXPLANATION OF GOSPELS AND OF CATHOLIC WORSHIP. LAMBERT-BRENNAN. Paper, $0.35; cloth, *net*, $1.00.
EXPLANATION OF THE MASS. COCHEM. *net*, $1.00.
EXPLANATION OF THE HOLY SACRAMENTS. ROLFUS. *net*, $1.00.
FINGER OF GOD, THE. BROWN, M.A. *net*, $1.75.
FOLLOWING OF CHRIST, THE. Plain edition. With reflections. $0.55.
FUTURE LIFE, THE. SASIA, S.J. *net*, $3.00.
GENERAL CONFESSION MADE EASY. KONINGS, C.SS.R. Cloth, *$0.50.
GENTLEMAN, A. EGAN. *net*, $1.00.
GIFT OF THE KING. By a Religious. *net*, $0.75.
GOFFINE'S DEVOUT INSTRUCTIONS ON THE EPISTLES AND GOSPELS FOR THE SUNDAYS AND HOLY-DAYS. *net*, $2.00.
HANDBOOK OF THE CHRISTIAN RELIGION. WILMERS, S.J. *net*, ¶$2.50.
HINTS TO PREACHERS. HENRY, Litt.D. *net*, $2.25.
HOME VIRTUES, THE. DOYLE, S.J. *net*, $1.50.
HOME WORLD, THE. DOYLE, S.J. Paper, $0.35; cloth, *net*, $1.50.
IDEALS OF ST. FRANCIS OF ASSISI, THE. FELDER, O.M. Cap.-BITTLE, O.M.Cap. *net*, $4.00.
INTRODUCTION TO A DEVOUT LIFE. ST. FRANCIS DE SALES. *net*, $1.75.
LADY, A. BUGG. *net*, $1.25.

1

H-jroc

LAWS OF THE KING. By a Religious. *net*, $0.75.
LETTERS ON MARRIAGE. SPALDING, S.J. *net*, $1.75.
LITTLE ALTAR BOY'S MANUAL. $0.75.
LITTLE FLOWER'S LOVE FOR HER PARENTS, THE. SISTER M. ELEANORE, C.S.C., Ph.D. *net*, $0.20.
LITTLE FLOWER'S LOVE FOR THE HOLY EUCHARIST, THE. SISTER M. ELEANOR, C.S.C., *net*, $0.20.
LIVING FOR GOD. SISTER MARIE PAULA. *net*, $1.75.
MANUAL OF THEOLOGY FOR THE LAITY. GEIERMANN, C.SS.R. Paper, *$0.75; cloth, *net*, $1.50.
MASS-SERVER'S CARD. Per doz., *net*, $0.80.
MASS FOR CHILDREN, THE. REV. WILLIAM R. KELLY. List $0.32.
MIND, THE. PYNE, S.J. *net*, $2.00.
OUR FIRST COMMUNION. REV. WILLIAM R. KELLY. List, $0.32.
OUR NUNS. LORD, S.J. Regular Edition, $2.50; De Luxe Edition, *net*, $3.50.
OUR SACRAMENTS. REV. WILLIAM R. KELLY. List $0.60.
OUT TO WIN. Straight Talks to Boys on the Way to Manhood. CONROY, S.J. *net*, $2.00.
POETS AND PILGRIMS. BRÉGY. School Ed., *net*, $1.50; Decorative Ed., *net*, $2.50.
PRINCIPLES OF THE RELIGIOUS LIFE; or, AN EXPLANATION OF THE "CATECHISM OF THE VOWS." COTEL, S.J. *net*, $1.85.
QUEEN'S FESTIVALS, THE. By a Religious. *net*, $0.75.
RELIGION HOUR: BOOK ONE. HANNAN, D.D. List, $0.32; net to schools, $0.24.
SACRAMENTALS OF THE HOLY CATHOLIC CHURCH. LAMBING. Paper, $0.35; cloth, *net*, $1.00.
SHORT COURSE IN CATHOLIC DOCTRINE. Paper, *$0.20.
SHORT STORIES ON CHRISTIAN DOCTRINE. *net*, $1.00.

SIMPLE COURSE OF RELIGION. WEIGAND. *net*, price to schools per 100, $4.25.
SIX ONE-ACT PLAYS. LORD, S.J. *net*, $1.75.
SOCIAL ORGANIZATION IN PARISHES. GARESCHÉ, S.J. *net*, $3.25.
SOCIAL PROBLEMS AND AGENCIES. SPALDING, S.J. *net*, $2.50.
SOCIALISM: ITS THEORETICAL BASIS AND PRACTICAL APPLICATION. CATHREIN-GETTELMAN. *net*, $3.00.
SODALITY CONFERENCES. GARESCHÉ, S.J. *net*, $2.75. First Series.
SODALITY CONFERENCES. GARESCHE, S.J. *net*, $2.75. Second Series.
SPIRITISM: FACTS AND FRAUDS. BLACKMORE, S.J. *net*, $3.00.
SPIRITUAL PEPPER AND SALT. STANG. Paper, *$0.40; cloth, *net*, $0.90.
STORIES OF THE MIRACLES OF OUR LORD. By a Religious. *net*, $1.00.
SUNDAY-SCHOOL TEACHER'S GUIDE. SLOAN. net, $1.00.
TALKS TO BOYS. CONROY, S.J. Paper, $0.35.
TALKS TO NURSES. SPALDING, S.J. *net*, $2.00.
TALKS TO PARENTS. CONROY, S.J. *net*, $2.00.
TALKS WITH OUR DAUGHTERS. SISTER M. ELEANORE, Ph.D. Cloth. *net*, $1.50.
TALKS WITH TEACHERS. SISTER M. PAULA. *net*, $1.75.
TEACHER TELLS A STORY: BOOK ONE. HANNAN, D. D. List $2.00.
VOCATIONS EXPLAINED. Cut flush, *$0.25.
WAY OF INTERIOR PEACE. DE LEHEN, S.J. *net*, $2.25.
WONDERFUL SACRAMENTS, THE. DOYLE, S.J. *net*, paper, $0.35; cloth, *net*, $1.75.
WONDER DAYS, THE. TAGGART. *net*, $0.40.
WONDER GIFTS, THE. TAGGART. *net*, $0.40.
WONDER OFFERING, THE. TAGGART. *net*, $0.40.
WONDER STORY, THE. TAGGART. *net*, $0.40.

II. DEVOTION MEDITATION, SPIRITUAL READING. PRAYER-BOOKS

ABANDONMENT; or Absolute Surrender of Self to Divine Providence. CAUSSADE, S.J. *net*, $1.00.
BLESSED SACRAMENT BOOK. Prayer-Book by FATHER LASANCE. Im. leather, $2.75.
BOYS' AND GIRLS' PRAYER-BOOK. FINN, S.J. 27 colored illustrations, 22 in black and

white. Im. leather, round corners, limp, cut flush. Retail, $0.45. Other bindings up to $2.50.

CATHOLIC GIRL'S GUIDE, THE. Prayer-Book by FATHER LASANCE. Seal grain cloth, stiff covers, red edges, $1.75. Im. leather, limp, red edges, $2.00; gold edges, $2.50. Real leather, limp, gold edges, $3.00.

COMMUNION DEVOTIONS FOR RELIGIOUS. SISTERS OF NOTRE DAME. Imitation leather, *net*, $2.75; leather, $4.00.

CONVENT ECHOES. Devotional Verses. SISTER M. PARACLITA. *net*, $1.00.

EARLY FRIENDS OF CHRIST, THE. CONROY, S.J. *net*, $2.75.

EPITOME OF THE PRIESTLY LIFE, AN. ARVISENET-O'SULLIVAN. *net*, $2.50.

EUCHARISTIC PRIEST, THE. LEPICIER, O.S.M. *net*, $2.00

EVER TIMELY THOUGHTS. GARESCHÉ, S.J. *net*, $1.50.

FAIREST FLOWER OF PARADISE. LEPICIER, O.S.M. *net*, $1.75.

FOR FREQUENT COMMUNICANTS. ROCHE, S.J. Paper, *$0.20.

GO TO JOSEPH. LEPICIER, O.S.M. *net*, $1.75.

HER LITTLE WAY. CLARKE. *net*, $1.50.

HOLY HOUR, THE. KEILEY. 16mo. *$0.20.

HOLY HOUR OF ADORATION. STANG. *net*, $1.25.

HOLY SOULS BOOK. Reflections on Purgatory. A Complete Prayer-Book. By REV. F. X. LASANCE. Im. leather, round corners, red edges, $1.90; gold edges, $2.50; real leather, gold edges, $3.00.

IMITATION OF THE SACRED HEART. ARNOUDT. *net*, $2.00.

JESUS CHRIST, THE KING OF OUR HEARTS. LEPICIER, O.S.M. *net*, $1.75.

KEEP THE GATE. WILLIAMS, S.J. *net*, paper, $0.35.

LET US PRAY. LASANCE. Retail, $0.35.

LIFE'S LESSONS. GARESCHÉ, S.J. *net*, $1.50.

LIFT UP YOUR HEARTS. By REV. F. X. LASANCE. Im. leather, round corners, red edges, retail, $2.75; gold edges, retail, $3.25; Amer. seal, limp, gold side, gold edges, retail, $3.75; Amer. morocco, seal grain, gold roll, red under gold edges, retail, $5.00.

LITTLE COMMUNICANTS' PRAYER-BOOK. SLOAN. $0.60.

LITTLE FLOWER AND THE BLESSED SACRAMENT, THE. HUSSLEIN, S.J. *net*, $0.60.

LITTLE FLOWER TREASURY, THE. Edited by CARYL COLEMAN. Im. leather, fine grain, very flexible, round corners, red edges. Retail, $0.65. Other bindings up to $1.75.

LITTLE MANUAL OF ST. ANTHONY. LASANCE, *net*, $0.50.

LITTLE MANUAL OF ST. JOSEPH. LINGS. *net*, $0.50.

LITTLE MANUAL OF ST. RITA. MCGRATH. $1.25.

LITTLE MASS BOOK, THE. LYNCH. Paper, *$0.15.

MANNA OF THE SOUL. Vestpocket Edition. A little Book of Prayer for Men and Women. By REV. F. X. LASANCE. Oblong, 32mo. $1.00.

MANNA OF THE SOUL. A Book of Prayer for Men and Women. By REV. F. X. LASANCE. Extra Large Type Edition, 544 pages, 16mo. $1.90.

MANNA OF THE SOUL. Prayer-Book by REV. F. X. LASANCE. Thin Edition. Im. leather. $1.50.

MANNA OF THE SOUL. Prayer-Book by REV. F. X. LASANCE. Thin edition with Epistles and Gospels. $1.75.

MANUAL OF THE HOLY EUCHARIST. LASANCE. Im. leather, limp, red edges, *net*, $2.25.

MEDITATIONS FOR EVERY DAY IN THE YEAR ON THE LIFE OF OUR LORD. VERCRUYSSE, S.J. 2 vols, *net*, $6.50.

MEDITATIONS FOR THE USE OF THE SECULAR CLERGY. CHAIGNON, S.J., 2 vols. *net*, $7.50.

MEDITATIONS ON THE LIFE, THE TEACHING AND THE PASSION OF JESUS CHRIST. ILG-CLARKE. 2 vols. *net*, $5.75.

MEDITATIONS ON THE SUFFERINGS OF JESUS CHRIST. PERINALDO. *net*, $1.00.

MENDING THE NETS. MORNING STAR SERIES II. FEELY, S.J. *net*, $0.75.

MISSION REMEMBRANCE OF THE REDEMPTORIST FATHERS. GEIERMANN, C.SS.R. $2.00.

MOMENTS BEFORE THE TABERNACLE. RUSSELL, S.J. *net*, $0.90.

MORNING SACRIFICE, THE. MOFFAT, S.J. Retail, $0.15.

MY GOD AND MY ALL. A Prayer-Book for Children. By REV. F. X. LASANCE. Black or white, cloth, square corners, white edges, retail, $0.35. Imit. leather, black or white, seal grain, gold edges, retail, $0.70. Persian Morocco,

3

gold side and edges, retail, $1.25. Same, white leather, retail, $1.50. Celluloid, retail, $1.00; with Indulgence Cross, retail, $1.35.

MY PRAYER-BOOK. Happiness in Goodness. Reflections, Counsels, Prayers, and Devotions. By Rev. F. X. Lasance. 16mo. Seal grain cloth, stiff covers, $1.65. Imitation leather, limp, round corners, red edges, $1.85; gold edges, $2.25. Real leather, gold edges, $2.75.

MY PRAYER-BOOK. Extra Large Type Edition. By Rev. F. X. Lasance. Seal grain cloth, stiff covers, square corners, red edges, $1.85. Imitation leather, round corners, red edges, $2.25. Imitation leather, round corners, gold edges, $3.25. American seal, limp, gold side, gold edges, $4.00.

MYSTERY OF LOVE, THE. Lepicier, O.S.M. net, $1.75.

NEW MISSAL FOR EVERY DAY, THE. Complete Missal in English for Every Day in the Year. New Edition. With Introduction Notes and a Book of Prayer. By Rev. F. X. Lasance. Oblong, 32mo. Imitation leather, $3.00.

NEW MISSAL FOR EVERY DAY, (Student's Edition.) By Rev. F. X. Lasance. Retail $2.00.

NEW TESTAMENT. 12mo edition. Large type. Cloth, net, $1.75.

NOVENA IN HONOR OF SAINT THERESE OF THE CHILD JESUS. Coleman. net, $0.15.

OFFICE OF HOLY WEEK, COMPLETE. Latin and English. Cut flush, net, $0.65; silk cloth, net, $1.00; Am. seal, red edges, net, $2.25.

OUR FAVORITE DEVOTIONS. Lings, net, $1.50.

OUR FAVORITE NOVENAS. Lings. net, $1.50.

OUR LADY BOOK. By Rev. F. X. Lasance. Imitation leather, limp, round corners, red edges, $2.00. Morocco Grain. Imitation Leather, gold edges, $2.50. American Seal, limp, gold side, gold edges, $3.00. Rutland limp, red under gold edges, $3.75. Turkey Morocco, limp, gold roll, red under gold edges, $5.25.

PATHS OF GOODNESS, THE. Garesché, S.J. net, $1.50.

POLICEMEN'S AND FIREMEN'S COMPANION. McGrath. $0.60.

PRAYER-BOOK FOR RELIGIOUS. Lasance. 16mo. Imitation leather, limp, red edges, net, $2.50.

PRAYERS FOR OUR DEAD. McGrath. Cloth, $0.35; imitation leather, $0.75.

PRISONER OF LOVE. Prayer-Book by Father Lasance. Im. leather, limp, red edges, $2.00.

REFLECTIONS FOR RELIGIOUS. Lasance. net, $2.75.

REJOICE IN THE LORD. Prayer-Book by Father Lasance. $2.00.

ROSARY NOVENAS TO OUR LADY. Lacey. net, $0.15.

ROSE WREATH FOR THE CROWNING OF ST. TERESA OF THE CHILD JESUS, A. Clarke. net, $1.50.

SACRED HEART BOOK. Prayer-Book by Father Lasance. Im. leather, limp, red edges, $1.75.

SERAPHIC GUIDE, THE. $1.50.

SHORT MEDITATIONS FOR EVERY DAY. Lasausse. net, $1.50.

SHORT VISITS TO THE BLESSED SACRAMENT. Lasance. net, $0.50.

SOLDIERS' AND SAILORS' COMPANION. McGrath. Vest-pocket shape, silk cloth or khaki, $0.35.

SOUVENIR OF THE NOVITIATE. Taylor. net, $1.25.

SPIRIT OF SACRIFICE, THE. AND THE LIFE OF SACRIFICE IN THE RELIGIOUS STATE. Giraud. net, $3.00.

SPIRITUAL CONSIDERATIONS. Buckler, O.P. net, $1.00.

SUNDAY MISSAL, THE. Lasance, Im. leather, limp, red edges, $2.25.

TEACHINGS OF THE LITTLE FLOWER, THE. Garesché, S.J. net, $1.50.

THINGS IMMORTAL, THE Garesché S.J. net, $1.50.

THOUGHTS FOR TODAY. MORNING-STAR SERIES I. Feeley, S.J. net, $0.75.

THOUGHTS ON THE RELIGIOUS LIFE. Lasance. Im. leather, limp, red edges, net, $2.75.

THY KINGDOM COME, SERIES I. Moffat S.J. net, $0.30.

THY KINGDOM COME, SERIES II. Moffat. S.J. net, $0.30.

THY KINGDOM COME, SERIES III. Moffat, S.J. net, $0.30.

THY KINGDOM COME, SERIES IV. Moffat, S.J. net, $0.30.

TRUE SPOUSE OF CHRIST. Liguori. net, $2.00.

VALUES EVERLASTING, THE. Garesché, S.J. net, $1.50.

VIGIL HOUR, THE. Ryan, S.J. Paper, *$0.25.

VISITS TO JESUS IN THE TABERNACLE. Lasance. Im. leather, limp, red edges, $2.25.

VISITS TO THE MOST HOLY SACRAMENT. Liguori. net, $1.00.

WAY OF THE CROSS. Paper. *$0.08.

WAY OF THE CROSS, THE. Very large-type edition. Method of St. Alphonsus Liguori. *$0.20.

WAY OF THE CROSS. Eucharistic method. *$0.15.

WAY OF THE CROSS. Method of St. Francis of Assisi. *$0.15.

WITH GOD. Prayer-Book by Father Lasance. Im. leather. limp, red edges, $2.50.

YEARNING FOR GOD. Williams, S.J. net, $1.50.

YOUNG MAN'S GUIDE, THE. Prayer-Book by Father Lasance. Seal grain cloth, stiff covers, red edges, $1.75. Im. leather, limp, red edges, $2.00; gold edges, $2.50.

YOUR INTERESTS ETERNAL. Garesché, S.J. net, $1.50.

YOUR NEIGHBOR AND YOU. Garesché, S.J. net, $1.50.

YOUR OWN HEART. Garesché, S.J. net, $1.50.

YOUR SOUL'S SALVATION. Garesché, S.J. net, $1.50.

III. THEOLOGY, LITURGY, HOLY SCRIPTURE, PHILISOPHY, SCIENCE, CANON LAW

ALTAR PRAYERS. Edition A: English and Latin, net, $3.00. Edition B: German-English-Latin, net, $4.50.

ANNOUNCEMENT BOOK. 12mo. net, $4.80.

AUTOBIOGRAPHY OF AN OLD BREVIARY. Heuser, D.D. net, $2.00.

BAPTISMAL RITUAL. 12mo. net, $1.50.

BENEDICENDA. Schulte. net, $2.50.

BURIAL RITUAL. Cloth, net, $1.50.

COMBINATION RECORD FOR SMALL PARISHES. net, $8.00.

COMPENDIUM SACRÆ LITURGIÆ. Wapelhorst, O.F.M. net, ¶$3.50.

GENERAL INTRODUCTION TO THE STUDY OF THE HOLY SCRIPTURES. Gigot. net, ¶$5.75.

GENERAL INTRODUCTION TO THE STUDY OF THE HOLY SCRIPTURES. Abridged edition. Gigot. net, ¶$3.75.

HOLY BIBLE, THE. Large type, handy size. Cloth. $2.50.

HYMNS OF THE BREVIARY AND MISSAL, THE. Britt, O.S.B. net, $3.50.

JESUS LIVING IN THE PRIEST. Millet, S.J.-Byrne. net, $4.50.

LIBER STATUS ANIMARUM, or Parish Census Book. Large edition, size, 14x10 inches. 100 Families. 200 pp. half leather, net, $7.00; 200 Families, 400 pp., half leather, net, $8.00; Pocket Edition. net, $0.50.

MARRIAGE LEGISLATION IN THE NEW CODE. Ayrinhac, S.S. net, $2.75.

MARRIAGE RITUAL. Cloth, gilt edges, net, $2.50; sheepskin, gilt edges, net, $3.75.

MIND, THE. Pyne, S.J. net, $2.00.

MISSALE ROMANUM. Benziger Brothers' Authorized Vatican Edition. Black or Red Amer. morocco gold edges, net, $15.00; Red Amer. morocco, gold stamping and edges, net, $17.50. Red finest quality morocco, red under gold edges, net, $22.00.

MORAL PRINCIPLES AND MEDICAL PRACTICE. Coppens, S.J.-Spalding, S.J. net, $3.00.

OUTLINES OF JEWISH HISTORY. Gigot, D.D. net, $3.00.

OUTLINES OF NEW TESTAMENT HISTORY. Gigot. net, $4.50.

PASTORAL THEOLOGY. Stang. net, ¶$3.25.

PENAL LEGISLATION IN THE NEW CODE OF CANON LAW. Ayrinhac, S.S. net, $3.75.

PEW COLLECTION AND RECEIPT BOOK. Indexed. 11x8 inches, net, $5.75.

PREPARATION FOR MARRIAGE. McHugh, O.P. net, $0.40.

RECORD OF BAPTISMS. 200 pages, 700 entries, net, $7.00. 400 pages. 1400 entries, net, $10.00. 600 pages, 2100 entries, net, $12.00.

RECORD OF CONFIRMATIONS. net, $6.00.

RECORD OF FIRST COMMUNIONS. net, $6.00.

RECORD OF INTERMENTS. net, $6.00.

RECORD OF MARRIAGES. Size 14x10 inches. 200 pages, 700 entries, net, $7.00. 400 pages, 1400 entries, net $10.00. 600 pages, 2100 entries, net, $12.00.

RITUALE COMPENDIOSUM. Cloth, net, $1.50, seal. net, $3.00.

SPECIAL INTRODUCTION TO THE STUDY OF THE OLD TESTAMENT. Gigot. Part I, net, ¶4.75; Part II, net, ¶$5.00.

TEXTUAL CONCORDANCE OF THE HOLY SCRIPTURES. Williams. net, $8.75.

IV. SERMONS

EIGHT-MINUTE SERMONS. DeMouy. 2 vols., *net*, $5.50.
FUNERAL SERMONS. Wirth, O.S.B. *net*, $2.25.
HINTS TO PREACHERS. Henry, Litt.D. *net*, $2.25.
POPULAR SERMONS ON THE CATECHISM. Bamberg-Thurston, S.J. 3 vols., *net*, $7.50.
SERMONS. Canon Sheehan. *net*, $3.00.
SERMONS. Whelan, O.S.A. *net*, $2.50.
SERMONS FOR THE SUNDAYS AND CHIEF FESTIVALS OF THE ECCLESIASTICAL YEAR. Pottgeisser, S.J. 2 vols, *net*, $7.00.
SODALITY CONFERENCES. Garesché, S.J. *net*, $2.75. First Series
SODALITY CONFERENCES. Garesché, S.J. *net*, $2.75. Second Series.
THREE-MINUTE HOMILIES. McDonough. net, $2.00.

V. HISTORY, BIOGRAPHY, HAGIOLOGY, TRAVEL

AUTOBIOGRAPHY OF AN OLD BREVIARY. Heuser, D.D. *net*, $2.00.
CATHOLIC NURSERY RHYMES. Sr. M. Gertrude, M.A. Retail, $0.25.
CHILD'S LIFE OF ST. JOAN OF ARC. Mannix. *net*, $1.60.
HISTORY OF THE CATHOLIC CHURCH. Brueck. 2 vols., *net*, $5.75.
HISTORY OF THE PROTESTANT REFORMATION. Cobbett-Gasquet. *net*, $1.00.
HISTORY OF THE MASS. O'Brien. *net*, $3.00.
IDEALS OF ST. FRANCIS OF ASSISI, THE. Felder, O.M. Cap. *net*, $4.00.
ILLUSTRATED LIVES OF PATRON SAINTS FOR BOYS. Mannix. *net*, $1.25.
ILLUSTRATED LIVES OF PATRON SAINTS FOR GIRLS. Mannix. *net*, $1.25.
IMMOLATION. Life of Mother Mary of Jesus (Marie Deleuil-Martiny.) Laplace - Newcomb. *net*, $3.75.
IN THE WORKSHOP OF ST. JOSEPH. Heuser, D.D. *net*, $1.75.
LIFE OF CHRIST. Businger-Brennan. Illustrated. Half morocco, gilt edges. *net*, $18.00.
LIFE OF CHRIST. Cochem, *net*, $1.00.
LIFE OF THE BLESSED VIRGIN. Rohner. *net*, $1.00.
LIFE OF ST. MARGARET MARY ALACOQUE. Illustrated. Bougaud. *net*, $1.84.
LITTLE LIVES OF THE SAINTS FOR CHILDREN. Berthold. *net*, $1.25.
LITTLE PICTORIAL LIVES OF THE SAINTS. With 400 illustrations. *net*, $2.00.
LIVES OF THE SAINTS. Butler. Paper, retail, $0.35; cloth, *net*, $1.00.
LOURDES. Clarke, S.J. *net*, $1.00.
MARY THE QUEEN. By a Religious. *net*, $0.75.
MILL TOWN PASTOR, A. Conroy, S.J. *net*, $2.00.
OUR NUNS. Lord, S.J. *net*, $2.50.
OUR OWN ST. RITA. Corcoran. *net*, $2.50.
PASSIONISTS, THE. Ward, C.P. *net*, $5.00.
PATRON SAINTS FOR CATHOLIC YOUTH. By M. E. Mannix. Each life separately in attractive colored paper cover with illustration on front cover. Each 10 cents postpaid; per 25 copies, assorted, *net*, $1.75; per 100 copies, assorted, *net*, $6.75. Sold only in packages containing 5 copies of one title.
For Boys: St. Joseph; St. Aloysius; St. Anthony; St. Bernard; St. Martin; St. Michael; St. Francis Xavier; St. Patrick; St. Charles; St. Philip.
The above can be had bound in 1 volume, cloth, *net*, $1.00.
For Girls: St. Ann; St. Agnes; St. Teresa; St. Rose of Lima; St. Cecilia; St. Helena; St. Bridget; St. Catherine; St. Elizabeth; St. Margaret.
The above can be had bound in 1 volume, cloth, *net*, $1.00.
PICTORIAL LIVES OF THE SAINTS. With nearly 400 illustrations and over 600 pages, *net*, $5.75.
ROMA. Pagan, Subterranean and Modern Rome in Word and Picture. By Rev. Albert Kuhn, O.S.B., D.D. Preface by Cardinal Gibbons. 617 pages, 744 illustrations. 48 full-page inserts, 3 plans of Rome in colors. 8½x12 inches. Red im. leather, gold side. *net*, $18.00.
ST. ANTHONY. Ward. *net*, $1.00.
ST. JOAN OF ARC. Lynch, S.J. Illustrated. *net*, $3.00.

SHORT LIFE OF CHRIST, A. McDonough. Retail, $0.15.
SHORT LIVES OF THE SAINTS. Donnelly. *net*, $1.00.
STORY OF THE ACTS OF THE APOSTLES. Lynch, S.J. Illustrated. *net*, $3.50.
STORY OF THE LITTLE FLOWER, THE. Lord, S.J. Retail, $0.15; *net*, to Priests and Religious, $0.10.
WHISPERINGS OF THE CARIBBEAN. Williams, S.J. *net*, $2.00.
WONDER STORY, THE. Taggart. Illustrated Board covers, *net*, $0.40. Also an edition in French and Polish at same price.

VI. JUVENILES

FATHER FINN'S BOOKS.
Each, *net*, $1.25.
CANDLES' BEAMS.
SUNSHINE AND FRECKLES.
LORD BOUNTIFUL.
ON THE RUN.
BOBBY IN MOVIELAND.
FACING DANGER.
HIS LUCKIEST YEAR. A Sequel to "Lucky Bob."
LUCKY BOB.
PERCY WYNN; OR MAKING A BOY OF HIM.
TOM PLAYFAIR; OR, MAKING A START.
CLAUDE LIGHTFOOT; OR HOW THE PROBLEM WAS SOLVED.
HARRY DEE; OR WORKING IT OUT.
ETHELRED PRESTON; OR THE ADVENTURES OF A NEW COMER.
THE BEST FOOT FORWARD; AND OTHER STORIES.
"BUT THY LOVE AND THY GRACE."
CUPID OF CAMPION.
THAT FOOTBALL GAME AND WHAT CAME OF IT.
THE FAIRY OF THE SNOWS.
THAT OFFICE BOY.
HIS FIRST AND LAST APPEARANCE.
MOSTLY BOYS. SHORT STORIES.
FATHER SPALDING'S BOOKS.
Each, illustrated, *net*, $1.50.
THE INDIAN GOLD-SEEKER.
STRANDED ON LONG BAR.
IN THE WILDS OF THE CANYON.
SIGNALS FROM THE BAY TREE.
HELD IN THE EVERGLADES.
AT THE FOOT OF THE SANDHILLS.
THE CAVE BY THE BEECH FORK.
THE SHERIFF OF THE BEECH FORK.
THE CAMP BY COPPER RIVER.
THE RACE FOR COPPER ISLAND.
THE MARKS OF THE BEAR CLAWS.
THE OLD MILL ON THE WITHROSE.
THE SUGAR CAMP AND AFTER.
ADVENTURE WITH THE APACHES. Ferry, *net*, $0.75.
AS GOLD IN THE FURNACE. Copus, S.J. *net*, $1.00.
AS TRUE AS GOLD. Mannix. *net*, $0.75.
AT THE FOOT OF THE SANDHILLS. Spalding, S.J. *net*, $1.50.
AWAKENING OF EDITH, THE. Illustrated. Specking. *net*, $1.50.
BEST FOOT FORWARD, THE. Finn, S.J. *net*, $1.25.
BETWEEN FRIENDS. Aumerle. *net*, $1.00.
BISTOURI. Melandri. *net*, $0.75.
BLISSYLVANIA POST-OFFICE. Taggart. *net*, $0.75.
BOBBY IN MOVIELAND. Finn, S.J. *net*, $1.25.
BOB O'LINK. Waggaman. *net*, $0.75.
BROWNIE AND I. Aumerle. *net*, $1.00.
"BUT THY LOVE AND THY GRACE." Finn, S.J. *net*, $1.25.
BY BRANSCOME RIVER. Taggart. *net*, $0.75.
CAMP BY COPPER RIVER. Spalding, S.J. *net*, $1.50.
CANDLES' BEAMS. Finn, S.J. *net*, $1.25.
CAPTAIN TED. Waggaman, *net*, $1.25.
CAVE BY THE BEECH FORK. Spalding, S.J. *net*, $1.50.
CHILDREN OF CUPA. Mannix. *net*, $0.75.
CHILDREN OF THE LOG CABIN. Delamare, *net*, $1.00.
CLARE LORAINE. "Lee." *net*, $1.00.
CLAUDE LIGHTFOOT. Finn, S.J. *net*, $1.25.
COBRA ISLAND. Boyton, S.J. *net*, $1.25.
CUPA REVISITED. Mannix. *net*, $0.75.
CUPID OF CAMPION. Finn, S.J. *net*, $1.25.
DADDY DAN. Waggaman. *net*, $0.75.

DAN'S BEST ENEMY. Holland, S.J. net, $1.50.
DEAR FRIENDS. Nirdlinger, net, $1.00.
DEAREST GIRL, THE. Taggart. net, $1.50.
DIMPLING'S SUCCESS. Mul Holland. net, $0.75.
ETHELRED PRESTON. Finn, S.J. net, $1.25.
EVERY-DAY GIRL, AN. Crowley, net, $0.75.
FACING DANGER. Finn, S.J. net, $1.25.
FAIRY OF THE SNOWS. Finn, S.J. net, $1.25.
FINDING OF TONY. Waggaman. net, $1.50.
FIVE BIRDS IN A NEST. Delamare. net, $1.00.
FRED'S LITTLE DAUGHTER. Smith. net, $0.75.
FREDDY CARR'S ADVENTURES. Garrold, S.J. net, $1.00.
FREDDY CARR AND HIS FRIENDS. Garrold, S.J. net, $1.00.
GOLDEN LILY, THE. Hinkson. net, $0.75.
GREAT CAPTAIN, THE. Hinkson. net, $0.75.
HARMONY FLATS. Whitmire. net, $1.00.
HARRY DEE. Finn, S.J. net, $1.25.
HARRY RUSSELL. Copus, S.J. net, $1.00.
HEIR OF DREAMS, AN. O'Malley. net, $0.75.
HELD IN THE EVERGLADES. Spalding, S.J. net, $1.50.
HIS FIRST AND LAST APPEARANCE. Finn, S.J. net, $1.25.
HIS LUCKIEST YEAR. Finn, S.J. net, $1.25.
HOI-AH! McDonald. net, $1.50.
HOSTAGE OF WAR, A. Bonesteel. net, $0.75.
HOW THEY WORKED THEIR WAY. Egan. net, $1.00.
INDIAN GOLD-SEEKER, THE. Spalding, S.J. net, $1.50.
IN QUEST OF ADVENTURE. Mannix. net, $0.75.
IN QUEST OF THE GOLDEN CHEST. Barton. net, $1.00.
IN THE WILDS OF THE CANYON. Spalding, S.J. net, $1.50.
JACK. By a Religious, H. C. J. net, $0.75.
JACK-O'-LANTERN. Waggaman. net, $0.75.
JACK HILDRETH ON THE NILE. Taggart. net, $1.00.
KLONDIKE PICNIC, A. Donnelly. net, $1.00.
LAST LAP, THE. McGrath, S.J. net, $1.50.

LITTLE APOSTLE ON CRUTCHES. Delamare. net, $0.75.
LITTLE GIRL FROM BACK EAST. Roberts. net, $0.75.
LITTLE LADY OF THE HALL. Ryeman. net, $0.75.
LITTLE MARSHALLS AT THE LAKE. Nixon-Roulet. net, $1.00.
LITTLE MISSY. Waggaman. net, $0.75.
LOYAL BLUE AND ROYAL SCARLET. Taggart. net, $1.50.
LORD BOUNTIFUL. Finn, S.J. net, $1.25.
LUCKY BOB. Finn, S.J. net, $1.25.
MADCAP SET AT ST. ANNE'S. Brunowe. net, $0.75.
MAD KNIGHT, THE. Schaching. net, $0.75.
MAKING OF MORTLAKE. Copus, S.J. net, $1.00.
MAKING THE ELEVEN AT ST MICHAEL'S. Uniack. net, $1.50.
MAN FROM NOWHERE. Sadlier. net, $1.50.
MANGLED HANDS. Boyton, S.J. net, $1.25.
MARKS OF THE BEAR CLAWS. Spalding, S.J. net, $1.50.
MARTHA JANE. Speckling. net, $1.50.
MARTHA JANE AT COLLEGE. Speckling. net, $1.50.
MARY ROSE AT BOARDING SCHOOL. Wirries. net, $1.50.
MARY ROSE GRADUATE. Wirries. net, $1.50.
MARY ROSE KEEPS HOUSE. Wirries. net, $1.50.
MARY ROSE SOPHOMORE. Wirries. net, $1.50.
MARY TRACEY'S FORTUNE. Sadlier. net, $0.75.
MILLY AVELING. Smith. net, $1.00.
MIRALDA. Johnson. net, $0.75.
MOSTLY BOYS. Finn, S.J. net, $1.25.
MYSTERIOUS DOORWAY. Sadlier. net, $0.75.
MYSTERY OF CLEVERLY. Barton. net, $1.00.
MYSTERY OF HORNBY HALL. Sadlier. net, $1.00.
NAN NOBODY. Waggaman. net, $0.75.
NEW SCHOLAR AT ST. ANNE'S. Brunowe. net, $1.00.
OLD CHARLMONT'S SEEDBED. Smith. net, $0.75.
OLD MILL ON THE WITHROSE. Spalding, S.J. net, $1.50.
ON THE RUN. Finn, S.J. net, $1.25.
ON THE SANDS OF CONEY. Boyton, S.J. net, $1.25.

PAMELA'S LEGACY. TAGGART. *net*, $1.50.
PANCHO AND PANCHITA. MANNIX. *net*, $0.75.
PAULINE ARCHER. SADLIER. *net*, $0.75.
PERCY WYNN. FINN, S.J. *net*, $1.25.
PERIL OF DIONYSIO. MANNIX. *net*, $0.75.
PETRONILLA. DONNELLY. *net*, $1.00.
PICKLE AND PEPPER. DORSEY. *net*, $1.75.
PILGRIM FROM IRELAND. CARNOT. *net*, $0.75.
PLAYWATER PLOT, THE. WAGGAMAN. *net*, $1.50.
QUEEN'S PAGE, THE. HINKSON. *net*, $0.75.
QUEEN'S PROMISE, THE. WAGGAMAN. *net*, $1.50.
QUEST OF MARY SELWYN. CLEMENTIA. *net*, $1.50.
RACE FOR COPPER ISLAND. SPALDING, S.J. *net*, $1.50.
REARDON RAH! HOLLAND, S.J. *net*, $1.50.
RECRUIT TOMMY COLLINS. BONESTEEL. *net*, $0.75.
ST. CUTHBERT'S COPUS, S.J. *net*, $1.00.
SANDY JOE. WAGGAMAN. *net*, $1.50.
SCHOONER AHOY! MCDONALD. *net*, $1.50.
SEA-GULL'S ROCK. SANDEAU. *net*, $0.75.
SEVEN LITTLE MARSHALLS. NIXON-ROULET. *net*, $0.75.
SHADOWS LIFTED. COPUS, S.J. *net*, $1.00.
SHERIFF OF THE BEECH FORK. SPALDING, S.J. *net*, $1.50.
SHIPMATES. WAGGAMAN. *net*, $1.50.

SIGNALS FROM THE BAY TREE. SPALDING, S.J. *net*, $1.50.
STRANDED ON LONG BAR. SPALDING, S.J. *net*, $1.50.
STRONG ARM OF AVALON. WAGGAMAN. *net*, $1.50.
SUGAR CAMP AND AFTER. SPALDING, S.J. *net*, $1.50.
SUMMER AT WOODVILLE. SADLIER. *net*, $0.75.
SUNSHINE AND FRECKLES. FINN, S.J. *net*, $1.25.
TALISMAN, THE. SADLIER, *net*, $1.00.
TAMING OF POLLY. DORSEY. *net*, $1.75.
THAT FOOTBALL GAME. FINN. S.J. *net*, $1.25.
THAT OFFICE BOY. FINN, S.J. *net*, $1.25.
THREE GIRLS AND ESPECIALLY ONE. TAGGART. *net*, $0.75.
TOM LOSELY; BOY. COPUS, S.J. *net*, $1.00.
TOM PLAYFAIR. FINN, S.J. *net*, $1.25.
TOM'S LUCK-POT. WAGGAMAN. *net*, $0.75.
TRANSPLANTING OF TESSIE. WAGGAMAN. *net*, $1.50.
TREASURE OF NUGGET MOUNTAIN. TAGGART. *net*, $1.00.
TWO LITTLE GIRLS. MACK. *net*, $0.75.
UNCLE FRANK'S MARY. CLEMENTIA. *net*, $1.50.
UPS AND DOWN OF MARJORIE. WAGGAMAN. *net*, $0.75.
VIOLIN MAKER. SMITH. *net*, $0.75.
WHERE MONKEYS SWING. BOYTON, S.J. *net*, $1.25.
WINNETOU, THE APACHE KNIGHT. TAGGART. *net*, $1.00.
WHOOPEE! BOYTON, S.J. *net*, $1.25.

VII. COLORED PICTURE BOOKS FOR CHILDREN

CATHOLIC NURSERY RHYMES. SR. MARY GERTRUDE. Retail, $0.25.
LITTLE FLOWER'S LOVE FOR THE EUCHARIST. SR. M. ELEANORE. C.S.C. *net*, $0.20.
LITTLE FLOWER'S LOVE FOR HER PARENTS. SR. M. ELEANORE, C.S.C. *net*, $0.20.
MASS FOR CHILDREN, THE. KELLY. List, $0.32.
OUR FIRST COMMUNION. KELLY. List, $0.32.

OUR SACRAMENTS. KELLY. List, $0.60.
WONDER DAYS. TAGGART. *net*, $0.40.
WONDER GIFTS. TAGGART. *net*, $0.40.
WONDER OFFERING. TAGGART. *net*, $0.40.
WONDER STORY. TAGGART. *net*, $0.40.

VIII. NOVELS

ISABEL C. CLARKE'S GREAT NOVELS.
A CASE OF CONSCIENCE. *net*, $2.50.
Each, *net*, $2.00.

CASTLE OF SAN SALVO.
SELMA.
IT HAPPENED IN ROME.
VILLA BY THE SEA, THE.
CHILDREN OF THE SHADOW.

VIOLA HUDSON.
ANNA NUGENT.
CARINA.
  AUTOGRAPH FICTION.
  LIBRARY. Each, *net* $1.75.
AVERAGE CABINS.
THE LIGHT ON THE LAGOON.
THE POTTER'S HOUSE.
TRESSIDER'S SISTER.
URSULA FINCH.
THE ELSTONES.
EUNICE.
LADY TRENT'S DAUGHTER.
CHILDREN OF EVE.
THE DEEP HEART.
WHOSE NAME IS LEGION.
FINE CLAY.
PRISONER'S YEARS.
THE REST HOUSE.
ONLY ANNE.
THE SECRET CITADEL.
BY THE BLUE RIVER.
ANNA NUGENT. CLARKE. *net*, $2.00.
AVERAGE CABINS. CLARKE. *net*, $1.75.
BOY. INEZ SPECKING. *net*, $1.50.
BUT THY LOVE AND THY GRACE. FINN. *net*, $1.25.
BY THE BLUE RIVER. CLARKE. *net*, $1.75.
CABLE, THE. TAGGART. *net*, $2.00.
CARINA. CLARKE. *net*, $2.00.
CASE OF CONSCIENCE, A. CLARKE. *net*, $2.50.
CASTLE OF SAN SALVO. CLARKE. *net*, $2.00.
CHILDREN OF THE SHADOW. CLARKE. *net*, $2.00.
CHILDREN OF EVE. CLARKE. *net*, $1.75.
CIRCUS-RIDER'S DAUGHTER. BRACKEL. *net*, $1.00.
CONNOR, D'ARCY'S STRUGGLES. BERTHOLDS. *net*, $1.00.
DEEP HEART, THE. CLARKE. *net*, $1.75.
DENYS THE DREAMER. HINKSON. *net*, $1.00.
DION AND THE SIBYLS. KEON. *net*, $1.00.
ELSTONES, THE. CLARKE. *net*, $1.75.
EUNICE. CLARKE. *net*, $1.75.
FABIOLA. WISEMAN. Paper, $0.35; cloth, *net*, $1.00.
FABIOLA'S SISTERS. CLARKE. *net*, $1.00.
FALSE GODS. WILL SCARLET. *net*, $1.00.
FAUSTULA. AYSCOUGH. *net*, $2.00.
FINE CLAY. CLARKE. *net*, $1.75.
FOR BETTER FOR WORSE. SCOTT, S.J. *net*, $1.75.
FORGIVE AND FORGET. LINGEN. *net*, $1.00.

GRAPES OF THORNS. WAGGAMAN. *net*, $1.00.
HEIRESS OF CRONENSTEIN. HAHN-HAHN. *net*, $1.00.
HER JOURNEY'S END. COOKE. *net*, $1.00.
IDOLS; OR, THE SECRET OF THE RUE CHAUSSE D'ANTIN. DE NAVERY. *net*, $1.00.
IN GOD'S COUNTRY. BOYTON, S.J. *net*, $1.25.
IN GOD'S GOOD TIME. ROSS. *net*, $1.00.
IN SPITE OF ALL. STANIFORTH. *net*, $1.00.
IT HAPPENED IN ROME. CLARKE. *net*, $2.00.
KELLY. SCOTT, S.J. *net*, $1.75.
KIND HEARTS AND CORONETS. HARRISON. *net*, $1.00.
LADY TRENT'S DAUGHTER. CLARKE. *net*, $1.75.
LIGHT OF HIS COUNTENANCE. HART. *net*, $1.00.
LIGHT ON THE LAGOON, THE. CLARKE. *net*, $1.75.
"LIKE UNTO A MERCHANT." GRAY. *net*, $1.00.
MARCELLA GRACE. MULHOLLAND. *net*, $1.00.
MARIQUITA. AYSCOUGH. *net*, $2.00.
MIRAGE. SPECKING. *net*, $1.50.
MISS ERIN. FRANCIS. *net*, $1.00.
MISSY. SPECKING. *net*, $1.50.
MONK'S PARDON, THE. DE NAVERY. *net*, $1.00.
MY LADY BEATRICE. COOKE. *net*, $1.00.
NO HANDICAP. TAGGART. *net*, $2.00.
ONLY ANNE. CLARKE. *net*, $1.75.
PASSING SHADOWS. YORKE. *net*, $0.80.
POTTER'S HOUSE, THE. CLARKE. *net*, $1.75.
PRISONERS' YEARS. CLARKE. *net*, $1.75.
PROPHET'S WIFE. BROWNE. *net*, $1.00.
REST HOUSE, THE. CLARKE. *net*, $1.75.
ROSE OF THE WORLD. MARTIN. *net*, $1.00.
RUBY CROSS, THE. WALLACE. *net*, $1.00.
RULER OF THE KINGDOM. KEON. *net*, $1.50.
SECRET CITADEL, THE. CLARKE. *net*, $1.75.
SECRET OF THE GREEN VASE. COOKE. *net*, $1.00.
SELMA. CLARKE. *net*, $2.00.
SHADOW OF EVERSLEIGH. LANSDOWNE. *net*, $1.00.
SO AS BY FIRE. CONNOR, *net*, $1.00.
TEMPEST OF THE HEART. GRAY. *net*, $1.00.

TEST OF COURAGE. Ross. *net*, $1.00.
TRESSIDER'S SISTER. CLARKE. *net*, $1.75.
TURN OF THE TIDE, THE. GRAY. *net*, $1.00.
UNBIDDEN GUEST, THE. COOKE. *net*, $1.00.
UNDER THE CEDARS AND THE STARS. CANON SHEEHAN. *net*, $3.50.

URSULA FINCH. CLARKE. *net*, $1.75.
VILLA BY THE SEA, THE. CLARKE. *net*, $2.00.
VIOLA HUDSON. CLARKE. *net*, $2.00.
WAY THAT LED BEYOND, THE. HARRISON. *net*, $1.00.
WHOSE NAME IS LEGION. CLARKE. *net*, $1.75.